USING SOCIAL MEDIA EFFECTIVELY IN THE CLASSROOM

Blogs, Wikis, Twitter, and More

Edited by Kay Kyeong-Ju Seo

Routledge
Taylor & Francis Group

NEW YORK AND LONDON

First published 2013
by Routledge
711 Third Avenue, New York, NY 10017

Simultaneously published in the UK
by Routledge
2 Park Square, Milton Park, Abingdon, Oxon OX14 4RN

Routledge is an imprint of the Taylor & Francis Group, an informa business

Library of Congress Cataloging in Publication Data
Seo, Kay.
    Using social media effectively in the classroom : blogs, wikis, twitter, and more /
    Kay Seo.
    p. cm.
    Includes bibliographical references and index.
    1. Internet in education. 2. Social media. 3. Education—Effect of technological
    innovations on. I. Title.
    LB1044.87.S46 2012
    371.33'44678—dc23
    2012006904

ISBN: 978-0-415-89679-5 (hbk)
ISBN: 978-0-415-89680-1 (pbk)
ISBN: 978-0-203-10149-0 (ebk)

Typeset in Bembo and Stone Sans
by EvS Communication Networx, Inc.

Printed and bound in the United States of America on sustainably sourced paper by
IBT Global

CONTENTS

Contributors   *vii*
Preface   *xiii*

UNIT I
Planning a Socially Enriched Learning Environment   **1**

1 Analysis in Virtual Worlds: The Influence of Learner
   Characteristics on Instructional Design   3
   Aimee deNoyelles

2 Blurring the Lines: Teacher Insights on the Pitfalls and Possibilities
   of Incorporating Online Social Media into Instructional Design   19
   Thomas Highley and Kay Kyeong-Ju Seo

3 Analysis of Second Life as a Delivery Mechanism in EFL Education   34
   Kay Kyeong-Ju Seo, Noah Kreischer, and Muruvvet Demiral

UNIT II
**Developing Powerful Instructional Strategies
with Social Media**   **45**

4 Designing Recorded Voice Reflection as a Pedagogical Strategy   47
   Dana A. Tindall

5 Live in Your World, Learn in Ours: Virtual Worlds … Engaging
   the New Generation of Students!   62
   Elizabeth M. Hodge and Sharon Collins

6 Developing a Wiki for Problem-Based Online Instruction and Web
   2.0 Exploration   80
   Teresa Franklin and Briju Thankachan

7 Learning and Teaching as Communicative Actions: Social Media as
   Educational Tool   98
   Scott J. Warren and Jenny S. Wakefield

UNIT III
Teaching Successfully with Social Media   **115**

8 Everyone's All a-Twitter about Twitter: Three Operational
   Perspectives on Using Twitter in the Classroom   117
   Matthew Krüger-Ross, Richard D. Waters, and Tricia M. Farwell

9 Online Videos in the Classroom: Exploring the Opportunities and
   Barriers to the Use of YouTube in Teaching Introductory Sociology   132
   Nick Pearce and Elaine Tan

10 A Framework to Enrich Student Interaction via Cross-Institutional
    Microblogging   147
    Suku Sinnappan and Samar Zutshi

UNIT IV
Assessing Instructional Effectiveness with Social
Media   **167**

11 Designing Assessments for Differentiated Instruction Using Social
    Media Applications   169
    Seung H. Kim and Ying Xie

12 VoiceThread® as a Facilitator of Instructional Critique   190
    Jamie Smith and Teresa Franklin

13 Is There (Still) a Place for Blogging in the Classroom?: Using
    Blogging to Assess Writing, Facilitate Engagement, and Evaluate
    Student Attitudes   207
    Tricia M. Farwell and Matthew Krüger-Ross

Index   *223*

CONTRIBUTORS

Sharon Collins is a Project Manager at East Carolina University. She is the Director of the Early College High School program, Second Life administrator, and iWebFolio administrator. Collins has 20 years of experience in education and IT as well as 10 years of experience with the federal government in academic computing, federal grant, strategic planning, innovative technology application, and university-wide technology deployment. She also has extensive, expert experience in virtual worlds, specifically Second Life. She was part of the Collaborative Distance Learning Technologies grant with ECU. She co-authored the book *The Virtual Worlds Handbook: How to use Second Life and other 3d Virtual Worlds*, was recently published in the Merlot JOLT, and has been published in other works regarding distance education.

Muruvvet Demiral is a Ph.D. student in Instructional Systems Technology at Indiana University. She earned her Master's degree in Instructional Design and Technology from University of Cincinnati. Her research interests are designing online learning environments, integrating technology in education, and pre-service teacher education.

Aimee deNoyelles, Ed.D., is an instructional designer at the University of Central Florida, engaging in the support and professional development of faculty who teach online. deNoyelles earned her Ed.D. in Curriculum and Instruction with a specialization in Instructional Design and Technology from the University of Cincinnati. Her current research interests include avatar-mediated communication, immersive technology and presence, and virtual social identity.

Tricia M. Farwell, Ph.D., is an assistant professor in the School of Journalism in the College of Mass Communication at Middle Tennessee State University. She has served in leadership roles for AEJMC and the Entertainment and Sports Section of PRSA. Her research interests include gender issues in mass communication and applications of social media in education. She is the author of *Love and Death in Edith Wharton's Fiction.*

Teresa Franklin, Ph.D., Professor, Instructional Technology, is a 30-year veteran of teaching and learning through the integration of technology in math and science. Research interests include: mobile technologies, virtual learning environments, and game development for digital learning. Dr. Franklin has significant journal publications and textbooks that integrate technology into science and math including *Teaching Science for All Children (5th ed.), Virtual Games and Career Exploration* and *The Mobile School: Digital Communities Created by Mobile Learners.*

Thomas Highley is a 20-year veteran of the public school classroom, as well as adjunct professor in the middle level education program at the University of Cincinnati. Highley received his Masters degree in Instructional Technology in 2002 and is currently pursuing his doctorate in literacy. Highley's research interests include issues of access and equity in public school applications of digital technology, as well as the influence of online social media on comprehension in middle level and secondary public school classrooms.

Elizabeth M. Hodge, Ph.D., is currently an Associate Professor in the College of Education and Assistant Chair in the Department of Business and Information Technologies Education at East Carolina University. Dr. Hodge has taught graduate and undergraduate business, marketing, management, finance, web design, and information technology courses utilizing Virtual Environments. In addition, Dr. Hodge has published several research papers on the use of emerging technologies (Web 2.0 and beyond). She has co-authored the *Virtual Worlds Handbook* and provided several international and national seminars surrounding the integration of virtual environments for teaching and learning.

Seung H. Kim, Ed.D., is currently an Associate Professor in the College of Education and Program Director of Instructional Technology Master's program at Lewis University. She earned her Ed.D. in Instructional Technology at the University of Houston. She has expertise in the areas of technology integration into curriculum, instructional design, web/multimedia development, interactive graphics, online learning, and teacher education. Her current research includes studies on the effect of students' use of technology on their social/emotional network and investigating teachers' use of emerging Web 2.0 technology in instruction.

Noah Kreischer is an Information Technology Analyst in the Faculty Technology Resources Center (FTRC) at the University of Cincinnati. He provides support and training to faculty members on various educational technologies, mainly Blackboard. Noah earned his MEd in Instructional Design and Technology from the University of Cincinnati. His research interests are focused on the improvement of online education through instructor training and certification.

Matthew Krüger-Ross is a graduate research and teaching assistant in the Instructional Technology program at North Carolina State University. He also assists with professional development for the North Carolina Virtual Public School's STEM faculty and staff. His research interests include philosophy of education and technology as well as applications of emerging technologies to teaching and learning.

Nick Pearce is a doctoral student in curriculum theory and implementation at Simon Fraser University in Burnaby, British Columbia, Canada. He received his BS in Middle Grades Education and MS in Instructional Technology at North Carolina State University in Raleigh, North Carolina. Matthew also assists with professional development for the North Carolina Virtual Public School's STEM faculty and staff. His research interests include philosophy of education and technology as well as applications of emerging technologies to teaching and learning.

Kay Kyeong-Ju Seo, Ph.D., is an Assistant Professor of Instructional Design and Technology at the University of Cincinnati. Seo earned her Ph.D. in Instructional Technology from Utah State University. Her research interests revolve around promoting social cognitive development in 3D immersive virtual worlds, designing constructivist instructional approaches with online social media, inspiring diversity and equality in online social environments, and integrating technology in K–12 and teacher education.

Suku Sinnappan, Ph.D., has extensive experience in Web 2.0 research and development. He is currently a Senior Lecturer at the Faculty of Higher Education, Swinburne University of Technology. He obtained his doctorate in Interactive Marketing from University of Newcastle, Australia, in 2004. His current research interests involve E-learning, Crisis Communication, and online consumer behavior.

Jamie Smith is an instructor and doctoral candidate in the Instructional Technology program at Ohio University. She has a background in K–12, having taught elementary, middle, and high school in Ohio and Florida. She is currently teaching both undergraduate and graduate courses in the Patton College of Education at Ohio University and working on a variety of research projects focused on the integration of free and open source technology into a variety of learning environments.

Elaine Tan is a learning technologist in the Computing and Information Service of Durham University. She is completing a Ph.D. in technology enhanced learning at Lancaster University and her research interests surround the adoption of technology to support teaching practice by early career staff.

Briju Thankachan is a doctoral student in Instructional Technology at Ohio University. His research focuses on ICT integration in developing countries, open source adoption of software and social networking. Presentations include: Association for Educational Communications and Technology (AECT) Conference, *Implementation and Evaluation Process of the IT @ School Project, Kerala, India: A Case Study* and Mid-Western Educational Research Association (MWERA), *Comparative Study on the Impact of Google Earth and Maps or Atlas on Student Learning.*

Dana A. Tindall is the Associate Director for Learning Environments at Xavier University in Cincinnati, Ohio. He works in the area of faculty development particularly with the implementation of successful online pedagogical strategies. His research interests are in online learning and the use of recorded audio, the use of online social networking tools and reflective practice.

Jenny S. Wakefield works as a Web Developer and Instructional Designer at the University of Texas at Dallas and is a Ph.D. learner and Research Assistant at the University of North Texas in the College of Information. She holds a Master of Science in Computer Education and Cognitive Systems. Her research focuses on instructional design, social networks learning, and virtual worlds. She has been on the editorial board for several books.

Scott J. Warren, Ph.D., is an Associate Professor of Learning Technologies at the University of North Texas. His research examines the use of emerging online technologies such as digital learning environments and educational games and simulations. His early work included creating the Anytown world to support writing, reading, and problem solving. His current work includes The 2015 Project and Refuge alternate reality game courses that use social media to support game play and learning.

Richard D. Waters, Ph.D., is an assistant professor in the School of Management and the University of San Francisco, where he teaches nonprofit organization marketing and public relations, fundraising, and nonprofit organization management. His research interests include relationship management between organizations and stakeholders, the development of fundraising theory as it pertains to charitable nonprofits, and the use of Web 2.0 technologies by nonprofit organizations. He is a former fundraising practitioner and consultant to healthcare organizations in Northern California. His research has been published in nonprofit management and public relations journals.

Ying Xie, Ph.D., is an Assistant Professor in the Graduate Department of Educational Leadership and Instructional Design at Idaho State University. She earned her Ph.D. in Instructional Systems from the Pennsylvania State University. Her current research focuses on design-based research, the integration of emerging technologies and creation of cognitive tools to promote reflective thinking, higher-order learning, and knowledge construction.

Samar Zutshi, Ph.D., completed his Masters in Information Technology and Ph.D. from Monash University in Australia, where he taught at the Faculty of Information Technology. Samar has also worked as a software developer and IT trainer. Since 2008 Samar has been a lecturer in Information Systems at Swinburne University of Technology, teaching both on-campus and online. His research interests include content-based image retrieval, independent learning and the use of technology in education. He is a Program Director at Swinburne Online, a joint initiative in tertiary online learning by Swinburne University of Technology and the job hunting website company, Seek.

PREFACE

The rapid expansion of social media such as blogs, wikis, Twitter, and virtual worlds is dramatically transforming the way we teach our students. With highly accessible, network-based mechanisms, these technologies are more than ever empowering students to create, customize, and share content online. This change opens up new opportunities for us to implement socially enriched pedagogies as it allows for diverse means to facilitate student interaction and effective ways to manage collective knowledge. For example, a three-dimensional online virtual world offers an immersive environment to mirror the real world and provides rich social cues to help students build connections with others and accomplish a collaborative task in real time.

This book aims at exploring the educational potential of these powerful technologies and offering practical guidelines for designing a socially empowered learning environment. Given the growing role of social media in education, it is integral for educators to gain insights on how to effectively utilize a variety of social media for instructional purposes and how to solve common issues that may arise so that students can become more engaged in learning and have positive educational experiences. To make a valuable contribution to this quest, this book provides creative, unique insights into the design of instruction by discussing how to best support learners with these user-centered technologies and addressing any trends and issues that may come with these new approaches.

This book presents innovative strategies and significant issues to be taken into considerations in the process of designing a social media enriched environment. Four major design phases are discussed in an orderly manner:

Unit 1: Planning a Socially Enriched Learning Environment
Unit II: Developing Powerful Instructional Strategies with Social Media
Unit III: Teaching Successfully with Social Media
Unit IV: Assessing Instructional Effectiveness with Social Media

Unit 1 addresses the importance and effect of analyzing learner characteristics, learning contexts, teacher attitudes towards media, and delivery mechanisms at the planning stage to inform subsequent design decisions. Unit 2 discusses new considerations for designing student activities and developing instructional strategies to effectively use social media in the teaching and learning process. Unit 3 introduces successful cases to implement social media in instruction and explores potentials and barriers of using the tools in the classroom. Unit 4 presents creative approaches to utilize social media to assess instructional effectiveness and elicit positive learning outcomes.

Designed to provide a practical guidance and a framework for decision making in the process of instructional design, this book can enable instructional designers, college professors, and K-12 pre-service and in-service teachers to tap into these powerful technologies, redefine and reinforce teaching methods, and facilitate interactive, meaningful learning for students.

Planning a Socially Enriched Learning Environment

1

ANALYSIS IN VIRTUAL WORLDS

The Influence of Learner Characteristics on Instructional Design

Aimee deNoyelles

Introduction

Social media applications have not only gained incredible popularity in the online sector, but have also transformed the lives of those using them. Tools such as blogs and wikis are the products of a significant shift in online activity and agency from developer to user (Kaplan & Haenlein, 2010). The new and interesting ways in which people project their identities and interact are enabled by the ability of social media to allow users to create, edit, and share their own content. This open-ended platform supports instant communication to be perpetually shaped by users in a public sphere, producing a sense of individual and collective agency (Dieterle & Clarke, 2009) and opportunities for identity projection (boyd, 2007).

Recognizing the power of social media to transform learning, educators are now integrating it in instruction. Certainly, the features of social media complement the constructivist philosophy of teaching and learning, allowing learners to create, co-create and share knowledge with a global audience beyond classroom walls. In addition, social media has tremendous popularity in learners' social lives. Objectivist approaches to learning run counter to the social activities that most learners pursue in their personal lives.

While the integration of social media in education could support powerful learning opportunities, concerns remain. Although popular among learners' lives, personal use does not automatically guarantee being prepared to use them for educational purposes. It is unclear if there are certain learner characteristics that are advantageous toward learning through social media. Concerning instruction, there is no inherent objective embedded in social media, so it can be a challenge for educators to structure interaction and design instruction.

Since these applications are newly emerging, educators are rarely formally trained on their effective use. Although becoming more prominent, research is still limited and focused more on best practices.

Virtual Worlds: Unique Social Media

The focus of this chapter is on virtual worlds, three-dimensional online spaces in which users, represented by simulated bodies called avatars, navigate and interact with others in real time. They are unique from other social media in that they resemble massively multi-player online role-playing games (MMOR-PGs). However, they share the defining feature of social media by enabling user-centered creation of content and social interaction. Some researchers have argued that virtual worlds represent a step beyond social media and are places in their own right, inhabited by people (Boellstorff, 2008; Colby, 2010). Through avatars, users experience a sense of heightened presence in the space, promoting a feeling of immersion. Common ground can be created and sustained with others, eliciting co-presence, a perception that the user is really with others (Jarmon, 2009).

Although virtual worlds share similarities with MMORPGs, the fundamental features more reflect social media. While games contain embedded objectives for the user to achieve, virtual worlds like Second Life® (n.d.) are inherently social and open-ended. In contrast to an MMORPG in which avatars are characters, the avatar is intended to represent the user in a virtual world. This creates a powerful learning opportunity to feel immersed in an environment beyond classroom walls.

Virtual Worlds in Education: Promises and Concerns

Virtual worlds pose exciting possibilities in education by offering a sense of unique place and presence. A primary reason for incorporating virtual worlds in education is the distinctive ability to simulate authentic learning settings that are impractical to provide in traditional classroom settings (Gee, 2007). Space can be customized to fit specific learning objectives. Learners can actively create and display their own knowledge to the online community in multiple ways, such as exhibits, embedded media, discussions, and performances. Learners can communicate and collaborate with others while being immersed in a shared space.

There are also concerns with integrating virtual worlds in educational settings. Like other social media, there is no inherent objective, although objectives can be built in. The space was originally constructed for social purposes rather than educational. In addition, some virtual worlds such as Second Life® are public. With the capability of avatars to look much different from their users, anonymity, privacy and safety issues arise.

Significance of Analysis in Instructional Design

For these reasons, the analysis phase of instructional design is especially significant in this environment. Which learner characteristics are relevant to identify and gauge? Compared to other kinds of social media, virtual worlds are not nearly as popular; only around 10% of teenagers and 4% of adults use them (Lenhart, Kahne, et al., 2008). While social media is used equally by gender, games are a gendered activity (Carr, 2005). Young men are much more likely to engage in multi-user video games, which closely resemble environments such as Second Life® (Lenhart, Jones, & Macgill, 2008; Williams, Consalvo, Caplan, & Yee, 2008). In a national survey, Lenhart et al. (2008) found that boys play video games more often and longer than girls, and play a wider variety of games. Since boys and men are likely to be more familiar with embodying and interacting through avatars, along with navigating within a 3D space, it is possible that this prior experience will grant them privileged access to virtual worlds. However, virtual worlds are more open-ended and social, and the focus is on education, so the experience is not identical.

One key need in this area is to better understand what learner characteristics and contexts emerge as important in this online space. Since it is a type of social media, will students be familiar with its' features? Since it resembles games, is it possible that gamers (more likely to be men) will have advantaged access? Since it is open-ended, how should the virtual world space be designed to support learners? If learners and context are understood in greater detail, the chances for effective, consistent, accessible instruction and learning are improved.

In this chapter, the first phase of the instructional design process is explored. While the identification of learning objectives is a crucial task, the primary attention will be on the influence of learner characteristics and the selection of learning context on instructional design. Through research data and a review of literature, considerations are shared for analysis of learners and contexts in this unique environment. If educators know which characteristics to identify, they can take advantage of the technology's promises, remove barriers before they are created, and design powerful instruction to support learners. The remainder of the chapter is organized by (a) a review of relevant literature, (b) description of the research data, (c) identification and discussion of the four learner characteristics, and (d) conclusion.

Review of Literature

This review of literature concerns virtual world instructional design, particularly the analysis phase. While only a few articles specifically address instructional design in virtual worlds, other articles suggest underlying principles that may inform instructional design. Gaps and limitations are explored.

For the articles that addressed instructional design in virtual worlds, typical principles were identified. For instance, Wang and Hsu (2009) prompt educators to consider their target learners and assess their needs. Aspects like content knowledge, technical affordances, and individual motivation are all relevant. They also recommend gauging students' prior experience with virtual worlds, in order to help determine background knowledge and motivation in this setting. Since none of their participants had prior experience with Second Life®, it influenced the design of activities, focusing more on supporting them to actively participate and interact. Mayrath, Traphagan, Heikes, and Trivedi (2009) also recommend gauging existing Second Life® skills because it helps educators design activities around them. Students in their class enjoyed the virtual world activity if it existed within their technical skills and abilities. deFreitas, Rebolledo-Mendez, Liarokapis, Magoulas, and Poulovassilis (2010) recommend matching activities with learner specifics, such as competencies. Mayrath et al. (2009) mention that some students excelled at building in Second Life® right away, while others did not. A deeper understanding of learner characteristics may help educators predict which students are likely to technically excel in virtual worlds.

Personal expectations about the virtual world impact the degree of participation as well. For instance, deFreitas et al. (2010) found that gamers were accustomed to high quality of graphics. The virtual world did not meet their expectations, resulting in a negative impact on participation and learning. Not explored in the literature, women may be more likely to avoid social interactions in the virtual world (Dumitrica & Gaden, 2009; O'Connor, 2009). Sometimes women report being harassed in the virtual space (Collins, personal communication; Taylor, 2008). Still, a common theme in these studies is that students prefer socially interactive activities over individual ones. For example, students in Mayrath et al.'s (2009) study preferred role-play activities over building activities because of the level of social interaction experienced.

Not surprisingly, support emerged as a theme in the literature. Wang and Hsu (2009) emphasize the importance of multiple kinds of support. While technical support emerged in their study, they also supported students to use the communication tools and actively participate in Second Life®. The instructor designed a sequence of activities to support students to gain competence in these areas.

Learner characteristics inform the design of virtual world learning context. Mayrath et al. (2009) suggest that if learners are new to Second Life®, the activities can be initially simple and gradually grow more technically complex. For instance, role-play activities are technically simpler than building activities, so it may support novices to begin there. In addition, the real world context cannot be ignored, as learners are always situated there.

While the existing literature proposes implications, there are still questions to pursue. First, only a few articles specifically focused on instructional design in virtual worlds. While some characteristics have emerged such as technical skill, more research needs to be conducted on analyzing learners and contexts.

For instance, gender and gaming experience are factors that are hinted at, but not fully explored. It would be helpful to be better able to identify students who may have a higher likelihood of harboring negative personal expectations about virtual worlds. In addition, few studies acknowledge the full context of the user, namely the real world location. This omission is problematic and may not capture the complexity of the experience. In a classroom, surely the physical presence of peers will influence how students construct their avatars and interact with others in the virtual world environment. It is important to better understand how these contexts shift in order to better support students as they negotiate between the two.

Keeping in mind trends about gaming, no studies have specifically documented men and women in a virtual world for education. For example, Edirisingha, Nie, Pluciennik, and Young (2009) explored the experiences of college students in Second Life®, but no mention was made concerning gender. In the case of a female student who wanted to run away from a virtual stranger, they explained that she was a "newbie" and just coming to terms with her own virtual identity. While this could certainly be a factor, as literature does support it, this interpretation alone ignores the larger context of this particular student who has lived a lifetime of gendered identity.

The research data explained in the following section aim to address some of these gaps and limitations concerning learner characteristics and learning contexts in virtual worlds.

Research Data

In addition to a consideration of the literature, identification of learner characteristics and contexts largely stems from a two-phase research study conducted by the author. Participants were drawn from two face-to-face sections of an undergraduate course called "Communication and Technology," taught by the same teacher at a large midwestern university. In both sections, Second Life® was selected to enhance course material and address learning objectives. The main purpose of using Second Life® was to explore theories of communication exhibited outside of the classroom walls and to experience how communication is influenced through innovative applications such as virtual worlds. The two phases, including research designs, methods, and data analysis are described below.

Phase One

There were a total of 21 participants, including 13 women and 8 men. These students were unaware of the virtual world component before enrolling in the class. Students met in a computer lab to use Second Life® for weekly class activities, most which occurred in the university's private space (called "an island"), which largely resembled the real campus. First, there was a basic orientation to Second Life®, in which topics such as avatar customization and navigation were addressed by an expert in the computer lab. Students also customized dorm rooms they shared with others on the virtual campus. Regarding course content, students explored areas and interacted with others outside of the university's island with the purpose of observing and analyzing instances of communication. For the last session, they interacted with a guest speaker in the lecture hall on the island. Students' experiences were documented by the snapshots they took in Second Life®, along with blogs on the class website.

A qualitative stance was adopted, since the intention was to identify emerging themes from the data. The main objective of this phase was simply to better understand how college students used Second Life® to interact and learn in an educational setting. Multiple sources of data were collected to account for what was happening in the virtual world and the physical classroom. A survey was distributed to collect demographic information such as age, gender, and previous experience with games and Second Life®. Five observations were conducted in the computer lab. A total of 82 blog entries were collected, with the teacher providing a specific prompt for reflection. From the pool of students who consented to being interviewed at the end of the course, three women and one man were selected at convenience. The interview addressed areas like technical skill, assignments, and assessment of virtual worlds for learning.

Regarding analysis, grounded theory techniques were employed (Corbin & Strauss, 2008). The data were open coded at the time of collection, which informed the interview questions. Two demographic factors dramatically emerged as significant in virtual world learning: gender and personal gaming experience. There were disparities in the virtual world experience, concerning women in particular. The design and development of the course in Phase Two was influenced by these findings in Phase One.

Phase Two

In this phase that occurred the following year, 14 women and 13 men agreed to participate. Unlike the previous section, Second Life® was used for three consecutive sessions instead of weekly. The teacher's selection of activities was influenced by the findings from Phase One. Along with a basic orientation to the virtual world, there was a collaborative scavenger hunt and a traditional classroom meeting with three distanced guest speakers. The design of the island included clearer navigation and a shop intended for avatar customization. Students were also given a list of landmarks, so they could travel (teleport) to teacher-selected spaces in Second Life®.

Since women's experiences and gaming experience emerged as areas of concern in Phase One, the guiding question concerned how women negotiated their identities and interacted with others in a Second Life® learning community. Instead of an open-ended qualitative focus, a relational stance was used to better understand how women related to their contexts. Although the focus was on women, men were also included in the study as they were a factor in the class that cannot be separated from the context. To gauge personal gaming experience, a more comprehensive demographic survey was developed and distributed, inquiring about lifelong experience and attitudes about games and virtual worlds. Along with observations of each class, students also published one blog related to their Second Life® experiences. From the women participants, a sample was selected that represented a range of personal gaming experiences, since this also emerged as significant in Phase One. From this range, four women were interviewed at the beginning and end of the course.

Interviews were analyzed using a relational tool called the Listening Guide. Interviews are transcribed and "listened to" from multiple perspectives such as plot, self, themes, and interaction of themes (Raider-Roth, 2005). It is important to acknowledge the researcher's social position within the context of the study and the larger context of the world (Clarke, 2006). For instance, I exist not only as a researcher, but a person—more specifically a White, young, middle-class American heterosexual woman student who has a penchant for virtual worlds. Because of these overlapping affiliations, I am personally grounded in particular contexts that will inevitably affect how I select and interpret the data. The data that emerges from this qualitative, relational study is acknowledged and accepted as subjective.

Learning Characteristics

Based on research data and previous literature, four learner characteristics emerge as critical to identify before designing and developing instruction in a virtual world. The characteristics are: (a) technical skill in virtual worlds; (b) beliefs about the nature of the virtual world; (c) personal gaming experience; and (d) gender. In this section, each characteristic will be addressed, supported by examples from research and literature. Implications about the design of the learning context are considered and practical suggestions are proposed to design instruction that supports all learners in virtual worlds.

Technical Skill in Virtual Worlds

Virtual worlds are technically more complex than other kinds of social media. The learning curve required for Second Life® has been documented by many (Collins, personal communication; Mayrath et al., 2009; Sanchez, 2007). One consistent theme in the literature is that learners often report technical difficulties when participating in Second Life®, resulting in frustration (Mayrath et al., 2009; Sanchez, 2007). In this study, one's technical skill regarding virtual worlds significantly impacted participation in critical areas including avatar customization, interaction, and agency.

Concerning avatar customization, Falloon (2010) concluded that when students could project personal and social identity through avatar appearance, they perceived more agency. In Second Life®, there are many features to customize, such as body, clothes, and accessories. In this study, students who could not technically customize their avatars experienced diminished feelings of identity. For instance, Jalen wanted to change her avatar's strapless shirt to something she would typically wear on campus, but she did not have confidence in her ability to do so; "I have something on and it's showing up, so I'm just gonna leave it." As Chelsea explains, "I want them [peers] to see a reflection of me." For some, technical skill prevented this. Less technical competence also affected perception of co-presence. For instance, when Sasha accidentally removed her avatar's pants and did not know how to reattach them, she isolated her avatar from the rest of the group (Figure 1.1). This supports the idea that one must feel control over the avatar in order to feel agency in the environment (Kennedy, 2006; Taylor, 2006). Not feeling personally represented by one's avatar significantly affects the quality of learning and interaction in virtual world activities.

Similar to the results of Mayrath et al. (2009), building and shaping content was considered difficult for most students. Some could not interact with objects, such as media or note cards, which impacted learning. The ability to customize the personal space of the dorm room was also affected. While some students had very personalized rooms in which peers visited often, others' rooms were bare because they did not know how to collect or edit objects. This inability affects presence and co-presence.

Navigation and interaction is also impacted by technical skill. To fully participate in learning activities, one must move her avatar throughout the virtual space and travel ("teleport") to other areas. Some students experienced problems with knowing where their avatars were located, producing feelings of disorientation. During the scavenger hunt, in which student pairs collected objects in Second Life®, some had difficulties keeping up with their partners. Ramona notes the complexity of communicating with her partner, navigating through the space, and actively participating in the activity. Chelsea recalls the challenge of multiple channels of communication; "I didn't know how to *fly*, I didn't know how to *land*. I would be trying to ask him a question but then he also would be sending me messages like, 'I'm going here' and he'd be gone. But I still don't know what's going on!" This stands in contrast to technically skilled Marla who says, "It was pretty simple to navigate, it's not really hard to figure out what we are supposed to be doing." Concurrent with the findings of Mayrath et al. (2009), some learners caught on more quickly than others.

The technical abilities of students must be considered in the design of the learning context in virtual worlds. Technical support must be offered in each session, in the computer lab and "in-world" as well. In the second section,

FIGURE 1.1 Technical difficulties with the avatar potentially cause social embarrassment.

a paper-based tutorial was distributed containing screen shots of the virtual world, which helped students with the basics. An interactive tutorial "in-world" also allows students to review the basics on their own as many times as they need. In addition, scaffolds can support all students. For example, Marla, who was technically skilled, shares, "Second Life® gave you way too many options like, how far I want my eyes apart. Really, is that necessary? I started getting really tired, it's not really easy." It is helpful to offer some already-made avatars in which students can make simple modifications. Concerning navigation, the second section was given landmarks to certain areas in their inventories, which simplified traveling. Mary shares, "Once you figure out how to navigate, I felt more comfortable in Second Life®."

Beliefs of Nature of the Virtual World

Since virtual worlds are places and people are represented by bodies, it elicits a complex experience. While students' technical skills are frequently mentioned in literature, a factor that is often omitted is students' perceptions of the virtual world which are likely to influence how they will participate and learn in this environment (deFreitas et al., 2010). In the study, there was a wide variation in the ways that students perceived Second Life®. This strongly affected how they participated, projected identity, and interacted.

Some students, particularly those new to virtual worlds and games, harbored hesitancies in participating in the virtual world. Unlike other social media, Second Life® was often compared to the real world. Chelsea writes in her first blog, "I was skeptical when I heard we were going to be going into Second Life®. My first thought was, why wasn't real life good enough?" Most hesitations concerned the avatar-mediated social interactions they expected to encounter. Chelsea shares, "This is kind of weird … I feel, use Skype or something and actually see their faces, but they choose to use avatars, which I'm still trying to figure out." Bayne (2008) suggests that the emotional hesitations often experienced in virtual worlds are due to the "peculiar commingling between the familiar and the unfamiliar … a crisis of the proper and natural" (p. 198). Jalen explains, "You can dress however you want, talk to people, I mean you can create these identities that no one would ever know." Mary says, "When you're behind that avatar, you're not really yourself, you know? Because you're in the computer and you're a different character …" Not surprisingly, students with this view of avatars were often less connected to their own avatar and were less likely to interact with others.

Because virtual worlds are places inhabited by people, social and cultural practices exist. While many real world social practices are emulated in a virtual world (avatars maintaining personal distance from each other, for example), there are some major differences. Boellstorff (2008) explains, "Actual world sociality cannot explain virtual world sociality … it develops on its own terms" (p. 63). In some cases, students expressed an interest in forging social connections with others, but did not know how to establish relations. For instance, during Jalen's visit to an island, she was "sad" that no one talked to her, explaining, "I felt uneasy about approaching another avatar and making conversation because I didn't really know what to talk about. In real life, it seems a lot easier to make small talk." Georgina shared, "I would feel uncomfortable just flying up to someone who I do not know and have a random conversation with them." While having "random conversations" with people in the real world is not typical, it is accepted and expected in the virtual world.

For students less familiar with virtual settings, virtual world interactions were usually interpreted the way they would be if they occurred in the real world. When interactions closely resembled the social context of desirable real world interactions, most reported feeling more immersed and empowered in the environment. For instance, Chelsea and Ramona both view the virtual class session as a highlight, in part because they were familiar with the avatars in the space and knew the social norms of the classroom. They preferred to interact with avatars who they knew in real life, especially with avatars that looked like their real counterparts. Real modes of communication like voice were interpreted as a direct link to the person's real life identity. Ramona finds that voices brought a "human aspect to a virtual world" and was more "personal" and "meaningful." Uma adds, "SL became a new place to me and seemed more real when voice was added." Carr, Oliver, and Burn (2008) found that voice is a tool for self-disclosure and promotes trust.

In addition, the more realistic the environment was, the more comfortable novices were. When Jalen describes her visit to a fantastical place in Second Life®, she says, "My initial reaction was a little uneasy. It looked very fairytale-ish, and I thought I would meet a lot of weird people." Reflecting on the university space, Sasha explains, "It's more realistic when it's on campus." While Chelsea was comfortable on campus, she became anxious when she explored houses in Second Life®, fearing that she would "get caught and really be in trouble." In Second Life®, it is socially acceptable to explore others' homes, but since Chelsea is applying real world norms to this situation, she feels distress.

It is tempting to assume that students will quickly "get" virtual worlds, much as the "get" other kinds of social media. However, learning the culture and social practices of the virtual world is much like learning the culture of another land. My research, along with literature, suggests that since the nature of virtual worlds is unique to both social media and MMORPGs, it is important to acknowledge this in the beginning. How do the students conceive the term "virtual world"? Is an avatar a user representation or a character? Ramona conceives Second Life® in the first interview, "I think it's like a game where you can create a character and like have it do things but that's really all I know about it." It is important for the educator to gauge these perceptions before virtual world activity commences. During instruction, student-composed blogs or journals help capture unspoken perceptions and beliefs about the virtual world, and also helps develop their personal understanding. Harriet, who initially said that Second Life® "rubs me the wrong way," wrote in her last blog, "I suppose that in writing this blog, I have now found the good in SL, to an extent."

It also helpful to introduce students to the culture of the virtual world. For example, Jalen was unsure what to discuss and how to approach others. This subject can be addressed in the classroom before it happens. Better understanding of these social practices will give the students more confidence to act within the virtual world. It will also help them interpret the interactions more accurately. Engaging in a role play scenario with trusted classmates may help facilitate this practice. Time and practice support technical competence and knowledge of virtual world norms, so one visit to the virtual world is not likely to be sufficient (Dumitrica & Gaden, 2009; O'Connor, 2009). For instance, Chelsea explains in her final interview that she now understands why people use virtual worlds; "It is more personal to have your own person there." Students that are already familiar with virtual worlds may not need this amount of time to develop understanding.

Personal Characteristics: Gaming Experience and Gender

Two personal characteristics emerged as significant in influencing technical skill and beliefs of the virtual world: personal gaming experience and gender. These two are related, in that men tend to have more gaming experience. In both phases of this study, 100% of men but only around 16% of women had substantial gaming experience. This supports the statistics found in many gaming studies. While gender alone does not determine how students will fare in Second Life®, there is a relationship with games that cannot be overlooked.

Students with substantial gaming experience exhibited high technical skill in Second Life®. Avatar customization, navigation, and interaction were not an issue technically. While this is a positive, they often had extra time waiting for others to catch up. This led to "goofing off" in the virtual world. They also were not threatened or unsure of the nature of the virtual world, and picked up the cultural practices quickly. Familiar spaces, like the classroom or campus, did not support them as much. Marla complains, "We didn't do much, we mostly stayed on campus. I can walk around in real life. The classroom is kind of boring because you just sit and listen." Regarding dorm rooms, Jon said, "At first, I put in a bed. Then I thought, why am I doing this? I can do this in real life." Gamers were more interested in challenging and experimenting with social norms. In contrast, non-gamers perceived the fantastical items as not real enough. For example, customizing typical dorm rooms makes Lindsey feel "at home" and a place she can call "her own."

While privileged in technical access, gamers did not have an advantage in an educational setting. They were unfamiliar with an environment that resembled a game but that did not have built-in objectives. They were also not used to using an environment similar to a game in an educational rather than a personal setting. While non-gamers experienced issues with technical skill, they did not have the prior experience of games to influence their conception of Second Life®. Some non-gamers grasped the potential of it, such as Ramona who explains, "It's a virtual community where you can be someone you decide to create ... I understand you can even get jobs here." Chelsea has the idea of revisiting real places in Second Life®: "I was thinking even like going in Second Life® to visit Costa Rica, like that would be so fun to see the virtual places of where I've actually been."

Gender emerges as an important element mainly due to the gendered nature of avatars. Because the women in the two sections all customized their avatars as women, they judged their interactions as a woman would in the "real world." Since the majority of the women were not familiar with the gaming context, they felt like women in a strange place (Dumitrica & Gaden, 2009). When interactions were judged as atypical or undesirable by real world standards, some of the women reported distressing psychological conditions such as anxiety, avoidance, and intimidation. Namely, the majority of interactions with strangers were met with some element of discomfort. This is exemplified in Ashley's blog, in which she describes her interpretations of her independent experience in Second Life®:

> I came to a bridge with a creepy looking avatar standing at the other end of bridge. I was pretty intimidated by his appearance (yes, I realize he is made up) but anyone who looked the way he did in real life, I would be sketchy of as well. I did not approach him and talk to him, but I did manage to get him included in a snapshot I took of me, the bridge, and creepy avatar man [Figure 1.2].

Ashley's selection of words throughout this story reveals her gendered experience of this interaction, which Dumitrica and Gaden (2009) describe as "a discomfort and a fear that was both familiar and less so …" (p. 10). While women gamers reported less troubling feelings, it is critical to keep in mind that the majority of women students are likely to not have extensive gaming experience.

FIGURE 1.2 Applying real world social norms to virtual interactions can produce "real" distress.

Conclusion: Implications for Practice

Before designing instruction in a virtual world, it is important to gauge students' technical abilities, beliefs of the nature of the virtual world, personal gaming experience, and gender. Having a better understanding of these characteristics helps an educator prepare learners and helps them design a suitable context and scope of activities. In this section, some implications are offered about collecting information of these characteristics and strategies and decisions to make.

A comprehensive survey can capture a lot of information on a learner's technical skill in virtual worlds, beliefs, gaming experience, and gender. For the first course section in this study, a survey item was posed: "Do you have previous experience with Second Life?®" This question proved insufficient to gauge ability or experience, since some explained later they had only used it once. Some contextual factors that are critical to identify include how long they have used it, how often they participate, who they participate with, and what they do while they are there. This also applies to gaming experience. In line with previous gaming research, while the majority of the women in the study participated in games at some point, they tended to play games that did not resemble Second Life®, played less often than men, and often played individually. Knowing these factors ahead of time can help an educator prepare students for the unique and complex interaction that virtual world learning requires.

Virtual world beliefs can also be gauged through a survey. For example, one of the questions asked students to select words they associated with gaming, such as exciting, scary, and time consuming. The answers can help an educator anticipate the initial reaction to virtual worlds and open up an opportunity for group discussion. As stated before, having students compose blogs to document their virtual world experiences serves to make their thinking and beliefs visible to others.

There are many implication of the selection of learning contexts. The main suggestion is to provide a range of options for learners to choose, based on their individual skill, beliefs and experience. Scaffolding learners with avatar customization and navigation can guide everyone, but helps novices in particular. Although virtual worlds afford contexts that are impractical in a traditional classroom, this study suggests that designing familiar spaces may support novices. However, those with more gaming experience may need to be challenged with more complex, "unusual" environments. If they are able to achieve the learning objectives in either kind of space, it is important to let them choose. It is also helpful to include a range of communication options, including voice, for those who prefer it.

It is important to note that as a user spends more time in the virtual world, they build competence in technical ability and social expectations. Concurrent with the findings of Mayrath et al. (2009), it is helpful to structure activities carefully to support that progression. At first, tasks can be smaller and stay within the familiar spaces of campus with familiar people, and then steadily increased to the public areas of the virtual world. As students incrementally gain both technical and worldly social competence, they will likely feel more confident in exploring unfamiliar places and engaging in new situations. Therefore, more complex visits can be envisioned and forged with each class session. It is also important to be aware of the real life context of the learners. If they access a virtual world together in a computer lab, they can receive more technical support. However, it may distract them from the true immersive experience a virtual world can offer.

In conclusion, the complexity of virtual worlds offers both unique advantages and concerns. Although students may be skilled with some kinds of social media in their personal lives, it does not automatically mean they will be effective learners in virtual worlds. While instructional design principles still apply such as gauging learner characteristics and selecting learner contexts, the nature of virtual worlds complicate the decisions a designer must make. This research indicates that women may be less inclined to engage with virtual worlds. While we live in an era where technologies are seen as equal access, it is still critical to acknowledge that video gaming continues to be a gendered practice (Jenkins & Cassell, 2008). It is likely that there will be some students who are novices to virtual worlds and games, and some who are more experienced. Designing a variety of spaces and activities for students to engage is important to support all learners.

References

Bayne, S. (2008). Uncanny spaces for higher education: Teaching and learning in virtual worlds. *ALT-J: Research in Learning Technology, 16*(3), 197–205.

Boellstorff, T. (2008). *Coming of age in Second Life: An anthropologist explores the virtually human.* Princeton, NJ: Princeton University Press.

boyd, d. (2007). Why youth (heart) social network sites: The role of networked publics in teenage social life. In D. Buckingham (Ed.), *MacArthur Foundation Series on Digital Learning – Youth, identity, and digital media volume* (pp. 119-142). Cambridge, MA: MIT Press.

Carr, D. (2005). Contexts, gaming pleasures, and gendered preferences. *Simulation & Gaming, 36*, 464–482.

Carr, D., Oliver, M., & Burn, A. (2008, November). *Learning, teaching, and ambiguity in virtual worlds.* Paper presented at the Second Life ReLive08 Conference, London.

Clarke, A. E. (2006). Feminisms, grounded theory, and situational analysis. In S. Hesse-Biber (Ed.), *Handbook of feminist research: Theory and praxis* (pp. 345–370). Thousand Oaks, CA: Sage.

Colby, R. (2010, March). *Research agents in the World of Warcraft.* Paper presented at the Conference on College Composition and Communication, Louisville, KY.

Corbin, J. M., & Strauss, A. L. (2008). *Basics of qualitative research: Techniques and procedures for developing grounded theory* (3rd ed.). Thousand Oaks: Sage.

deFreitas, S., Rebolledo-Mendez, G., Liarokapis, F., Magoulas, G., & Poulovassilis, A. (2010). Learning as immersive experiences: Using the four-dimensional framework for designing and evaluating immersive learning experiences in a virtual world. *British Journal of Educational Technology, 41*, 69–85.

Dieterle, E., & Clarke, J. (2009). Multi-user virtual environments for teaching and learning. In M. Pagani (Ed.), *Encyclopedia of multimedia technology and networking* (2nd ed., Vol. II, pp. 1033–1041). Hershey, PA: Information Science Reference.

Dumitrica, D., & Gaden, G. (2009). Knee-high boots and six-pack abs: Autoethnographic reflections on gender and technology in Second Life. *Journal of Virtual Worlds Research, 1*(3), 3–22.

Edirisingha, P., Nie, M., Pluciennik, M., & Young, R. (2009). Socialisation for learning at a distance in a 3-D multi-user virtual environment. *British Journal of Educational Technology, 40*, 458–479.

Falloon, G. (2010). Using avatars and virtual environments in learning: What do they have to offer? *British Journal of Educational Technology, 41*(1), 108–122.

Gee, J. P. (2007). *What video games have to teach us about learning and literacy.* New York: Palgrave Macmillan.

Jarmon, L. (2009). An ecology of embodied interaction: Pedagogy and homo virtualis. *Journal of Virtual Worlds Research, 2*(1), 3–9.

Jenkins, H., & Cassell, J. (2008). From quake grrls to desperate housewives: A decade of gender and computer games. In Y. B. Kafai, C. Heeter, J. Denner, & J. Y. Sun, (Eds.), *Beyond Barbie and mortal kombat: New perspectives on gender and gaming* (pp. 5–20). Cambridge, MA: MIT Press.

Kaplan, A., & Haenlein, M. (2010). Users of the world, unite! The challenges and opportunities of social media. *Business Horizons, 53*(1), 59–68.

Kennedy, H. (2006). Illegitimate, monstrous and out there: Female Quake players and inappropriate pleasures. In J. Hollows & R. Moseley (Eds.), *Feminism in popular culture* (pp. 183–202). Oxford, UK: Berg.

Lenhart, A., Jones, S., & Macgill, A. R. (2008). *Adults and video games.* Retrieved from http://www.pewinternet.org/Reports/2008/Adults-and-Video-Games.aspx

Lenhart, A., Kahne, J., Middaugh, E., Macgill, A. R., Evans, C., & Vitak, V. (2008). *Teens, video games, and civics.* Retrieved from http://pewinternet.org/Reports/2008/TeensVideo-Games-and-Civics.aspx

Mayrath, M. C., Traphagan, T., Heikes, E. J., & Trivedi, A. (2009). Instructional design best practices for Second Life: A case study from a college-level English course. *Interactive Learning Environments, 19*(2), 125–142.

O'Connor, E. (2009). Instructional and design elements that support effective use of virtual worlds: What graduate student work reveals about Second Life. *Journal of Educational Technology Systems, 38*, 213–234.

Raider-Roth, M. B. (2005). *Trusting what you know: The high stakes of classroom relationships.* San Francisco: Jossey-Bass.

Sanchez, J. (2007, June). *A sociotechnical analysis of Second Life in an undergraduate English course.* Paper presented at the World Conference on Educational Multimedia, Hypermedia and Telecommunications 2007, Chesapeake, Virginia. Retrieved on January 21, 2009, from http://research.educatorscoop.org/ed-media.htm

Second Life. (n.d.). Available from http://www.secondlife.com

Taylor, T. L. (2006). Play between worlds: Exploring online game culture. Cambridge, MA: MIT Press.

Taylor, T. L. (2008). Becoming a player: Networks, structure, and imagined futures. In Y. B. Kafai, C. Heeter, J. Denner, & J. Y. Sun (Eds.), *Beyond Barbie and Mortal Kombat: New perspectives on gender and gaming* (pp. 51–66). Cambridge, MA: MIT Press.

Wang, S. K., & Hsu, H. Y. (2009). Using the ADDIE model to design Second Life® activities for online learners. *Tech Trends, 53*(6), 76–81.

Williams, D., Consalvo, M., Caplan, S., & Yee, N. (2008). Looking for gender: Gender roles and behaviors among online gamers. *Journal of Communication, 59*, 700–725.

2

BLURRING THE LINES

Teacher Insights on the Pitfalls and Possibilities of Incorporating Online Social Media into Instructional Design

Thomas Highley and Kay Kyeong-Ju Seo

Introduction

Over the years, classroom teachers have seen the rise and fall of a number of educational initiatives that promised to remake public schools. Most recently, the incorporation of Web 2.0 programs and online social media has emerged as the most promising tool for reinventing public education. These interactive technologies have promised to bridge the gap between home and schools, raise academic performance, and level the playing field for all students, regardless of ethnicity or income level (The New London Group, 1996). Recent research supports the stance that these tools have the potential to enhance literacy and learning across diverse student populations, calling for the use of interactive social media as a means of preparing students for the 21st century (Greenhow, Hughes, & Robelia, 2009).

The assumption that digital media is the answer to the many problems facing schools is worthy of skepticism. Too often, we have counted on new educational initiatives to solve complex educational problems, ignoring their place in instructional designs. As a result, many of these programs fail. Without a thorough analysis of instructional problems and an adequate instructional design, digital learning initiatives may be doomed to join past programs on the educational scrapheap.

Millennials and the Potential of Social Media

Over the past 10 years, rapid growth has radically changed the way we interact with the Internet and with each other. Today, the Internet is production oriented, emphasizing interactive, collective modes of online collaboration and creation. This type of Web 2.0 interaction reflects a movement away from proprietary conceptions of web content. However, generational differences may impact our adoption of this production mindset.

Young learners of the new millennium embrace these newer modes of online communication more readily than their elders. Many Millennials have grown up with interactive programs such as Facebook®, Twitter®, and MySpace®, identifying them as the social tool of choice. Of course, this adoption is not homogenous across populations. Poverty affects the access to and frequency with which some young people access these online communities (Hargittai, 2010; Martin & Robinson, 2007).

There is a gap between older and younger users of digital media. In fact, educational consultant Marc Prensky (2009) coined two descriptive labels to address this division. Prensky identifies Millennials as "digital natives," due to their early and constant exposure to digital media. Older users are assigned the less glamorous distinction of "digital immigrant," reflecting their late arrival to digital shores. Though these labels have since been reframed, a clear generational gap exists influencing the usage of digital tools.

Youth affinity for online networking has attracted the attention of big business and social media sites have become an avenue for marketing products and services. Corporations carry Facebook connections on their websites, but marketing to these audiences is becoming ever more subtle. Facebook advertising has become adaptive, changing to match the content of online posts.

Use of online social media in education seems a logical next step. This assumption is supported by research. In several studies, rich experiences with online social networking promised improved educational achievement, student engagement, and collaboration (Greenhow & Robelia, 2009).

However, although well-designed research studies support the incorporation of social media, few educators have blended online social media into their instructional planning (Greenhow, Walker, & Kim, 2010; Tan, & Libo, 2009; Warschauer, 2007). So, why do teachers resist?

One might assume that age is a factor. However, teacher resistance is not solely dependent on age. Some pre-service teachers with backgrounds rich in social media report they do not see the benefit of using online social media in their classrooms (Lei, 2009). This was supported in a recent survey of 30 pre-service teachers at the University of Cincinnati. After developing educational online social media sites for use within their lesson plans, most students noted that they did not think they would use social media in their own teaching. This raises some important questions regarding the role of online social media in instructional design.

Incorporating Social Media into Instructional Design

Technology implementation in schools is generally ill planned. Spurred by promises of quick results, commercial and web-based programs are quickly incorporated, ignoring the analysis of learners, educational constraints, or timelines (Wang & Hsu, 2009). It is essential for educators to view use of digital tools within instructional design frameworks.

The analysis phase is most vital in designing classroom instruction. Considering the needs and characteristics of the learner, as well as the skills and knowledge necessary for learning tasks, provides a foundation for the instructional goal. Analysis of the instructional goal should include assessment of the learning domains (intellectual, psychomotor, verbal, and attitudinal) and the skills relevant to those domains (Peterson, 2003, p. 229). The constraints and contexts surrounding the instruction and performance settings must also be considered. Further, a needs analysis should assess the content of learners' knowledge, what they want to learn, and why they need to learn it (Wang & Hsu, 2009, p. 79).

To better understand the teacher's planning process when incorporating online social media, interviews were conducted with several Midwest public school educators. Their responses regarding planning for and implementing online social media illustrate the potential benefits of online social media, while highlighting the importance of analysis in instructional design.

Methods

In planning for online social media use, several questions were considered. First, what instructional problems lend themselves to online interaction? Second, what skills and understandings are essential to student use of online social media? Third, what constraints or limitations hinder online social media integration?

Initially, interview questions were generated and a mass recruitment email sent to several suburban school districts in the Midwest. This geographic area was chosen based on the researcher's knowledge of educational standards in the Midwest and the researcher's practitioner status. This status facilitated the recruitment of teaching professionals and encouraged participant responses.

Inclusion criteria included five or more years of service teaching in public schools, as well as experience with Web 2.0 and online social media in the classroom. Based on these criteria, three teachers were chosen from two separate districts. Participants were provided a list of questions ahead of time. Interviews were conducted in teacher classrooms during planning periods, where they were video recorded and later transcribed.

After transcription, data was open coded and analyzed, using an inductive analysis model. This model helped identify salient themes from the contextualized phenomenon of planning for and implementing online social media in the classroom by close analysis of qualitative data (Hatch, 2002). After analysis, the interviews were then crystallized into a narrative format. Summaries of these interviews are provided below, followed by a discussion of salient trends.

Findings

Alicia: Exploring World Literature with Online Social Media

Background. Alicia has taught high school English for 13 years in the same high school she attended as a student. She considers herself a lifelong learner and values new innovations in teaching. With the development of online social networks, Alicia was eager to pull this media into the classroom. Alicia stated, "A teacher has to constantly be willing to adapt to the times … and meet students where they live."

Alicia teaches in a technology rich classroom. Net books are available for student use, however, the computers are the property of the school district, which permitted individual teachers to acquire them through a lengthy and competitive application process; Alicia's passion for educational innovation was rewarded with a grant that funded the purchase.

Alicia's passion for technology is personal, as well professional. "I find that the things that get my attention also get the attention of my students. Initially, I tried using wikis, but I don't use that anymore. I was, however, amazed at how students responded to the online collaboration wiki use provided. I immediately had kids contributing who would have otherwise been quiet in class." This early work was beneficial in scaffolding for use of new online media. "The wikis were exciting to create, but now I use more current online social media, like Twitter, Skype, and Ning."

Alicia uses her school Ning® site as a place for class collaboration. Much like Facebook, Ning users can add videos, forums, blogs, photos, etc. This familiarity is crucial for the Facebook generation, creating a digital bridge between the home and the classroom.

As mentioned previously, Alicia uses Web 2.0 technologies to personally connect with the world, using Twitter daily. This program has become increasingly important as a teaching tool. Alicia's Twitter feed is connected to her school Ning site. Tweeting each morning, Alicia comments on daily happenings for her classes. Alicia usually hears from her students throughout the day on Twitter, occasionally tweeting back. "I want to provide an online environment where students can feel competent and collaborative. I read all of their posts, and sometimes respond to their Twitter discussions."

Alicia's Tweets are public, and she often gets feedback from other teachers, not just locally, but internationally, as well. "Several teachers from other countries have been following my Tweets for a while. I get a lot from their input, especially for my world literature class." Alicia's participation in professional online learning networks has enriched her practice and established connections with teachers around the globe.

Planning and Implementation. Alicia described her lesson planning process as organic and interwoven with online social media. Reflecting aspects of the

Understanding by Design process of Wiggins and McTigue, Alicia starts planning with state standards in mind, establishing essential questions and understandings, working backwards to incorporate online social media into her lessons. A good example of this technique is evident in her unit planning for the play *Master Harold and the Boys*.

Alicia teaches a world literature course for high school seniors. Collaborating with a senior world history teacher, they identified connections in the standards for both 12th grade literature and 12th grade world history under the theme, *Voices of the Young*. "This unit was based on the objectives for the course, which are intended to make connections between world literature and the student's world through writing and discussions. I use online social media to explore student connections to the content."

Alicia began her study of the play *Master Harold and the Boys* the day after Martin Luther King Day. After viewing Martin Luther King's "I Have a Dream" speech, a class discussion developed regarding global racism. Alicia next posed the driving question, "Has King's dream been realized?" Using journaling, small group sharing, and large group discussion, relevant questions were developed for the Ning site. "It was important that this be a very organic discussion. From our discussion of Dr. King, the Ning site asked for examples of the sort of racial issues we deal with here at school." The unifying theme provided context and relevance for the online discussions that followed.

This led to a focus on South African Apartheid, which is central to the play. Online sources were used to investigate the background of the play's author, Athol Fugard. Fugard's experience as a young South African living under Apartheid was essential to the study. "This not only provided context for reading, but tied into the universal theme of our unit, *Voices of the Young*. At this point, we were reading and watching scenes from the play *Master Harold* and using the Ning to discuss the issues and events."

Alicia's Ning was an arena for correspondence. Students posted two questions daily regarding relevant issues from the reading and also responded. Alicia noted that the tone of classroom responses is somewhat different from informal online exchanges. "There is a distinction between purely social and academic language. Although Ning looks a lot like Facebook, it's really more of an edu-social network."

When posting, grammar and sentence structure are not initial concerns, but, when the ideas are developed into extended responses, revision for spelling and punctuation matter. Alicia uses online rubrics as a means of assessment. Informal online posts count as quiz grades and serve as prewritings for extended responses. All evaluation of written work is rubric based and all rubrics are posted on the Ning.

Alicia scaffolds student understanding by posting links to related content. In this unit, for example, she posted links to articles on Apartheid, a video link to an interview with Fugard, maps of South Africa, and other relevant resources. Sometimes, exploration of these resources was optional; sometimes required.

Regardless, evaluation rubrics clarified requirements. This sort of public, distributed, collective sharing replaces traditional closed forms of assessment. As Alicia noted, "The idea that students today would hand in work to a single source (the teacher) that would then just die in a folder is unfathomable to me."

For Alicia, posting online is only a part of the conversation; replies to postings are what drive online learning. "Students are required to respond to a number of posts. Sometimes I'll say 'read over everybody's postings and pick ten people to respond to.'" To facilitate discussions, Alicia uses a "validate and contribute" approach to online discussion. In this approach, responses to online comments must acknowledge the other person's point and then extend the discussion, making use of links, comments, and questions. "Responding to another writer's posting extends the discussion and builds reflection." Additionally, Alicia pulls in expertise from outside the classroom to participate on the Ning site. She encourages students to email working writers with their questions. "This shows that students have power. But the teacher still has an important role in helping facilitate more professional online writing."

A blurring of the lines emerges regarding the roles of teachers and students. "Students contact me all the time with links or videos or information from the Web that not only expands the knowledge of the class, but mine, as well." This sort of co-learning is inherent in use of online social media.

Obstacles and Limitations.   Although Alicia values the use of online social media in her classroom, she made it clear that she is not the norm. Repeatedly, Alicia noted that many teachers view the blurring effect regarding the roles of student and teacher as problematic. "There are some people who think that by utilizing these Web 2.0 tools, you may not be maintaining some level of propriety. Many teachers used to believe that use of online social media was pandering to the wasteful behavior of the students. Or worse, we were just trying to entertain them." These preconceptions have led to resistance from school staff and administration. "A lot of the early resistance was based on a negativity and belief that our job as teachers was to get them away from Internet distractions. Now, there is a fear that by using online social media to make these connections, we are blurring the lines between not just teacher and student, but home and school, as well. This may make some teachers uncomfortable about the student/teacher relationship." It is worth noting that the attempt to blur the lines between home and school, often referred to as "bridging the gap," has been endorsed in much of the research literature.

Even as the divisions between home and school become less distinct, some schools still block social media sites. Alicia noted that this sort of "protection" denies students much needed guidance: "Denying access to online social media is mostly fear based. But it is essential that we overcome this fear. As teachers, we should model with and for students how to contribute real insight in their online writing. Teachers can enrich online discussions. Without guidance, student will continue to post online static like, 'I just drank a Mountain Dew.' This type of writing does not add anything to the debate; it's draining it."

Benefits of Online Social Media in the Classroom.   Alicia's classroom is an excellent example of how integration of online social media can create relevant learning environments. However, it should be noted that the analysis phase seemed lacking in Alicia's planning. As online social media reframes the teacher role, planning for successful online interactions requires more robust analysis. According to Alicia, redefining teacher/student roles is a step in the right direction: "It is a charade to pretend that we as teachers have fuller access to information than our students. But I do feel we have such an important role in helping our students to think deeply." Still, a thorough learner analysis would create a more dependable design framework.

Terri: Authentic Encounters in Foreign Language through Online Social Media

Background.   For Terri, integrating online social media into her Spanish classroom is a natural step in her development as an educator. A 20-year veteran of both the middle school and high school, Terri has continually sought to incorporate relevant engagements. Like Alicia, Terri is always searching for more innovative practices for her classroom, and sees a close relationship between her students and herself. As she put it, "I need to be challenged and keep learning, as well."

Terri's interest in Web 2.0 technologies was sparked by a visit from educational technology guru Will Richardson. A vocal proponent of bridging the gap between students' home and school life, Richardson's focus on using digital media to connect schools with broader communities had a major impact on Terri. "I've always enjoyed technology and it was clear that this was the right time to start pursuing it in my teaching. I wanted to expose my students to communication that was more real; more authentic." Terri was especially excited about the opportunity to experience Spanish in its actual use: "The traditional Spanish classroom treats language as more isolated, rather than what you would find in a real dialogue. Using Web 2.0 tools allows students to experience Spanish as it's used in the real world."

Terri noted that she depends on some online tools more than others. "I've been doing this process for five years, so I know what tools work and what don't. I've pared down the programs that I use in class, like Ning and Voice-Thread®." Terri's Ning site is used for writing and responding to threaded discussions. Songs and videos are also incorporated into the Ning, as well as news from Spanish speaking countries. However, VoiceThread® is a favorite classroom tool, as its multimodal platform sparks engagement. On VoiceThread®, pictures are uploaded to the site, allowing for comments to be posted around the picture, either in print text, audio, or video formats. "I first had the students post a picture of themselves as little kids on VoiceThread®, which they then described." Terri appreciates the multi-modal aspect of the site. "What I love is the audio and video component to posting replies." Terri notes that the personal aspect of classroom use of social media is at the heart of its appeal. "The sharing component of social media is so valuable. Anyone can view the pictures, and I can see the response of the class immediately."

Terri uses other Web 2.0 and proprietary programs. "Flickr® is another great tool I use. We post images from the students to demonstrate vocabulary. Kids can post their pictures and other students can comment on the photo in Spanish, but it's much more authentic. It's their own family, and they are remembering things that happened and commenting on them. There is a sense of ownership in what they build into the class." This use provides a relevant bridge between home and school.

Planning and Implementation.   Terri noted that everything she plans for class, with or without online social media, is standards based: "There's not a single thing we do in here that deviates from the standards." Using the standards as a jumping off point, Terri's planning process is based on the development of three to five core activities in each lesson. "I try to include one speaking piece, at least, based on partners and conversation. I've been encouraging them to ask follow up questions to make the conversation authentic." However, Terri noted that partner interactions in Spanish can be difficult: "This is tough, because some students have a hard time carrying on a conversation in English."

For Terri, online social media has not really changed her planning process. "It has become second nature to include online social media as an aspect of class. And the use of online social media can be included at all phases of planning, depending on what you want to do in your lesson." As Terri pointed out, online social media broadens the audience for learning. "Face-to-face class time is very valuable, but the online environment provides a larger audience. In the childhood picture activity, everyone was conversing about the personal connection to the pictures. I think the more personal the content, the more the kids seem to relate to it." Terri views her lesson planning as a hybrid of online and in-class activity. "Just being online, we wouldn't get the oral practice we need. The online social media is important, but so is the interactive class time. It's a blend."

Planning for assessment with online social media is also varied. "I don't always evaluate everything online. It depends on the assignment." Further, Terri noted that offering choice in assessment and assignment is valuable for students.

Obstacles and Limitations.   Though Terri is an active user of Web 2.0 and online social media in her classroom, she highlighted several important considerations for planning. Surprisingly, overestimation of student abilities is one of them. "One false assumption I had was that all students would be able to jump right onto the online social media site and go. But, no. Even though this is the digital generation, students do not instantly make that transition from Facebook to other forms of online social media. The bulk of them need help using it."

Given the amount of time they spend online, it might be assumed that students should be able to transition from one form of social media to another intuitively. However, in class application, some students seek teacher help immediately. This lack of transference hinders classroom use, as teachers must facilitate online interactions.

Another consideration in planning for use of online social media involves cost. Terri pointed out that free online programs often alter access privileges or shift to a fee-based model once the program has established its success. This can be particularly tough for cash strapped schools. "The issue of access to free programs is a problem. You'll use one and then it's taken down, or they start charging you to use it. You have to be flexible and knowledgeable about emerging technologies."

A perfect example of this need for flexibility occurred during a Ning collaboration Terri conducted with a school in California. Students from both schools met on Terri's Ning site to collaboratively research Hispanic musical genres. However, as the project neared completion, Ning changed its access rules, limiting the number of students who could participate per class. As a result, the project could no longer be conducted as planned. Though other online social media sites might be investigated to overcome this obstacle, staying on top of emerging media can be exhausting. Terri noted, "I went through a two-year period where I immersed myself in online social media, but I had to pair that down in order to not burn out."

The time spent working with online social media can become difficult to measure. Terri said, "The time frame of teaching has gotten blurry. My workday used to end at 3:00, but now, with Twitter and Ning and the other types of online social media I use at school, I seem to be working later hours at home." As with other teachers, Terri interacts with professional learning networks, as well as monitoring student interactions: "I've gotten lots of great ideas, but you have to know when to turn the computer off. "

Finally, as with Alicia, Terri sees teacher resistance as a major obstacle. With some hesitation, Terri shared her frustration in spreading online social media use in her school, noting that no other foreign language teachers valued or used online social media in their classrooms. Further, Terri noted that her administration did not support the classroom use of social media until recently, fearful of the outcomes and effectiveness of online practice.

Of course, anyone who has spent much time in the classroom knows the glacial pace of innovation in schools. It often seems we are preparing our students for the world of the past, rather than demands of the future. Although we share frustration at the slow progress of educational innovation, it is essential that teachers like Terri feel supported by administration if their productive and progressive practices are to gain ground.

Derek: Online Social Media as Mass Media

Background.   Derek came to education as a second career, having spent the first 15 years of his professional life in public broadcasting. Derek also considers himself a lifelong learner, recently earning awards and university recognition for his master's work. Entering the high school classroom, he first taught junior and senior English, but eventually moved into teaching video production and photography. Derek remains committed to the potential of student collaboration, seeing his work in media as an extension of his work in communication, evolving from print-based to digital formats. His mindset provides a sharp contrast with the school's previous instruction on media: "In the old video production class, the teacher came from a shop background, and taught the course focused on basic skills and tools. My approach is all about communication."

Planning and Implementation.   Communication is at the heart of Eric's planning, as well. "Communication courses are about developing your own voice. Multimodal voices are a part of that. What we've considered as text is changing to include anything that carries a message, like with ESPN's show Sports Center or the cable news channels. They mix all kinds of texts to tell their stories: video, audio, graphics, side and bottom tickers. It's all part of the same message, though."

In Derek's planning, he maps out his lessons thoroughly ahead of time, to "avoid wandering." He noted that the syllabus itself is a planning tool he uses as a scaffold: "In using technology, like with other disciplines, you have to build on foundational skills." Although he noted that he will change pace and sequence occasionally, the overall workflow is articulated in his syllabus. "My classes are always based on a series of media productions that start simple and become increasingly more complex."

As with most teachers, state standards come into play in Derek's planning, but less so than in most core classes. Since photography and video production are not core classes, Derek feels he has more flexibility. Derek "weaves" English content standards into the class plans, focusing again on the strong connection between print and digital communication. "It's kind of ironic that the standards in technology should be out of date in an age where technology is important, especially to policy makers." Derek enjoys some freedom by working outside of the academic core, but sees the impact of standardization on other teachers. "It gets to the point where they cannot step outside the charted workflow."

The relevance of Web 2.0 and social media as a bridge to student learning is important to Derek: "I currently use Web 2.0 applications in my broadcasting classes; mostly wiki. Of course, for a while, it was tough because the firewalls wouldn't let you get to any sites, but that's changing. In the last month, YouTube has become available, which is wonderful. We post our newscast on YouTube to allow for comments and interaction." Derek's point echoes the recent movement to open up access to online sites, as schools realize the potential of online interaction.

Derek particularly likes the collaboration social media sites afford. This interest led him to initiate interdisciplinary collaboration between school departments: "My classes are all team based, but the kids bring assignments from other classes that we blend into our own work. For example, kids may be working on a story in their 3rd period journalism class, but they can transfer that information into my 4th period video projects." Derek noted that this interdisciplinary collaboration only happens periodically, but he felt it made the work seem more authentic and purposeful.

Derek's favorite Web 2.0 site was the Independent Student Media site (ISM). On this site, students could post their self-made documentaries or short subjects to the website "screening room." Students and instructors from across the country could then post their opinions and comments on the video. In fact, professionals from the film community often provided feedback for student work.

Derek demonstrated a production created by his students the previous year. Created as an interdisciplinary project with the school's health department, the film blended aspects of dramatic performance with student interviews, and music on the subject of school violence and bullying. The film pulled together several modes of communication to make a relevant commentary on a subject relevant to school communities. Already an important project for the school, publishing it to the ISM site provided valuable feedback and critique from a national community of student filmmakers. A number of constructive comments were made regarding technical execution, topicality, and performances, as well as suggestions for improvements from professionals in the field. "What really made this cool was professional cinematographers had access to the site and would review and comment on the strengths and weaknesses of the projects," Derek noted. This online apprenticeship model let students see their work as authentic and public.

However, Derek sees the development of online social media as the most promising current channel for collaboration and publishing. "I think we need to find more meaningful exchanges through Web 2.0 and social media to get student work out there. I want my students to develop a voice and become good critical consumers of media, but, for that to happen, their work needs to be published and seen by others." As he pointed out, when news is produced and shared as social media, it can open an interactive online dialogue with the viewers. Online social media also prepares student filmmakers for a broader audience. "We now post our newscast on YouTube to allow for comments and interaction."

Obstacles and Limitations.   Unfortunately, as in Terri's case, a lack of funding interfered with the continued use of the ISM site, as it eventually moved from a free to a fee-based format; one had to pay for member status to post or comment. As noted earlier, this sort of shift is a frustrating obstacle in planning for successful online participation in cash strapped schools. As Terri noted, "The cost issue interfered with the use of the site. The product licensing may be initially free, but it eventually costs." The need to fund these kinds of online interactions brings public funding of education to the forefront. "Without public support of school innovation, it will be difficult to model these kinds of authentic online interactions." On the benefits of school privatization, Derek stated, "If that were the case, access to products like ISM would be the norm. But we don't have that level of funding because our business is education."

Beyond funding, Derek viewed school leadership as a formidable obstacle to broad use of online social media: "Nervous administrators and reluctant school boards have been our biggest limitation to real progress. The history of admin toward social media has usually been negative. They see it as risky. So, without their backing, this kind of use is not going to happen." Derek's comment echoes the fear that many school leaders share regarding online sharing.

Derek also emphasized the threat resistant teachers pose to the wide spread use of social media. Derek noted age as a factor, but not in the traditional sense: "Some teachers are intimidated. I used to think this intimidation was age related, but it's different. Some of the younger teachers have less comfort with using online social media than some of our older, more seasoned teachers. Of course, many of these young teachers went through their whole lives in public school without real use of technology." Here, Derek highlights a disturbing fact: for many pre-service and entry-level teachers, there has been no modeling of how to use digital technology or social media as an instructional tool. For some new teachers, social media is not perceived as an academic strategy. According to Derek, "They can Twitter on their smart phone, but they can't see how this kind of communication would be used in the classroom. This sort of shift requires leadership at the administrative and board level to support online social media use in the classroom, and staff training in the best way to use it." To a degree, Derek understands the resistance some teachers demonstrate: "Of course, I initially thought Twitter was useless, but tell that now to the people in Egypt." Derek's reference to the role of online media in the recent revolution that toppled Egyptian President Hosni Mubarak is clear. Online social media has established itself as a powerful agent of change.

For Derek, however, the most important role of online social media is in bridging the gap between home and school use. "I still find a divide—a gulf—between the young person's use of social media and the classroom potential.

Currently, our most robust online resources are being used for very trivial entertainment. But, most of these very powerful programs are forbidden in our schools." By excluding these sites from the instructional setting, we send the tacit message that social media lacks credibility, even as social networks promise the potential for major social change. "I think this is coming full circle. When kids realize there is a motivation for using social media for intellectual growth, they'll come back to it."

Discussion

Framed by the analysis phase of the ADDIE model, several salient themes emerged from the interviews. First, the interviews sought to identify the perceived instructional problems that drove teachers to incorporate online social media into their plans. Based on the data, problems seem to revolve around the need for facilitation of collaborative and authentic student interactions. This reflects a need for student empowerment in use of social media. As Alicia pointed out in her interview, she hoped to create an online environment "where students can feel competent and collaborative," developing an online voice that is both personal and collective. This is supported by Derek's statement that "Communication courses are about developing your own voice. Multimodal voices are a part of that." In this setting, the teacher's role is more of facilitator than instructor, blurring the lines between social and academic interactions.

The second question focused on the skills students need for successful interactions with online social media. The learner's ability to transfer digital skills is most important, as all teachers interviewed addressed the importance of scaffolding computer skills for student online social media interactions. Terri was most outspoken about the need for teacher facilitation with interactive online programs, noting the importance of direct instruction in use of online social media. The assumption that young learners bring sufficient competence with online interactions may be overestimated. Terri noted, "Students do not instantly make the transition from Facebook to other forms of online social media." Teachers must facilitate these engagements.

Perhaps the most pertinent area of questioning explored constraints and limitations. The interviews echo that resistance from teachers and administrators is based on a reluctance to release or reevaluate power structures in school settings. In essence, schools are divided in the acceptance of online social media as a teaching tool, as some view online social media as a threat to existing teaching roles.

This resistance is echoed by school administration. Based on the danger of misperception, administration often resists full support of online social media, fearing it will blur the traditional roles of the past. Also, given budgetary constraints, administrators struggle to justify the costs of proprietary programs and technologically rich classrooms.

As discussed above, the data reveals several common themes regarding the potential, limitations, and obstacles in involving online social media in the design of classroom instruction. Specifically, a strong belief in the value of social media as an authentic, collaborative multi-modal learning tool is essential, both from staff and administration. Further, teachers must resist the assumption that all digital natives share expertise in digital online interactions, as there are gaps in computer knowledge and access.

The data also strongly supports the assertion that many teachers are fearful of the blurring teacher/student roles inherent on social media use. This seems a dominant factor in teacher resistance. Clearly, any efforts to support online social media integration in public schools must address this issue. These obstacles certainly present challenges to the implementation of social media in the classroom.

Conclusions

As noted in the interviews, the lines between teacher and student are beginning to blur. However, the greatest challenge to the success of online social media in the classroom does not lie in the teacher's acceptance or rejection of digital interaction. It lies in the absence of solid instructional designs. Here the lines between planning and instructional activity are blurring more than teacher roles.

The consequences of rushing to implement social media without a proper instructional design are beginning to emerge. Studies on laptop programs emphasizing one-to-one use reflect little improvement in standardized test scores (Warschauer, 2007). This point was echoed in a recent *New York Times* cover story, noting that, though engagement with digital technology was high, there was little growth in scores for schools where use of digital technology had become the overwhelming norm (Richtel, 2011). Though filled with promise, the success of these new educational technologies depends on thoroughly planned and executed instructional designs.

As noted previously, many educational programs have failed to meet the diverse needs of modern classrooms. Given the potential of online social media, schools must focus on principles of integrated design. Sound instructional design is like a road map. However, without a clear direction and a firm educational plan, educators and students may find themselves lost in an ever-blurring digital landscape.

References

Greenhow, C., Hughes, J. E., & Robelia, B. (2009). Learning, teaching, and scholarship in a digital age: Web 2.0 and classroom research—What path should we take now? *Educational Researcher, 38*(4), 246–259.

Greenhow, C., & Robelia, B. (2009). Old communication, new literacies: Social network sites as social learning resources. *Journal of Computer-Mediated Communication, 14*(4), 1130–1161.

Greenhow, C., Walker, J. D., & Kim, S. (2010). Millennial learners and net-savvy teens? Examining Internet use among low-income students. *Journal of Computing in Teacher Education, 26*(2), 63–68.

Hatch, J. A. (2002). *Doing qualitative research in educational settings*. Albany, NY: State University of New York Press.

Hargittai, E. (2010). Digital na(t)ives? Variation in Internet skills and uses among members of the "Net Generation." *Sociological Inquiry, 80*(1), 92–113.

Martin, S., & Robinson, J. (2007). The income digital divide: Trends and predictions for levels of Internet use [Quantitative Study]. *Social Problems, 54*(1), 1–22.

Lei, J. (2009). Digital natives as preservice teachers: What technology preparation is needed? *Journal of Computing in Teacher Education, 25*(3), 87–97.

Peterson, C. (2003). Bringing ADDIE to life: Instructional design at its best. *Journal of Educational Multimedia and Hypermedia, 12*(3), 227–241.

Prensky, M. (2009). H. sapiens digital: From digital immigrants and digital natives to digital wisdom. *Journal of Online Education, 5*(3), 9.

Richtel, M. (2011, September 3). In classroom of future, stagnant scores. The *New York Times*, p. A1.

Tan, L., & Libo, G. (2009). From print to critical multimedia literacy: One teacher's foray into new literacies practices. *Journal of Adolescent & Adult Literacy, 53*(4), 315–324.

The New London Group. (1996). A pedagogy of multiliteracies: Designing social futures. *Harvard Educational Review, 66*(1), 60–92.

Wang, S. K., & Hsu, H. Y. (2009). Using the ADDIE model to design Second Life activities for online learners. *TechTrends, 53*(6), 76–82.

Warschauer, M. (2007). The paradoxical future of digital learning. *Learning Inquiry, 1*(1), 41–49.

3

ANALYSIS OF SECOND LIFE AS A DELIVERY MECHANISM IN EFL EDUCATION

Kay Kyeong-Ju Seo, Noah Kreischer, and Muruvvet Demiral

Introduction

Second Life® is an online 3D virtual world that integrates social networking tools that allow for interaction among its users. It allows users to interact with each other synchronously through the use of an avatar, or virtual representation of themselves. They can use text chat, audio, share images and videos and even explore the virtual environment together. In addition, Second Life® allows its users to create the world they live in. Users can create buildings, move land, and interact with objects and other users. Many educational institutions have even taken to Second Life® and recreated their institutions in the virtual world; one university has reconstructed many of its iconic architectural buildings on their own Second Life® "island." By creating an institutional island for the university, they provide a gathering space for any of their students and instructors.

Second Life® has many potential uses in education. It can be used to recreate environments and provide a virtual representation of real-life learning. For example, Mahon, Bryant, Brown, & Kim (2010) point out the potential of using Second Life® to produce simulations that enable pre-service teachers the chance to practice classroom management in a virtual environment. By creating a virtual classroom, pre-service teachers can have classroom management practice without entering an actual classroom. Additional applications could include the use of Second Life® for medical and health education (Boulos, Hetherington, & Wheeler, 2007) or using Second Life® to connect English as a Foreign Language (EFL) students with their American counter-parts (Wang, Song, Stone, & Yan, 2009).

The focus of this chapter is to analyze the use of Second Life® in an EFL program. The possible uses of a technology such as Second Life® seem nearly endless and possibly overwhelming for instructors and instructional designers. As such, we intend to focus on one possible use of the tool based on typical goals for an EFL program. For example, Wang et al. (2009) used Second Life® for an EFL program in China with the goal of improving language proficiency and their students' listening and questioning abilities. Second Life® poses a unique opportunity in language learning as it integrates synchronous audio, visual, and social networking capabilities. In the EFL program in China, the researchers were able to connect Chinese students with their American counterparts at another institution. Through their interactions, the students were able to conduct interviews, lectures, group discussions, and virtual tours or presentations. This provided the students with the opportunity to not only improve their language abilities, but to also increase their cultural awareness by sharing with foreign students.

While Second Life® may sound like an exciting opportunity for EFL or foreign language learning, it is important that instructional designers analyze their needs and ensure that the technology is a proper fit for their lesson. More specifically, analyzing the environment will ensure the designers understand what benefits the technology has to offer and what barriers may prevent students from reaching specified goals.

Analysis

In order to develop quality instruction, the designer must conduct a needs analysis according to their target audience first. According to Wang and Hsu (2009), analysis should "include an assessment of the content of the learners' knowledge, what they want to learn, and why they need to learn it. In addition, the analysis should include their learning characteristics, motivation, technology affordance, and learning goals" (p. 79). In the case of Second Life® in an EFL program, analysis becomes extremely important to determine the best method of design and whether or not it is an appropriate delivery mechanism.

Analyze the Audience

Analyzing the learners may be considered the most important aspect of the analysis phase because the very base of instruction relies on learners. Before designing any instruction, the designer must know who their audience is. He must consider the learners' previous knowledge, levels of experience, relevant socio-economic or cultural backgrounds, their expectations for instruction, and any other relevant characteristics. In the EFL case provided, the designer has already chosen Second Life® as a possible delivery mechanism and knows it will be applied to an EFL program. Relevant information in this case would include the students' ability and comfort level with the use of technology, specifically using the Internet and interacting in a 3D environment. In addition to specific skills, the designer must also consider student perceptions toward Second Life®, their level of comfort or self-confidence, and motivations to use the technology.

Furthermore, the designer must consider the students' language skills. Are their language skills at a level where they can use the various aspects of the technology? For instance, can they read and write English, and at what level? A possible example is the students' need to use a search tool where results may be presented in English. If the students are expected to partake in such activities, do they have the ability to do so? Additionally, learner motivation needs to be an important consideration. The designer must understand what is motivating the students to learn English as a foreign language and how that motivation will move them to use technologies such as Second Life®.

In the article by Wang et al. (2009) regarding an EFL program in China, the authors and researchers designed a survey in order to gauge the students' readiness to use Second Life®. The use of preliminary surveys is a good way to learn more about the audience in order to design effective instruction. Surveys will allow the designers to learn about students' prior knowledge and experience, motivation, and, in this case, perceptions toward Second Life® that may have not been known otherwise.

Identify Goals and Objectives

Throughout the instructional design process, it is important for designer to consider and modify the main goals and objectives for instruction. The designers must analyze their goals and narrow down the objectives to better understand and predict the expected outcomes for learning. In the case of using Second Life® for EFL programs, the main goal or objective is to teach English as a foreign language. As the designer gains further understanding about his students, he may modify the goal to include the students' characteristics and needs. For example, through the use of surveys, the designer may have learned that all of the students participating in the lesson have had prior experience using Second Life®. This would allow the instructor to focus more on the content of the lesson and not on how to use the technology. Thus, the overall goal for instruction may be to teach English as a foreign language by connecting students with native English speakers through the use of online virtual reality. Further objectives could then focus on student behaviors in Second Life® and not just where and when to click.

One of the objectives mentioned in the case regarding the EFL program in China was to see the effects of Second Life® on oral proficiency (Wang et al., 2009). When taken further, this could also include other important language aspects in addition to the ability to speak in a foreign language. For instance, the objective could be to gauge the students' oral proficiency by observing their ability to listen, read, write, and speak in English. If the main goal is to connect

EFL students with native English speakers and observe their oral abilities, Second Life® may be a good choice as it offers virtual interactions that allow the use of both written and spoken word.

Consider Delivery Options

Second Life® provides many opportunities and channels for the users to communicate. Users have the ability to use text chat, audio, share images and videos, create and interact with objects, the environment, and each other. Due to the sheer number of options available to the users, instructors of EFL programs who choose Second Life® as a delivery mechanism must understand, analyze and select the appropriate communication channels offered. For example, in the instance of learning another language, text-based delivery will help the learners improve their reading and writing skills. Whereas the primary use of audio will allow them to improve their listening and speaking abilities. For this reason, the designer must analyze the options available and decide which methods would be appropriate for which circumstances.

When using Second Life® for an EFL program, there are many different ways to deliver instruction. For example, students from different countries could meet in Second Life® and travel to different locations, such as U.S. landmarks recreated in the virtual environment. The students could then share information about the landmark by explaining its history and showing additional images and videos they have collected. Activities like these would help students not only practice their language skills, but improve their communication skills as they explore new areas.

Identify Constraints

Constraints come in all shapes and sizes. As a part of the analysis phase, it is important to identify constraints and determine if they can be overcome or if they will results in changes to how the instruction is delivered. The use of Second Life® in an educational setting provides many constraints that need to be identified. Not only are there constraints to the technology itself, but there may be constraints based on the learners and their ability to use and access the technology. Earlier it was mentioned that the use of surveys was a good method in identifying students' prior knowledge and gauging their abilities in Second Life®. This may also reveal the students' perceptions towards Second Life® and whether or not it is an appropriate delivery mechanism. If students have some moral opposition to virtual reality that was not known before, the use of such tool may not be appropriate.

Furthermore, Second Life® itself can create barriers to instruction. Second Life® is an online community that allows many different people from all over the world to have access. Having such a large user base may expose students to unnecessary risk. Second Life® has been the focus of many ethics and psychology researchers. Some believe that virtual crimes committed in Second Life® should also be considered real crimes as they have affects on a real person's life (Sipress, 2007). Furthermore, incidents of harassment and virtual attacks have taken place where a user's avatar has been taken over and caused to simulate insidious acts (Wang & Braman, 2009). Aside from the risks associated with the online community, psychologists have often wondered how the use of avatars affects student behavior. Similarities do exist between the virtual and the real, however, some believe the use of an avatar allows students to alter their persona and behave in ways that they would not do normally in regular face to face contact (Gajendra, Sun, & Ye, 2010). When designing an EFL program, student interaction is a key ingredient. If students are not behaving the way they would in regular face to face meeting with native speakers, then students may not reach the full objectives outlined by the designers.

Identify Assessment Strategies

Assessment is an important strategy for instructional designers which helps them understand if the goals and objectives are being met. As part of the analysis phase it is a good idea to also determine ways to measure success and determine if the learners are meeting the stated objectives. This can be done at any point during the instruction and in many different formats.

Using Second Life® in an EFL program, assessment strategies need not be limited to memory recall and oral performance. Language learning also includes reading, writing and even listening skills. Perhaps the students can be given a set of instructions in both written and spoken English directing them through a virtual scavenger hunt. By completing the hunt, the students will demonstrate their reading and listening skills. Furthermore, the students themselves could even be charged with the task to create their own scavenger hunt. Then, they could serve as guides to help the other students navigate through their hunt and answer questions from the other students in English. Most importantly, during the analysis phase of the design process, instructional designers should gather information about the students, the environment and the delivery mechanism in order to determine the possibilities for assessment before selecting the most effective methods.

Determine Timeline

Before actively engaging in the design of instruction, designers need to determine an appropriate timeline. They must determine how much time should be spent on the design and development of instruction, when the instruction is to be deployed, and for how long the students will be involved in the lesson. Sometimes these determinations are not always up to the designers, but are directed by guiding institutions providing education. Therefore, designers need to take these constraints into consideration. Knowing how long they have to spend on each activity, designers need to decide what areas require more focus. For example, when designing an EFL program using Second Life®, the designers may need to decide how much time can and should be spent instructing students on the use of the technology. If the students reveal they have had little to no interaction with Second Life®, the instructor may need to spend more time providing lessons on the technology. Having more time spent on the use of technology means less time is being spent on the actual instruction. However, by knowing these timeline restrictions, the designer may also find clever ways to introduce assessment or learning opportunities during Second Life® instruction. For example, the process of designing one's avatar provides many prospects to learn valuable vocabulary. Furthermore, if additional time is being spent instructing students on the use of the technology, the designer should also include assessments that measure the effectiveness of additional instruction and whether or not is helped the student reach their objectives.

Identify Pedagogical Considerations

Pedagogy is an important consideration for all instruction regardless of the delivery mechanism chosen. Designers must know and understand their audience in order to determine the best methods of instruction and how the students will best learn the material. In an EFL environment vocabulary and dialogue are important tools for language learning. The use of Second Life® will allow students to connect with their foreign counterparts and engage in self-directed dialogue and conversation. However, there can also be value found in producing daily conversations. For instance, the instructors may assign common expressions and conversations for the students to practice, which may not happen naturally through Second Life®. For example, a person from China traveling to the United States may need to learn how to ask for and locate a taxi. This may be a task given to EFL students to practice in a virtual environment such as Second Life® to help mimic what may happen in a real-life situation. Practicing such dialogues in a virtual environment with other students from different countries may produce more effective results than would recitation of lines from a text to fellow EFL students.

Key Findings

In the Chinese EFL program discussed in Wang et al.'s (2009) article, the researchers faced many unpredicted challenges that may have been avoided had a thorough analysis been completed. For example, the program faced some technical difficulties and failures with Second Life® being used at the proposed learning sites. This led to their recommendation that "researchers test the technology prior to the start of each EFL program activity at each of the sites" (p. 17). This type of technology testing could be completed during the analysis phase of the design process. If analysis is not completed, it is argued that unexpected software issues could arise during instruction (Sanchez, 2009).

When selecting an intensive technology as a delivery mechanism, such as Second Life®, it is imperative that the technology be understood; not just for is capabilities, but for it requirements on systems and hardware. A system like Second Life® cannot be used on any computer with any Internet connection, and as Sanchez (2009) indicated, "the software required to run Second Life® was very computer-processor-intensive and required a persistent and fast internet connection" (p. 30). Certain levels of capabilities must be maintained before such a delivery mechanism can be used. Once it is determined what those minimum qualifications are, the chances of technical failure can be drastically reduced. Otherwise, students may have difficulty to completing their assignments due to technical issues.

Although interface and navigation issues were not stated in Wang et al.'s (2009) article, it does not mean that anyone who uses Second Life® as a delivery mechanism for instruction would not be faced with such issues during the instruction. Many existing studies related to the topic point out that students struggle with navigation and using the interface of Second Life®. For instance, based on the results of a survey conducted by Jarmon, Traphagan, and Mayrath (2008) students tend to disagree that using Second Life® is easy. As a result, it is important to consider possible issues that can emerge during instruction. Therefore, analysis becomes necessary in order to prepare for possible issues and devise alternate solutions to solve any problems that are encountered.

Aside from the technical aspects of Second Life®, there are a number of safety concerns that need to be analyzed and considered carefully. According to Schiller (2009), it was determined that "instructors should be aware of the potential harm and unexpected incidents that students might encounter in Second Life" (p. 378). Second Life® is a users' community that provides access to anyone with the ability to use the software, It then allows those users to have a false name and to design their own virtual representation of themselves, whatever that representation might be. As such, there can be a number of issues that present themselves when users feel they can behave in a manner that is both virtual and disguised by an avatar. There are many examples of harassment, hacking, or virtual sabotage that has taken place inside Second Life® and has arguably affected real lives outside of the simulation (Sipress, 2007). Knowing the risks of using a technology like Second Life®, the designers must considered these risks as a part of the analysis phase and determine if the use of such a delivery mechanism is worth the risks and/or are there ways to reduce or avoid such risks. In the case of Second Life®, some may argue both are true. The ability to connect students from across the world to learn and practice their language learning through virtual reality allowing for audio, video, text chat, and the ability to manipulate interpersonal distance has obvious benefits for language apprehension. Furthermore, the risk can be reduced by controlling the environment within Second Life®. As a precaution to reduce possible risks, instructors need to be careful when choosing a location to send their students (Schiller, 2009). Moreover, users can create their own islands and allow access to the island be invitation only.

Another finding regarding the use of Second Life® for educational lessons was the discovery that using complex, highly interactive technology across continents requires a considerable amount of preparation time. Preparation for activities using a program such as Second Life® includes more than simple lesson plans, but involves analyzing, testing, and training users on the technology. Designers must be sure to include these additional activities in their preparation time. Schiller (2009) recommended that instructors also consider the time it will take students to complete each task assigned to them. If a designer decides that Second Life® is a perfect tool for her lesson without taking the time to consider and plan for technical and safety concerns, the resulting lesson could be rife with disaster. Students may get hung up on the technology and spend too much time learning the tools rather than actually participating in the lesson. Furthermore, they could access the system, be guided to an unidentified or poorly researched location only to find inappropriate material and interactions that could either pose as a distraction or cause harm to the students. Therefore, analysis of Second Life® and it capabilities and requirements becomes a crucial step in the design process.

Important Considerations

Second Life® provides an enormous opportunity for language learners as it allows for people all over the world to connect and communicate with one another. Having the ability to connect across the globe allows people to practice their language skills and learn from native speakers in their home countries. Connecting with native speakers in an environment that allows for communication through multiple channels brings language learning to a new level. As a result, Second Life® can be considered an emerging technology that can support and develop new methods of language learning. As this trend continues, there are some important considerations that will need to be further explored.

In the Wang et al. (2009) study, learning and research took place over the period of one academic term. In terms of language acquisition, learning often takes places over many terms or even years before students feel they have reached any level of fluency. As such, it is important to consider how valuable a short-term study is in regards to language learning in Second Life®. Second Life® is an immersive technology that provides stimulation for multiple channels. It can be enjoyable software that can lead to endless amounts of exploration and play. As such, we need to consider the impact of the software on overall learning. If students are simply enthralled with the technology, it may become difficult to measure if higher level learning is taking place. For this reason, it will become important to include Second Life® in longer term studies so that learning can be measured over time.

It is also important to determine whether or not the language skills learned inside Second Life® can be transferred to the performance context of interacting in person. According to Junglas, Johnson, Steel, Abraham, and Mac Lough-lin (2007), behaviors inside Second Life® may not be the same as behaviors in person. While learners may be comfortable interacting with on another inside Second Life®, the environment is virtual and students may hide behind their avatars. As a result, when faced with real life interactions, the students may have a hard time communicating. As more language learning takes place inside Second Life®, it will be important to consider the transferability of these skills.

Furthermore, with many language programs, cultural considerations will need to take place. For instance, if the students are using Second Life® to learn Portuguese, they will need to carefully select the individuals that they will be interacting with as it relates to the performance context. For example, if students enroll in a short language program to prepare them for a trip to Brazil, then interacting with Portuguese speakers from Portugal may not provide much value. Language learning has many cultural implications as one's cultural can strongly influence their speech. As a result, instructional designers and instructors must consider the performance context and select the appropriate group with whom they will interact.

Conclusion

Second Life® is a powerful tool that allows people from all walks of life to connect across continents and communicate through a variety of methods. The technology can be simple to use by exploring the site and meeting other users or it can be complex where participants can build the virtual world around them. The endless number of possibilities is what attracts education to use such a tool so it can be molded into existing curriculum. However, when using such a technology it is important to analyze it thoroughly and ensure that it is used in a way that benefits the participants and avoids issues that may harm the students or their learning.

In using Second Life® for language learning, the ability to connect with other students who are native speakers has a clear advantage over interactions with non-native speakers. In addition, Second Life® allows those interactions to include multiple channels of communication, through audio or text, and it uses the virtual world to try a replace what is not really present. For example, Second Life® has a number of pre-programmed gestures to help simulate body language, such as laughing, that would normally take place in real face-to-face conversations. It has even been pointed out by Yee, Bailenson, Urbanek,

Chang, and Merget (2007) that Second Life® users may even reproduce their interpersonal distances as they would in normal conversation, providing a link between the virtual and real. While studies are still being done regarding the psychological behavior of Second Life® users, there appears to be some clear advantages for using the software in language learning. Second Life® allows language learners to connect with people from the target language, it allows them to practice their speech and writing abilities, and to imitate what takes place during regular conversations using virtual reality.

Despite the many advantages for language learning in Second Life®, a very important consideration that needs to be taken into account is the technology. Second Life® is a very resource intensive tool that requires a certain level of understanding, expertise, and even minimum levels of available technology. Users must be comfortable with using a computer, navigating the Internet and trouble-shooting technical issues. They must also have good equipment and high speed Internet access that has little to no interruptions in service. Furthermore, they must understand the concept of virtual reality and have some level of exposure to such an environment. Without these core competencies, the amount of language learning will be reduced as issues relating to technology or expertise will deviate from the time spent on the lesson.

In addition to addressing technology issues and competency levels, instructional designers and instructors must also consider the virtual environment. Second Life® has the potential to expose students to people or areas of poor morality and malicious intent, such as harassment or virtual attacks on avatars and/or environments. As a result, steps must be taken to minimize these types of distractions and to ensure the students' safety. Providing students with their own space that has limited access to only the participants involved is an important first step. If students are to explore other areas of the virtual world as a part of their learning, these sites must be visited in advance and evaluated based on their exposure to other users and the possibility for attacks or other distractions. For example, Wang et al. (2009) suggest that selecting a site by the sea may seem attractive, but it may also contain jumping dolphins which would provide an un-needed distraction.

Overall there are many advantages and drawbacks for the use of Second Life® in language education. What is important is that proper analysis and considerations are taken into account. When Second Life® is chosen as a delivery mechanism, it is important to consider how instruction will be designed. Regardless of the environment in which instruction is conducted, a design process should be followed to make sure instruction is organized and meaningful. In order for quality language learning to take place students need to be comfortable with the technology, provided adequate resources to troubleshoot the technology, and be guided to areas that are deemed safe and free from distraction. If all of these requirements are met, then Second Life® could prove to be a very beneficial tool for learning a foreign language.

References

Boulos, M. K., Hetherington, L., & Wheeler, S. (2007). Second Life: An overview of the potential of 3-D virtual worlds in medical and health education. *Health Information & Libraries Journal, 24*(4), 233–245.

Gajendra, S., Sun, W., & Ye, Q. (2010). Second Life: A strong communication tool in social networking and business. *Information Technology Journal, 9*(3), 524–534.

Jarmon, L., Traphagan, T., & Mayrath, M. (2008). Understanding project-based learning in second life with a pedagogy, training, and assessment trio. *Educational Media International, 45*(3), 157–176.

Junglas, I. A., Johnson, N. A., Steel, D. J., Abraham, D. C., & Mac Loughlin, P. (2007). Identity formation, learning styles and trust in virtual worlds. *The DATA BASE for Advances in Information Systems, 38*(4), 90–96.

Mahon, J., Bryant, B., Brown, B., & Kim, M. (2010). Using second life to enhance classroom management practice in teacher education. *Educational Media International, 47*(2), 121–134.

Sanchez, J. (2009). Barries to student learning in second life. *Library Technology Reports, 45*(2), 29–34.

Schiller, S. (2009). Practicing learner-centered teaching: Pedagogical design and assessment of a second life project. *Journal of Information Systems Education, 20*(3), 369–381.

Sipress, A. (2007). Does virtual reality need a sheriff? Reach of law enforcement is tested when online fantasy games turn sordid. Retrieved from http://www.washingtonpost.com, p. A01.

Wang, C. X., Song, H., Stone, D. E., & Yan, Q. (2009). Integrating second life into an EFL program in China: Research collaboration across continents. *TechTrends, 53*(6), 14–19.

Wang, S. K., & Hsu, H. Y. (2009). Using the ADDIE model to design second life activities for online learners. *TechTrends, 53*(6), 76–81.

Wang, Y., & Braman, J. (2009). Extending the classroom through second life. *Journal of Information Systems Education, 20*(2), 235–247.

Yee, N., Bailenson, J. N., Urbanek, M., Chang, F., & Merget, D. (2007). The unbearable likeness of being digital: The persistence of nonverbal social norms in online virtual environments. *Cyber Psychology & Behavior, 10*(1), 115–121.

UNIT II

Developing Powerful Instructional Strategies with Social Media

4

DESIGNING RECORDED VOICE REFLECTION AS A PEDAGOGICAL STRATEGY

Dana A. Tindall

Social Media and Reflective Practice

Web 2.0 social media has the opportunity to change education, but in spite of a great range of teaching and learning possibilities, institutional adoption has lagged. Many students have grown up with Web 2.0 social media applications and are familiar with podcasts and social networking, but many institutions still wonder how to adopt these tools (Barnes & Tynan, 2007). Web 2.0, a term first used in 2004, describes a new way to utilize the World Wide Web as a platform where content and applications are not created and published by individuals alone, but are instead continuously modified by all users in collaboration (Kaplan & Haenlein, 2010). The Web honors multiple forms of intelligence (Brown, 2000). Pictures, audio, video, and hyperlinks to other online resources make Web 2.0 into a network of multiple information dissemination that goes beyond just text. Knowledge is stored, retrieved, created, or amended digitally online in a variety of media forms easily found by a user. Dohn (2009) refers to Web 2.0 as "certain forms of activities or practices ... not a binary function, but rather a question of degree" (p. 345). It is then essentially a framework and flexible modality for interaction and shared thinking, and can be considered to be a technology for holding and distributing interaction. Aside from only student-to-student interaction, social media offers the opportunity for student-to-instructor interaction. Students may provide a variety of media for instructor review and feedback. Beyond just online fulfillment of assignments, students may also use social media as a communication tool to provide proof of personal reaction, opinion, and reflection. Social media tools form a conduit for reflective activity in a very rich form.

Although the definition and concept of the term *reflection* is hazy (Atkins & Murphy, 1993), reflection describes a way of making sense or adapting internally to the world around us, and as such is a form of learning. An overarching theme is that internal conceptual change occurs as a result of reflection. Boud (2001) states, reflection is "a process of turning experience into learning, that is a way of exploring experience in order to learn new things … it involves exploring messy and confused events and focusing on the thoughts and emotions that accompany them" (p. 10). John Dewey defines reflective thinking as "active, persistent and careful consideration of any belief or supposed form of knowledge in the light of the grounds that support it and the further conclusions to which it tends [that] includes a conscious and voluntary effort to establish belief upon a firm basis of evidence and rationality" (Dewey, 1997, p. 6). If this is the case then learning is the dynamic act of sense-making, and is ongoing as we move through the contextual experiences of our lives. Learning is defined as the process of revised interpretation of experience, which guides understanding appreciation and action (Mezirow, 1990).

Reflection is a learning experience but is also part of the internal life narrative. It is the element of a story, a narrative where meaning concerning the ways in which we react to stimuli and the way we lead our lives is constructed. Those internal narratives, reflective elements included, are where experiences are tied together and sense is made. We create a story of our life, and as Daniel Pink (2005) states: "stories are how we remember" (p. 99). Storytelling is the act of stringing together, relating incidents, and making arguments (Conrad, 2008). Reflection then can be a process of reconciliation and making sense through an internal storytelling process that may also contain elements of emotion.

Reflection not only provides a deeper version of our own life story but it also informs our philosophy of life through learning. This learning in turn informs future reaction to contextual stimuli and continually shapes our perceptions. It can be considered a guidance tool that forms a path for life activities, and consequently helps through social contact to shape the life, reflections, and story paths of those who may surround and interact with us. Alexandra (2008), an ethnographic researcher, examined a case in which Irish immigrants manipulated multimedia to digitally document their personal stories. Her study discusses considered and adapted reflections of past experiences successfully represented in multimedia, which provided complex testimonials to garner empathy from an external audience. The immigrant's complex process for creating their reflections was involved, their reflection included thoughtful choices for media representation, and the process was critical in nature and transformative for the creators. It then provided a rich narrative of the immigrant's experience for the external audience. Observers of these reflective stories become intellectually and emotionally charged and in turn become reflective. The element of emotion then must be considered as part of the reflective experience.

As humans we are somewhat, for better or worse, guided by emotion that also plays an important part of our reflective process. We cannot ignore the role of emotion as a factor in our thoughts and cognitive processing (Baumeister, Vohs, DeWall, & Zhang, 2007). It is part of our daily lives and is deeply ingrained in the process of the daily living experience. Feelings, acknowledged or not, because they are part of our cognitive processing are a factor in the reflective process. When we recount our experiences to others, either informally or in a formal context such as in educational interaction, an element of emotion will likely be present. We understand this emotion through the spoken word by way of inflection, choice of wording, and structure of our story-conveying utterances.

Oral stories and the associated background reflective activity can and has traditionally, via transcription been converted into a symbolic tool such as text which holds that knowledge accessible via the act of reading over a period of time. We are organisms with several senses; memory and narrative contain elemental artifacts of our sensory perceptions, which are bound to our understanding of the world. Multiple sensory inputs are a part of our daily experience, and remembrance of those elements is included into our life story and subsequently our reflective activity. Reflection can involve a complex version of interpretive remembering, with defined experiences in collective formats that include sight and sound and elements of emotion all rolled into a rich internal narrative. Oral stories and reflection can, via a transcription, be converted into a tool such as text that holds knowledge accessible over a period of time. Reflection can go beyond commonly used text representation. The power of the spoken word may be converted in other ways through now available technologies that permit reflective narrative to be provided in a multimedia sense somewhat similar to the case cited above. The recording of the spoken word digitally holds the same knowledge and validity as it would be transcribed into text. It can be a record of knowledge accessible over time, but can also include added emotional elements exemplified through the primal power of articulated sound. Through recorded sound an observer may detect an implicit deeper meaning in reflection by way of inflection, choice of wording and sentence structure, which provides rich additional insight into the thought process, problem solving, and the reflective transformational learning process.

Recorded audio reflection can thus be considered an educational tool to be used as a strategy for learning. The interactive and now practically ubiquitous tools provided by social media found on the internet provide a natural format for educators to access the reflective process of the student in a much richer form than just text. The perception of emotion presented vocally can become part of the assessment strategy. An educator by way of listening to a reflective assignment may judge content as well as voice inflection to detect the impact of a lesson or contextual immersion upon their students.

Web 2.0 and Audio Recording Modalities

We can communicate rich content through our voices; it seems fitting that technology tools for recording and holding this audio should be taken advantage of for teaching and learning strategies. The voice, as stated, can carry emotion and the addition of any emotive content expressed with voice inflection gives an instructor an advantage in assessing the content and depth of the student's reflective reactions to a contextual experience or any learning materials presented to them. This vocal ability goes well beyond text, where emotion can only be expressed by a learned competency of written language skills. The grammatical dexterity and vocabulary skills of some students may not match the emotion they attempt to communicate in reflection. Reflection is above all a thoughtful personal reaction to a stimulus, and through voice nuance an instructor might be able to discern aspects of a student's thought processes and associated emotional communication that can be easily lost because of lacking written rhetorical skills.

Instructor choices and consideration of pedagogical strategy design must be taken into account, as there are several types of technologies and unique protocols for usage of audio recording as a reflective modality. Three pertinent features to the use of digital audio recording in education are podcasts, blogs, and voice discussion boards.

Podcasts

Podcasts are essentially recorded audio material used for a variety of means. Podcasting is of recent interest to educators because it gives them the ability to record lectures and instructions for students to download and use on their portable computer devices or mobile phones (Abedin, 2011). Podcasts are commonly and largely objectivist in nature; knowledge exists outside of the student and is transferred from the external into the mind of the student rather than being constructed from within. Podcasts, like lectures, seek to transfer knowledge to learners in an efficient, effective manner (Hannafin, 1997). This is not to say podcasts must be narrative nature. They can contain edited audio from a wide variety of sources all produced to create an interesting knowledge artifact from which a learner may construct their own meaning. Podcasts may additionally be used as a container for active reflective thought created by the student while immersed in a contextual environment. They can be used as a container for a summative transformative reflection as well. Any podcast can be recorded and contained on a computer or on a mobile recording device, such as a personal digital assistant (PDA), digital audio recorder, or even a cell or smart phone. There is a plethora of free and for purchase audio editing programs available for download via the Internet. Many computer operating systems come with at least a rudimentary audio recording and editing program where collected audio reflections may be turned into a suitable audio document for sharing online either with the public, or for educational purposes with the instructor or class peers. Podcasts of reflections are essentially recorded audio journals, rich with personal data such as descriptions, analysis, and reflection complete with voice inflection that suggests emotional reaction. Once created a recorded reflective podcast must have then a container in which it may be archived and appropriately shared.

Blogs

One Web 2.0 modality that may function as the container for audio reflection is a blog. A blog can be described as an online forum for collection of personal writing, interactive discussion, and for educational journalistic activities such as reflection. Because they are digital, blogs can contain or link to almost any kind of digital artifact including audio recordings of reflection. In a sense then a blog is a repository of digital materials and is presented to the observer in ordered fashion. Where a podcast functions as a single stand-alone entity, a blog instead is instead a collection of digital entities that may include a recording such as a podcast. Blogs come in many forms, all available online, and can be held by a single individual or a group either publically or privately. Though blogs usually are free of cost, and easily obtained, there are some drawbacks and concerns for instructors to consider when using blogs found on the internet. Highest among these is the privacy of the student.

One very useful feature, and a factor both pro and con in using blogs for education, is the ability to collect comments which may form useful feedback, and spur critical discussions among the audience of classmates or even the public at large if so desired. The instructor however must weigh the positive with the potential for the negative; this same capability may attract derisive statements by the audience, which in turn may inhibit creation of further reflective content by the student creator. Just the anticipation of having private thoughts and reflections exposed with student perceived lack of control to an audience of any type might inhibit the reflective process and a sharing of thoughts or emotions. That said, privacy, specifically visibility to an audience or the ability of that audience to post comments is a prime concern for the instructor in the course design process.

Voice Discussion Boards

Somewhat similar in form to a blog is a voice discussion board. Currently Wimba Voice Tools® provides this service which can be institutionally purchased and contained in a course management system (CMS). Like their text counterpart, they can be used as part of the pedagogical structure set up by an instructor in a CMS. Because it is contained within the CMS, it is shielded from the public so there is a measure of privacy assured. Wimba looks and functions very much like a common text-based discussion board, but has an audio recording function for posting which, if desired, may be accompanied by text in a single post. Technological issues can cause problems on occasion (Yaneske & Oates, 2010). Many times an instructor is ill prepared to deal with such issues. Wimba makes recording and posting audio reflection and comments a simple task for both the student and instructor. It assists the instructor in terms of technology; the recording and playback feature is contained within the voice discussion board interface, and only requires an external speaker and a microphone, a set of headphones with microphone, or the internal microphone and speakers commonly found on laptop computers. Should a student or instructor wish to record outside of the desktop interface, e.g., in the contextual environment, or elsewhere using a mobile audio recording device, they may upload that audio file within the above-mentioned graphic interface. In addition, Wimba also has a pre-use "wizard" function that can be run to make sure each student's hardware is working correctly prior to their recording and posting. Voice discussion posts can be listened and responded to by students or instructors by making their own audio recording using the same interface, and if desired the student can add an associated text reply. As an extra measure of privacy, the instructor also has an option to make the posts private thus shielding students from hearing each other's posts.

Listening to a voice post can take longer that reading a text post. Where an instructor may skim though words in a text post quickly, a voice post is delivered to the instructor in real-time. As an option, Wimba has designed the voice board to allow the instructor to set a time limit on the length of post in increments ranging from 15 seconds to 20 minutes.

CMS Containment Advantages

Many course management systems come containing a blog function, which may be set in a variety ways, either to be shared with a specified group of class peers or with an instructor alone. Most institutions limit access to the CMS to students and faculty only, thus confining any reflective activity to a shell of privacy that can be controlled at both the institutional level, and the course instructor level. The institutional CMS is, as a rule, held behind a secured authentication barrier where access is only given to members of the institution. Within that CMS itself, course materials access can be provided to groups such as course members or sub-groups. The instructor can decide specific permissions on what materials course members can access or comment upon, and can place even further access restrictions to elements such as the course blog. This granular security approach to access rights assures students that their reflective postings can be held privately and assures them of a safe environment to share personal thoughts and feelings. The CMS blog, because it is a tool that can hold a variety of multimedia, invites the possibility of additional media such as text, images, and video that may accompany a recorded voice reflection. The instructor using the CMS blog has a wide variety of multimedia design options for reflective activity within a course.

Case Strategies of Audio Recording

Social media tools are easily found and available for relatively simple application of voice reflection within the design structure of course curriculum. In order to discover their use in this manner, a literature search was done targeting empirical studies aimed at the use of audio by students as learning or reflective modality for course tasks including assignments, feedback, and instructor interaction. Key words such as: student-created, student podcast, audio recording, podcast, journal, Wimba, voice recording, and voice reflection, among others, were used singly and in various combinations. The primary search databases included: Academic Search Complete, ERIC, Education Research Complete, and Educational Administration Abstracts. Voice recording is used fairly frequently and understandably as an online tool for second language classes, but the literature to date seems to indicate it is very seldom studied as a tool specifically for reflective activity. Though reflection was not seen as a primary concern, recorded audio has been used in a few studies for facilitation of communication between student peers and between students and instructors. Two themes seem to dominate the literature in this area, one focuses on feedback and learning outcomes of the students, the other examines student preferences and comfort in voice recording.

Feedback Studies

Voice recording was used by instructors to post spoken comments and feedback to online students in a study by Ice, Curtis, Phillips, and Wells (2007). Though not directly studying audio reflection, this study was concerned with the empathetic effects of audio, and how audio feedback was found to be associated with retention of content and application of that content. The instructor in the study switched between text-based comments and digitally recorded audio feedback comments over the course term and provided feedback to students concerning their writing assignments. Analysis considered the learning outcomes by measuring the level and frequency of the taught teaching strategies found within the student final projects. A count of the number of the taught strategies used by students in their final assignments was found to be higher for those strategies taught using the audio feedback. A rather important finding was that vocal nuance was considered by the students to be an important factor in the audio feedback, and more helpful than text feedback in terms of outcomes. Data coming from 25 of 27 student interviews indicated preference for the audio feedback from instructors. Themes that stood out were the increase of understanding nuance in the feedback and a feeling of stronger involvement in the course, and instructor care.

Lai, Yang, Chen, Ho, and Chan (2007) had elementary school students in an intervention and control structure use a PDA as not only a field recording tool for both audio and imagery, but as a prompter toward individual learning. Their primary interest was how this modality affected learning flow; the study thrust being to determine the usefulness of mobile devices in experiential learning. One group of students on a botanical field trip was individually facilitated by technology: a PDA that is also equipped with a camera and voice recorder. The other group relied on text, paper, and pencil. Where the PDA group could record images and their voice, the other group could only take written notes and sketch pictures. Students found sound recording to strongly aid learning. Although the data for all the questions was not provided, Likert scale data from the preference questionnaire found students considered the functions of the PDAs, such as photo-talking and sound recording, make responding to prompts and learning more attractive and effective. Sound recording also strongly aids learning. T-tests applied to student outcomes show differences in the experimental student group using PDAs compared to the control group in pre- and post-testing significantly higher in terms of learning achievement.

Student Preference and Comfort

Marriott and Hiscock (2002) used Wimba voice discussion boards as an audio-posting option to study the viability of student audio summarization of course readings, the purpose of which was to stimulate discussion and better understanding. The study was run in consecutive terms of a course, with students in the first term having the option to post in audio or text. In the second term, the students were directed to post in audio, although the text option contained in the Wimba interface was still available to be used. The authors compared survey data to judge student perceptions in each term. Students did not seem to strongly mind posting by audio, and agreed that the voice forums were useful, although the general preference was to post in text. A few students noted perceptions of the voice board being a richer means of communication that allowed appreciation of natural and emotional content. The students cited self-consciousness, vocal fluency, and spoken errors as issues of concern. A concluding point made in this study is that students were not totally comfortable recording their voices.

This finding was noted as well in a study by Wei, Chen, Wang, and Li (2007) who studied voice postings via mobile phone to a special discussion board. The thrust of their study was on the usefulness and students perceptions of the technology. In the case of this study, students found the ability convenient, but were also not comfortable recording their voices. The authors believe the situation could be "alleviated after a period of adaptation" (p.136). A consideration not noted in either of these studies may be that the recorded audio was to be exposed to other students in the course and sensitivity to errors or vocal fluency problems observable to others may have been a factor causing discomfort. Yaneske and Oates (2010) using a small sample of language learning and teaching students also used Wimba. Students there found the human element of hearing tutors and other students gave them a feel of personal connection and found it easier to "identify their strengths and weaknesses" in audio feedback (p. 241). Again, as in the studies above, the students were not comfortable with the sounds of their own voices.

Jefferies and Hyde (2009) used a varying sample of self-selecting adult students in higher and continuing education. Volunteer adult students created periodic diary journals of their online learning experiences through a variety of electronic media means, including blogs, audio recording, and video recording over an 18-month period. Each 6 months students recorded their e-learning activity for a 5-day-period using their choice of recording modality ranging from text blogs to video camcorders. The primary focus of this study was on how the students use online learning tools in their courses. Of interest here, though a somewhat peripheral factor to the researchers, was the type of recording technology students gravitated toward over time. Information from the study showed the collection method used by students for the first iteration of diary journals to be relatively even between audio recording, web camera, and camcorder. Text blogs were also an option but were low in comparison. By the second iteration student using text blogs had fallen from three users to one. Camcorder and Web camera use decreased while audio recording usage increased. The authors cite the student perceived convenience and ease of use of digital voice recorders as being the cause of this change, but go no farther than that.

One notion that may be drawn from the cited studies is that voice recording was found to be convenient to students, aided in higher outcomes, and contained helpful voice nuance to aid in understanding. Though there may be some trepidation noted in recording one's own voice, this perceived discomfort was not debilitating even when the recordings were to be listened to by peers. The samples in all of these studies was not large and though there are somewhat common findings, a longitudinal study of student voice recording to replace what is normally text based interaction is missing in the literature. The literature to date also seems to be missing a specific focus on how audio recording may be used particularly for reflective purpose. Since voice inflection is seen as helpful in terms of personalizing the feedback and communicative aspects of online interaction, it seems a likely future study could also be helpful examining instructors level of perceiving and understanding the depth of instructional impact on a learner and how that might effect assessment.

Example Designs and Benefits

Because voice recording caters to situational immediacy as well as to the multi-tasking lifestyle of learners, contextual voice recording offers the option of spontaneous reflection from a learner. The student has the ability to quickly capture thought and emotion through the naturalness and primacy of the spoken word. This record of thought and emotion allows an instructor or others, including the recording student, to more easily examine learning and the reflective thought process through voice inflection, choice of wording, and relative conciseness of thought. Assigned reflection in contextual settings is a natural fit for audio recording of active and later critical reflection. This could be of use to instructors of Art, Architecture, History, Nursing, and Education, among many other disciplines, where field trips, projects, and other out of the classroom activities both short and long-term are part of the pedagogical strategy.

For an example, borrowing from a three-part strategy suggested by Boud, Keogh, and Walker (1985), students can be tasked to, on their own, visit a museum, school, hospital, or any other site specific to the course discipline. The assignment would ask for a blog post, either in text or audio prior to the experience to consider the task, and individual expectations for what the experience might hold in terms of learning. The instructor can mold this part of the assignment to a student's own needs and the context to which the student is to be exposed. This provides the instructor with an opportunity to collect a baseline of information from each student, perhaps information as to their current knowledge level, preexisting attitudes toward the context or subject matter, and level of commitment toward the assignment. The student is then sent into the contextual situation to record the sounds of that context, voice their reactions to, the environment and the experience, and actively consider their role related to the situation. The students could post this contextual recording to the blog or voice discussion board where they could listen to it again to refresh within their mind's eye the experience. For the student, this becomes a rich document that may be revisited again and again. The notion here being that the nuance in the recorded voice, particularly the recording made within the contextual setting can immediately remind the student of the moment, possibly bringing to internal eye a real-time remembrance of the sights, smells, and, of course, sounds of the moment. This can be useful to the student in recording or writing a final summative critical reflection. This design provides the instructor with a strong document of the experience as carried out by each student. The assignment additionally provides the instructor a formative assessment of the assignment or course design based upon qualitative data that can then assist with modification of the assignment, or modification of later course elements. Beyond being a tool for the fine-tuning the assignment efficacy, the instructor comes away with a rich empathetic record of the students learning process and the transformation that was brought on by the contextual experience, and with this he may assess the students' level of learning.

Project or problem-based learning tasks offer the ability to not only produce a product in accordance with an assignment, but to also audio record in a blog a reflective audio journal record of the process, including the difficulties and successes in the products creation. This seems a fitting assignment for business students or any student who will eventually be faced with committee work. This design example can be an organizational project task where a group of student peers form as members of a committee who collaboratively negotiate with each other to assign project roles, set agendas, create project timelines, and eventually create some product. As a final part of the assignment, each student records a self-assessment and project assessment reflection. The student on a regularly timed basis audio records a podcast, a journal reflection, which can contain consideration of the project progress, dynamics of group social interaction, and the concerns of each member, along with each student's perceptions of peer contributions. The instructor listening to these short podcast journal entries, aside from measuring progress, could detect in each student the voice nuance of excitement, joy, frustration, and even misery associated with each step of the committee process. This periodic audio journal reflection forms a cumulative document of minute details to help in creation of a final self-assessment reflection to be done by each student. Consistent with project-based and problem-based learning, the product and process is the assessment, both the group's, but also the individual's reflective journal. The final self-assessment reflection can contain edited-in excerpts of the earlier audio journal reflections if desired. This process, like the contextual example discussed above, provides the instructor with a rich document of the learning process by which to assess the student in a very granular fashion. This reflective learning has the possibility of being a touchstone reference for ongoing learning by the student.

Issues for Consideration

Technical and student support and the associated workload should be considered when using this strategy as part of a course design. Support of the student is of course paramount; when technical problems arise, dealing with errant technology gets in the way of learning. An instructor must give much thought to instructions and potential problems. Students must be trained in the use of the technology. Although many students are familiar with many social media tools, they might not be familiar with the tool the instructor chooses to use. Assuming that students are technically competent can be dangerous to successful outcomes. Explicit course software and hardware requirements should be provided for students. The instructor should consider providing easy to find tutorial information on how to use the technology. The tutorials can be as simple as text with image, or as complex as short videos modeling each step for the student.

Instructors should consider creating a frequently asked question (FAQ) document for self-help and problem rectification. A common approach is a special discussion board forum geared toward students helping each other. This gives the students a place to expose and solve technical problems within the course social context. For instructors it additionally alleviates the tiresome burden of answering the same technical questions over and over again via emails. It is not out of bounds for an instructor to leverage student technical knowledge for others self-help. Some students may have prior experience with a problem and can advise those in trouble. A "help" discussion forum then provides a place for frequently asked questions and advises instructors of trouble spots.

Besides providing a detailed assignment, the instructor should provide some form of a rubric listing expectations of the students for completing the assignment. Rubric items may include specific items to be addressed in a reflection, however providing a simple "recipe" of what is expected may not be the best approach; giving students a set of questions can disallow room for real reflection (Boud & Walker, 1998). The rubric should contain some firm rules to help the students with expectations on the mechanics of the assignment. Items to consider are the expected length of the recording, deadlines for posting, and acceptable language. Rules of courtesy should be delineated, especially the referral to, or treatment of other persons. This speaks specifically to making degrading, snide, or off-color comments about others in recordings. Though these items need not have any sort of point value they should be clearly communicated and enforced by some means.

Instructors providing assignments that allow students to upload audio recording from a device must consider what of the many audio file formats available are acceptable. Some audio recording programs on mobile devices may have proprietary file formats that do not necessarily play on all audio players or computers. Some computer audio recording programs may also use file formats that will not work on other programs, therefore the instructor for the reflective assignments should require a standard file format. This is particularly important as class members generally have differing computers and software configurations. The instructor may additionally want to provide links to websites where students can download free programs for editing audio files or converting existing files to the required formats. Consider technical support; inform students, though links to free programs are provided, that the institution and instructor take no responsibility for support or misuse of those programs.

Many students do not like the sound of their own voice as noted above, and may be uncomfortable listening to, or having others listen to them speak. It can be helpful to reassure a student that the same voice they have recorded and are hearing is the same one everyone else hears. Students may devise many methods for recording their voice, from speaking off the cuff all the way to writing the entire reflection down and reading it aloud. It may be a good idea for the instructor to acknowledge this and offer suggestions. Obviously, if a student is reading their reflection word for word, it cannot be considered a true audio reflection, it is just a recitation. The instructor in this case may want to advise students to perhaps consider what they would like to say, write down a few key words, or an abbreviated outline to help them keep on track while recording. It is important that the instructor let them know that perfectly clear speech void of any errors is not the thrust of the reflective recording assignment. Simple audio recording software, as well as Wimba Voice Boards®, have features for editing and correction. The instructor again should decide what is more appropriate in this case, great production or vocal spontaneity.

An important point stated earlier bears repeating; an instructor can read student posts very quickly but listening to audio posts must be done in real-time. In a class of 30 students, listening to audio posts of several minutes each will consume a great deal of time. This should be a real consideration when designing an assignment. The ability to capture the subtle nuance of a reflective voice stands in opposition to the ability to quickly read through a written reflection. The compromise lies within the maximum allowed length of the recorded reflection that must be weighed against what the instructor feels long enough to allow adequate time to discuss what students are being called upon to reflect.

Conclusion

Web 2.0 social media has opened possibilities for creative pedagogy that can provide meaningful learning for students of all ages. The spoken word as a communication tool provides us with a rich and emotion-laden means to express ourselves. The capabilities of modern software and social media bring the opportunity to express our thoughts orally in real-time and record ourselves for all time easily.

We are shaped daily by the world around us, and in the practice of that dynamic process we interact, learn, and are changed both by a reflexive activity but also by deeper and personal reflective activity. That reflective activity, often hidden, is that which often transforms us. It is learning, and as such has its place in education. Reflection can be provided in text, a symbolic language, but may now be oral, recorded digitally. Where text fluency and style depends upon the motor skill of writing, grammar, and the like, to symbolically represent thought and emotion, oral reflection instead makes use of more the primal language speaking skills, that do not necessarily depend upon those writing skills. The speaker by voice nuance communicates thought as well as emotional cues. This provides a rich and immediate understanding of the thought process involved in learning. We now have the technical advantage to take and save speech reflection and design its use to further and better assess learning.

There are a few studies that begin to examine the use of audio recording beyond just podcasts as a means of student-instructor, and student-student feedback and interaction. These studies though promising are limited and only begin to scratch the surface of the potential audio recording using social media can provide. Future course designs and research study should consider the use of audio as a reflective component. Inflection may be a component of reflection that presents greater student depth of experience for assessment by an instructor. This may particularly be the case when a student is a stronger speaker than writer.

There are newer social networking tools that appear online each day that may appeal to this type of study and pedagogical design. VoiceThread®, an online forum that can contain images, video as well as text and audio in a robust interactive discussion format, is just one of these. As education moves forward, it becomes important to us as educators to explore and to adopt social media using and mixing it with tried and true pedagogical devices such as reflection to create engaging learner-centered designs with meaningful outcomes both for the student and the instructor.

References

Abedin, B. (2011). Web 2.0 and online learning and teaching: A preliminary benchmarking study. *Asian Social Science, 7*(11), 5–12. doi:10.5539/ass.v7n11p5

Alexandra, D. (2008). Digital storytelling as transformative practice: Critical analysis and creative expression in the representation of migration in Ireland. *Journal of Media Practice, 9*(2), 101–112. doi:10.1386/jmpr.9.2.101_1

Atkins, S., & Murphy, K. (1993). Reflection: A review of the literature. *Journal of Advanced Nursing, 18*(8), 1188–1192. doi:10.1046/j.1365-2648.1993.18081188.x

Barnes, C., & Tynan, B. (2007). The adventures of miranda in the brave new world: Learning in a web 2.0 millennium. *ALT-J: Research in Learning Technology, 15*(3), 189–200. doi:10.1080/09687760701673568

Baumeister, R. F., Vohs, K. D., Dewall, C. N., & Zhang, L. (2007). How emotion shapes behavior: Feedback, anticipation, and reflection, rather than direct causation. *Personality & Social Psychology Review, 11*(2), 167–203. doi:10.1177/10888 68307301033

Boud, D., Keogh, R., & Walker, D. (1985). What is reflection in learning. In D. Boud, R. Keogh, & D. Walker (Eds.), *Reflection: Turning experience into Learning* (pp. 18–40). New York, NY: Routledge Falmer.

Boud, D., & Walker, D. (1998). Promoting reflection in professional courses: The challenge of context. *Studies in Higher Education, 23*, 191–206.

Boud, D. (2001). Using journal writing to enhance reflective practice. *New Directions for Adult & Continuing Education,* (90), 9–17.

Brown, J. S. (2000). Growing up digital. *Change, 32*(2), 10.

Conrad, D. (2008). Reflecting on strategies for a new leaning culture: Can we do it? *Journal of Distance Education, 22*(3), 157–161.

Dewey, J. (1997). *How we think.* Mineola, NY: Dover.

Dohn, N. (2009). Web 2.0: Inherent tensions and evident challenges for education. *International Journal of Computer-Supported Collaborative Learning, 4*(3), 343–363. doi:10.1007/s11412-009-9066-8

Hannafin, M. J. (1997, December). *The case for grounded learning systems design: What the literature suggests about effective teaching, learning, and technology.* Paper presented at ASCILITE '97. Retrieved from http://www.ascilite.org.au/conferences/perth97/papers/Hannafink/Hannafink.html

Ice, P., Curtis, R., Phillips, P., & Wells, J. (2007). Using asynchronous audio feedback to enhance teaching presence and students' sense of community. *Journal of Asynchronous Learning Networks, 11*(2), 3–25.

Jefferies, A., & Hyde, R. (2009). Listening to the learners' voices in he: How do students reflect on their use of technology for learning? *Electronic Journal of e-Learning, 7*(2), 119–126.

Kaplan, A. M., & Haenlein, M. (2010). Users of the world, unite! The challenges and opportunities of social media. *Business Horizons, 53*(1), 59–68. doi:10.1016/j.bushor.2009.09.003

Lai, C., Yang, J., Chen, F., Ho, C., & Chan, T. (2007). Affordances of mobile technologies for experiential learning: The interplay of technology and pedagogical practices. *Journal of Computer Assisted Learning, 23*(4), 326–337. doi:10.1111/j.1365-2729.2007.00237.x

Marriott, P., & Hiscock, J. (2002, October). *Voice vs. text-based discussion forums: An implementation of Wimba voice boards.* In E-Learn 2002 World Conference on E-Learning in Corporate, Government, Healthcare, & Higher Education. Proceedings, Montreal, Quebec, Canada.

Mezirow, J. (1990) *Fostering critical reflection in adulthood.* San Francisco, CA: Jossey-Bass.

Pink, D. H. (2005). *A whole new mind: Moving from the information age to the conceptual age.* New York, NY: Riverhead Books.

Wei, F., Chen, G., Wang, C., & Li, L. (2007). Ubiquitous discussion forum: Introducing mobile phones and voice discussion into a web discussion forum. *Journal of Educational Multimedia and Hypermedia, 16*(2), 125–140.

Yaneske, E., & Oates, B. (2010). Using voice boards: Pedagogical design, technological implementation, evaluation and reflections. *ALT-J: Research in Learning Technology, 18*(3), 233–250.

5

LIVE IN YOUR WORLD, LEARN IN OURS

Virtual Worlds … Engaging the New Generation of Students

Elizabeth M. Hodge and Sharon Collins

Introduction

Say the word "teaching" and images of classrooms with the teacher standing at the front of the room and students' sitting at desks is a traditional picture that would come to mind. Now, say the words "virtual world" and another image of computers and Internet-based instruction comes to mind. However, taking it a step further by saying "3D virtual world," a few people might conjure up images of an interactive environment or think of the movie *Avatar*, but in many instances they would not put teaching and 3D virtual worlds together as a concept that could be an effective way for instructing and learning to take place. However, in an effort to establish a successful global workforce, educators must realize the importance of infusing digital literacy skills within their curriculum (Kay & Honey, 2005). With the nationwide movement to capture more students through flexible online courses, blended learning and wholly online programs, higher education institutions are challenged to meet curricular and programmatic needs of a growing student population that is accustomed to interacting in a rich social media environment.

Throughout this chapter the authors will describe the use of the 3D virtual environment, Second Life®, as a social medium to immerse students in the learning process. Immersive learning spaces foster educational experiences through situated interactive activities, assessments, mentoring coupled with guided participation (Dede, 2009). Furthermore, two cases will be presented as examples for outlining outcomes, defining learning goals, designing student activities and developing instructional strategies that will enable student users to successfully interact and immerse themselves in the course content. The transformation that takes place will inspire educators to learn how to incorporate the compelling learning adventures that empower their students to be successful in our global workforce.

Theoretical Framework

Instructional design theories provide educators with a solid foundation for the teaching and learning process. However, today's digital native students follow a social learning participative motto of "We participate, therefore we are" (Brown & Adler, 2008, p. 18). This movement towards participatory learning has transformed the nature of current instructional models and theories. While there are many variations of each model, overall there are three main schools of thought that include behaviorism, cognitivism, and constructivism (Schuman, 1996). This chapter will focus on the use of constructivism which prepares the learner to solve problems given any type of situation.

Constructivism is the elimination of standardized curriculum. "Instead, it promotes using curricula customized to the students' prior knowledge. Also, it emphasizes hands-on problem solving" (Brooks & Brooks, 2001, p. 1). Constructivism also impacts other areas of instruction such as assessment. Many instructors are on onboard with this philosophy because of the new generation of learners. These learners expect immediacy and find much information on their own. Adapting to these learners is essential to teaching for the future. These students do not like to feel isolated in their learning, have access to immediate information, and expect the use of synchronous class sessions because they increase their ability to interact with other students. Constructivism in combination with immersive environments exemplifies this definition as learning is once again the responsibility of the student. The environments provide a sense of presence for the students and replace stagnant teaching with communication, movement, and immediacy. Students find the environment engaging, and it provides a means for the creation of a community. The combination of these theories does not take the instructor completely out of the classroom, but allows an instructor to define learning outcomes and shape the instructional design of a course to include communication, interaction, and learning. The inclusion of these elements will enhance the level of knowledge and applicability to applying abstract knowledge to complex situations that arise in real life. By fostering communication and interaction through collaboration, teamwork, feedback, engagement and constructivists learning activities, online course can alleviate students and instructors feelings of isolation. By utilizing this type of virtual infrastructure for teaching and learning, students collaborate through interactive activities creating a synthetic constructivist environment which provides a richer dynamic to leverage particular types of learning activities unlike those found in traditional face to face classes (Dede, 1995).

Many activities and simulations created in Second Life® implement a constructivist learning activity. Instructors can leverage the educational affordances of Second Life® and construct student knowledge through interactions with group members, objects, and collaboration (Girvan & Savage, 2010).

Design

Today's learners are socially engaged, which is an important element when designing courses that incorporate immersive environments According to Lave and Wenger (1991), educators need to explore the social relationships that develop between students who are involved in instructional interactions. Additionally, as more courses incorporate virtual environments, understanding the learning process and the dimensions of communication and interaction are inherent to the instructional design process. Swan and Shea (2005) summarized the learning process by stating that, "Knowledge ... is inseparable from practice, and practice is inseparable from the communities in which it occurs" (p. 241). To further emphasize the importance of interaction, Tennyson and Jorczak (2008) state that the interactive cognitive complexity is an integrative information processing model that proposes learning is the result of an interaction between internal and external variables. As a result, students learn through the affective and cognitive domains. Activities developed within virtual worlds provide educators with the ability to immerse students in environments that continually engage students in the learning experience, providing interaction within a community of learners to enhance self motivation. As a result, instructors must facilitate the various ways for students to interact and connect. For effective instructional interactivity to take place, the members of the learning community must fully participate (Bielaczyc & Collins, 1999). Notably, if knowledge is socially mediated by the instructor, a higher level of interaction evolves as student and teacher participate in discussions, collaborations, feedback, and shared content knowledge (Perraton, 1988).

The theory that students should gain a better understanding of learning from their experiences is not a new notion; in fact for several years educators have grappled with how to create learner centered environments that provides students with the ability to immerse themselves in real life situated problem-solving activities. The use of virtual worlds where students can immerse themselves into an artificially constructed environment where avatar's act out simulated scenarios or connect socially with classmates allows the students to apply abstract knowledge in authentic situated learning environments (Dede, 1992) These situation learning environments known as immersive environments provide the students with the impression that they are participating in a comprehensive, realistic experience (Dede, 2009). The immersion provides students with three types of experiences, which, in combination, create the immersive learning process, these include; sensory, actional, and symbolic factors (Lessiter, Freeman, Keogh, & Davidoff, 2001) Sensory immersion is the digital representation that Second Life® provides students through the design and development of objects that can be touched, heard, moved, and manipulated. Actional immersion in Second Life® allows avatars to experience through action (fly, walk, touch, edit, and manipulate objects and events that take place within the virtual space). Symbolic immersion involves an action that draws on a participant's beliefs, emotions, and values about the real world (Dede, Salzman, Loftin, & Ash 2000).

Many facets exist within the design of a course. These include learning outcomes, instructional goals, designing student activities, and developing instructional strategies that will enable student users to successfully interact and immerse themselves in the course content as well as deepen their understanding of the content. The heightened level of learning allows students to apply the content to real life situations. The instructor should focus on teaching, activities, and assignments that will achieve specific skills outlined in the revised Bloom's Taxonomy. The instructor should begin by asking "What is the content, and technology tool that will produce the level of thinking I wish to achieve in my lesson?" The revised Bloom's Taxonomy (2010) is a multi-tiered model for classifying thinking. Bloom's Taxonomy classifies student thinking into four distinct areas: (1) factual, (2) conceptual, (3) procedural, and (4) metacognitive. These four classifications correspond with the six cognitive levels of thinking complexity: (1) remembering, (2) understanding, (3) applying, (4) analyzing, (5) evaluating, and (6) creating.

When used in combination with the content evaluation process, instructors can determine the cognitive level the immersive lesson or assignment provides. Utilizing Bloom's Taxonomy allows instructors to address the level of alignment between standards, educational goals, assignments, and reflective practices with the institution's conceptual framework. Within the design phase, there are several factors to consider.

1. What are the student's computer literacy skills?
2. Are students digital natives?
3. Will students know how to access the course material?
4. Will students know how to use the virtual environment or will the instructor need to provide explicit directions?

When integrating a new tool, instructors must be visionaries, assessing the needs of the students as well as how the immersive environment will improve learning. In order to be successful, the instructor will need to create tutorials and utilize available resources to help the students be successful. The process is based on simple business concepts of knowing your customer, target market, and, in this case, the students. By providing structured training and facilitated open dialogue, coupled with hands-on interaction in-world, faculty and supporting staffs are better able to plan, build-out, and maximize the inherent academic capabilities that are characteristic of a virtual environment. Faculty must look at the numerous pedagogical methods and have brainstorming sessions to aid in planning and developing viable strategies for both current and future Second Life® classroom activities.

As virtual environments continue to gain interest at the university level, the biggest challenge during early inception is the faculty member's ability to fully understand SL's capacity as a teaching tool. Utilizing Second Life® as a teaching tool provides several possibilities for creating a learning opportunity online that replicates real life experiences. For example role playing is one type of activity that is easily constructed in a virtual environment that allows students aka avatars to immerse themselves in the learning experience and act out scenarios that will help provide them with hands on knowledge that can be implemented in future work related situations.

There are many suggested uses for Second Life® and some of these are listed below:

- Synchronous class meetings
- Office hours
- Project creations/displays
- Immersive simulations
- Field trips or web explorations
- Presentations
- Social interaction through learning communities
- Application and web sharing
- Medical simulations and training
- Business meetings and simulations
- Interdisciplinary projects
- Museums and gallery exploration
- Guest speakers
- Interviews

The list above demonstrates that there are a variety of uses for integrating SL virtual environment as an instructional technology tool for developing a teaching and learning space.

For example, librarians have created a presence in Second Life® using the virtual space as a reference desk. There are instructional rooms and links to academic journals and other research resources.

Case Scenario One: Personal Finance

Problem

With the rapid development of e-learning systems, some content management systems lack the cohesiveness to foster a community of learners. Many students become isolated during the completion of independent work and become disconnected in the learning process. Discussion threads and other avenues of technology that used to work are found to be repetitive and lack engagement. To overcome this challenge, pedagogical experts and technical support specialists collaborated on an innovative method for providing students with the ability to receive asynchronous and synchronous classroom instruction within the 3D virtual environment Second Life®.

Investigating many options, ECU determined this medium would be the best approach to delivery. The demand for the virtual space continues to grow as the element of the virtual world, Second Life®, offers additional opportunities to immerse students in learning through simulations, group activities, and a presence that makes students connected to the university. One of the projects, the virtual high school, has developed into a state-of-the-art delivery of course material involving 16-, 17-, and 18-year-old students in local high schools.

Objectives

1. To develop a community of learners through the use of virtual teams to learn personal financial concepts through game simulation competitions.
2. Virtual teams work asynchronously and synchronously to apply financial concepts to develop a financial budget, balance sheet, income statement, and financial ratios.
3. Virtual teams will present final financial spreadsheets; lessons learned and give a presentation in Second Life® to classmates. Following the presentation, students are to complete evaluation rubrics for each team member and a reflective blog based on game simulation experience and content learned
4. Individual team members will apply the concepts taught through the game simulation to develop personal financial goals for current, five and ten year increments. These goals will be shared during final presentation and culminating reflective blog.

Example

Students enrolled in a personal finance class were grouped together in virtual teams. The teams were provided with initial team building activities that required them to develop a connection by naming their team, constructing a virtual team t-shirt for their avatars to wear, and to decorate their student space in-world. The game simulation is comprised of four components.

1. As a team, students meet in-world to participate in the game simulation. The first phase is to login as your game avatar. The avatars line up at the game board and the game is turned on. Each team wears a HUD (Heads-Up Display), which allows them to read the personal financial questions and choose from a series of answers. The questions are made up of both multiple choice and true/false questions. When a team selects the correct

answer their avatar moves forward on the game board. The first team to win moves on to phase two.

2. Phase two consists of the winning team making the first selection on the "choice board". As the course is a personal finance class, student teams choose from a series of financial choices. The game consisted of four total choice board options. These included career, housing, automobile, and vacation. The choice board contains enough choices for each team to select after the completion of each game. The choices vary in costs. For example, the first choice allowed teams to choose between different careers, such as a nursing, computer programming, teaching, and others. Once they received the career chosen, financial data was provided to the team. The same was consistent with each choice board selection. Therefore when students selected a house, the team not only received the associated costs (mortgage, electric bill, water bill, etc.) that go along with traditional housing, but the teams also received houses within Second Life®. To complete the scenario, the students would place virtual objects in their houses such as furniture, televisions, and other items they felt they might need. These were also the team spaces where they uploaded financial documents and presentations to share with their classmates on virtual presentation boards such as a PresoMatic.

3. Following each choice board selection, teams were provided financial data that they had to input into a budget tracker, balance sheet and income statement. Through this process students learned about the personal financial planning process. The assignments focused on learning about budgeting, the differences between assets and liabilities as well as determining several financial ratios. The financial sheets were then required to be posted within Second Life® where students would share their data selection, evaluate their peers and complete a reflection utilizing the Simulated Linked Object Oriented Dynamic Learning Environment (Sloodle) Blog feature.

4. A final component to the entire simulation, which combines both real-time sessions and independent work, required teams to present to their classmates what they learned throughout the process. The team completed the work plan outlining which elements each team member would complete independently as well as which elements they would complete as a team. Following the presentations, students were also required to submit evaluations on their team members to ensure that each team member participated in the activity.

Technology Requirements and Visionary Development

The development of the game simulation required a team of technology experts and the design of the faculty vision. The following elements comprise the building of the simulation in Second Life®:

- Simulation Development—Second Life® Viewer, Scripting objects, object development, avatar creation, and storyboarding
- Instructor training
- Student instructions for completing the game
- Simulation Development
    - Storyboarding—The entire scenario had to be storyboarded by the technologists to be certain each step would achieve the faculty goal and also meet the requirements of the Second Life® viewer. This also required the beginning steps of flowcharting out the scripting element of the game board and the selection of the financial information and personal information the students received.
    - Second Life® Viewer—the game took advantage of the features of the Second Life® 2.0 Viewer, which needed to be installed on each computer performing the simulation
    - Object Development—The virtual objects had to be built using 3D virtual Second Life® tools. The Second Life® Viewer has built in tools to create and modify objects which then become "primitive shapes" or prims, a process known as "building". Once created, objects can be stored in the avatar's personal inventory, shared with other users, or placed somewhere within the 3D world. The prims can be linked together to form more complicated items. Each prim can have "textures" applied to the surfaces, and can contain scripts, animations, sounds, and other items inside.
    - Scripting—this element was one of the most complicated so that all elements of the game were automated except for the "Start" process, which had to be led by the avatar/person that created the script. A student worker within the (Information Technology and Computing Services (ITCS) team developed the scripts which were placed in all the virtual objects, essentially giving them life. The instructor created the quiz questions and these questions had to be built into the scripts.
    - Avatar Creation—the technology team created six avatars which represented the high school mascot of the student groups involved in the simulation. This involved replacing avatar skins and clothing and introduced an element of fun.
    - Instructor Training—the instructor had to be trained on the game so that tutorials could be created for the students.
    - Student Training and Object Construction—the students were not completely trained on the game so they would not see the questions beforehand, but they were given verbal instructions before the game began. Once the game was completed, the students went to the next simulation of "clicking" on the career board and receiving their careers, houses, and financial information that was placed into a NoteCard. The students stored the notecards in their inventory to use throughout the simulation. These particular students already knew how to build objects in Second Life® so they were able to enhance their houses with objects.

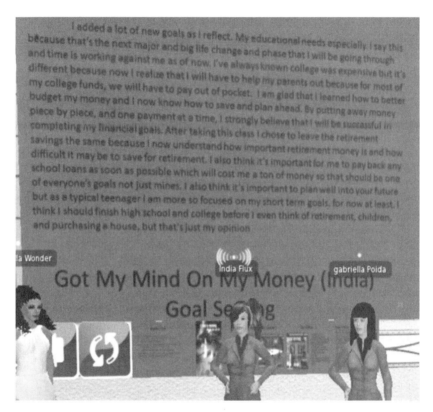

FIGURE 5.1 Students present the completed finance project to classmates within their virtual space, in this case it is the home they purchased and paid for during the financial simulation. The cost was calculated within the budget and income statement.

Outcomes

The power of the game simulation is based on the constructivist theory, which allows the student to take an active role and construct knowledge for themselves through problem-based learning, inquiry, and critical analysis (Concept to Classroom Learning Series, 2004). Through the use of virtual teams, problem solving, application to real life financial scenarios, peer evaluation and reflection the game simulation met all of Bloom's Taxonomy six cognitive levels of thinking complexity: (1) remembering, (2) understanding, (3) applying, (4) analyzing, (5) evaluating, and (6) creating.

1. Remembering: Students were required to study specific chapters in the course textbook and assigned readings regarding the personal financial process. Students would then use the material studied to answer the game board simulation questions as they competed against other virtual teams within Second Life®.

2. Understanding: To prepare for the game board simulation and following choice board game, students must understand the personal financial planning process concepts.

3. Applying: Once students completed each step of the game, they were provided financial data that had to be applied to financial worksheets.

4. Analyzing: The financial data required teams to analyze the information to form conclusions on whether they chose the appropriate data and inputted the material correctly into the financial worksheets.

5. Evaluating: The data had to be analyzed and evaluated to apply to the goal-setting activity, which was based on student's level of understanding of how assets and liabilities affect a student's net income.

6. Creating: Students were required to create a team project as well as individual elements which demonstrated their level of understanding, application, and reflection.

Future Implementation

Research demonstrates that experiences in game simulations enhance student's level of engagement in learning. As noted in the example above, the game-based simulation outlines the cognitive levels and expected outcomes that students should achieve. This personal finance project promotes career awareness as well as possible interest in the pursuit of science, technology, engineering, and mathematics. The instructional tools provided in the Second Life® virtual environment provide a viable means of communicating with students, capturing the interest of the multi-tasking, social networking students. Students

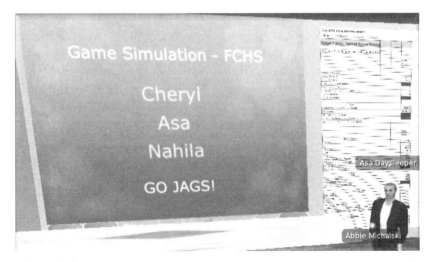

FIGURE 5.2 During presentation student demonstrates how they developed the financial spreadsheet and computed the calculations to complete the financial project.

take ownership by designing and building objects in Second Life® and through the use of tools built into Moodle®, a course management system designed by Martin Dougiamas and other open source creators. Moodle® is used by many universities, community colleges, and high schools that place an emphasis and focus on the use of constructivism. The success of this course and the simulations for the high school students lies in the collaborative efforts of the teachers, administration, admissions, and technical support provided by all participating institutions. Despite being physically separated, the students are actively engaged with each other and the professors via Second Life® using text chat and voice chat. The students are also exposed to guest lecturers and speakers which could not otherwise happen given the physical separation space. These guests are subject matter experts from businesses across the country as well as students from other countries. Using Second Life® provides the opportunity for cultural exchange and is an optimal delivery mode for learning other languages, business philosophies, and extends the classroom. This does not follow the typical examples and assignments used in the classroom which leave students uninvolved and not participating, creating a void in learning.

Although many K-12 institutions have yet to attain the level of technology implementation that institutions of higher education have achieved, it is easy to see how the personal finance game simulation can be changed to meet any content-based educational objective. It would be quite simple to change the context of the game once the initial platform was designed. For example, the financial game could be changed to a history game where students learn about different historical events and then construct the objects within Second Life®. The success of game-based simulation is through the teacher's visualization of how to incorporate learning within an immersive environment that allows students to construct knowledge for themselves through participation, interaction, and engagement in the virtual simulations.

Case Scenario Two: Classroom Management Simulation

Problem

With the current population growth and limited number of qualified teachers, public school systems struggle to fill current positions. In an effort to increase the number of qualified teachers available to enter the teaching workforce, East Carolina University developed a number of outreach programs. One of the issues facing teacher education programs is their inability to provide teacher education students with classroom experience. The current program offers three courses to pre-service teachers that provide classroom observations and teaching experiences. These courses include an introductory to teacher education course which allows students to observe teachers for a 16-week semester period. Two other courses are offered in conjunction, a Senior One

Instructional Methods course and the Senior Two Clinical Experiences course. Both of these courses offer students the opportunity to observe and teach classes at local school sites. The issue that remains is that these courses are not providing a variety of experiences for the pre-service teachers. Research indicates that most programs focus on providing declarative knowledge (knowing what) for specific program areas (i.e., reading, math, science etc.). Although declarative content knowledge (discipline specific) is important, teachers should also have the ability to implement procedural (knowing how) and conditional (knowing when) knowledge. To increase pre-service teacher's metacognitive abilities, the teacher education program needs to expose students to all three kinds of content knowledge: declarative, procedural, and conditional. By developing a baseline level of fundamental clinical experiences, pre-service teachers will have the opportunity to develop an inventory of instructional strategies and methods that can be utilized in their teaching career. Due to the nature of clinical school placements, it is difficult to assert that all students will receive the same level and type of experiences in the field. Therefore offering simulations within the Second Life® environment provides the students with the opportunity to advance their skills and to be exposed to a variety of situations and scenarios that occur on a daily basis in the classroom.

To offset the limited clinical teaching experience, East Carolina University developed classroom simulations in Second Life® that would expose students to a variety of instructional experiences. A teacher education best practices virtual conference was developed. The conference allowed students both within and outside of their discipline to discuss instructional methods that can be incorporated within the classroom. Offering the students the opportunity to connect and develop unplanned learning communities has been one of the small benefits of developing the simulation.

Objectives

1. To develop an immersive environment where pre-service teachers would take on the role of "teacher" and be exposed to a variety of classroom experiences.
2. To develop an immersive environment where pre-service teachers would take on the role of "teacher" and be exposed to a variety of instructional methods utilized by K–12 instructors.
3. To develop an immersive environment where pre-service teachers would be able to utilize problem-solving and critical thinking skills to evaluate challenges that arise during traditional classroom instruction.
4. To develop a community of learners through the use of a virtual conference where participants are able to share ideas and best practices.
5. Pre-service teachers are able to work asynchronously and synchronously to apply instructional method concepts to complete simulated activities.

6. Pre-service teachers are able to present "best practices" for lessons learned and give a presentation in Second Life® to classmates. Following the presentation, students are to complete evaluation rubrics for each team member and a reflective blog based on presentation and content learned.

Example

Pre-service teachers enrolled in the instructional methods course were asked to complete a short pretest quiz on classroom management behavior. The quiz was made available to student's using the Moodle® quiz feature. Following the quiz, a synchronous class was scheduled for students to attend where the instructor presented classroom management behavior methods within the Second Life® environment. Following the session, students also had the opportunity to view other presentations and videos that discussed the concept of classroom management behavior and strategies for K-12 instruction. The next phase was for the pre-service teachers to access a location (classroom) in-world where they would run through a classroom management simulation. The pre-service teachers logged in as their avatar and accessed the classroom. Once inside the classroom they sat at a teacher's desk, which started the simulation. The simulation controlled not only what their avatars heard, but also what they were viewing. This allowed different situations to arise during the class that their avatar (as teacher) would need to control. For example, at one point during the simulation a computer malfunctioned and the teacher would need to input into the chat feature of Second Life® how they would handle the situation and regain control of the class, now off task. Another scenario was when a student was viewing a Facebook page as opposed to working on their Word document. The avatar (teacher) would then have to present how the situation would be resolved in a real classroom. Once all the scenarios in the simulation had finished, the data that the avatar (teacher) inputted would automatically be sent via email to the faculty instructor for grading. Once each student had finished the classroom management simulation, a post-test quiz made available in Moodle®, on classroom management behavior was provided. The pre- and post-test scores were then analyzed to determine the level of increased learning based on the integration of the classroom management simulation.

Technology Requirements and Visionary Development

Second Life® is a software program that allows residents (users) to download the program for free. However the program does have some limitations that an instructor should be mindful of before developing an assignment, activity, or course that includes it. Second Life®, although free, does require a resident (when building) to lease or purchase land. In most cases, if you are an educational-based program, the best route to take is through the New Media

Consortium (NMC), which offers lease agreements, and technical support for a nominal fee. NMC Virtual World Services can be found at http://virtual-worlds.nmc.org/docs/services.pdf. NMC provides a variety of pricing options to meet every institutional or individual need. Another limitation that should be addressed by designers is the computer requirements for running the software. Although most up-to-date computers do not have issues with running it, residents should be made aware of the requirements, run tests, and have a backup plan for students. Information on current computer requirements can be found at http://secondlife.com/support/system-requirements/. For example, you could have students run the Phoenix or Firestorm viewer which allows them third-party access to Second Life®. On a final note most limitations arise from residents not participating in orientation sessions. The orientation sessions allow residents to become familiar with the environment, tools and controls that are available within the Second Life® program. If residents opt out of participating, they often become frustrated with learning the controls. We suggest that orientation be mandatory to alleviate frustration and allow for a smoother transition into the Second Life® activity.

The design and development of the classroom simulation required a team of technology experts and faculty vision. The following elements comprise the building of the simulation in Second Life®:

- Simulation Development—Second Life® Viewer, Scripting objects, object development, avatar creation, and storyboarding
- Instructor training
- Student instructions for completing the simulation
  - Storyboarding—The entire scenario had to be storyboarded by the technologists to be certain each step would achieve the faculty goal and react in the manner desired. This flowcharting included scripting/programming elements of the simulation which reacted immediately to the classroom disruptions occurring.
  - Second Life® Viewer—The simulation took advantage of the features of the Second Life® 2.0 viewer, which needed to be installed on each computer performing the simulation. Students could download this on their own laptops.
  - Object Development—The virtual objects were built using 3D Second Life® tools or by purchasing them from Second Life® MarketPlace with $Linden. $Linden is the SL currency used in-world (Hodge, Collins, & Giordano, 2011), which can be exchanged from any world currency. Objects are purchased from merchants in Second Life® and through Second Life® MarketPlace.
  - Scripting—This element is one of the most complicated as it is responsible for the simulations responding to all avatars; they must work smoothly. A student within the ITCS team developed the scripts, which were placed in all the virtual objects as in the game simulation.

Notecards had to be created as well as text that appeared in the chat window. For example, a chat showed the problem occurring in the classroom that the student needed to address.

- Avatar Creation —Each student used their own avatar for this simulation.
- Student Training—The students were trained on Second Life® through the use of PiratePort, the ECU orientation island. They also had additional training from the instructor and Second Life® technicians before the simulation began.

Outcomes

The use of the virtual environment Second Life® was integrated in the instructional methods course to immerse pre-service teachers in educational experiences that will arise in their real life classrooms on a daily basis. Furthermore, the variety of activities utilized through Second Life® provided the teachers with the ability to be exposed to diverse settings, students, instruction, and methods for improving teaching and learning. Based on the objectives listed above, the following outcomes were assessed.

1. Remembering, Understanding & Application: Pre-service teachers gained a higher level of understanding of the classroom management strategies that could be incorporated into their real life classrooms. They noted the immersion into the virtual classroom environment simulation as an excellent way for them to role play and formulate strategies for overcoming common classroom management and behavior issues.
2. Best Practices conference provided pre-service teachers with the following:
   a. Understanding & Analyzing: Exposure to new innovative teaching methods.
   b. Remembering: Awareness to new technologies that can be integrated into the classroom.
   c. Creating: Networking capabilities with other teachers "in the field" that have knowledge of both good and bad teaching practices.
   d. Creating & Applying: The use of the virtual classroom environment provided a location for pre-service teachers to communicate and interact with one another. They were able to discuss classroom challenges and issues that commonly arise in their schools.
   e. Applying: The conference offered a real life experience of presenting as opposed to attending a workshop. In most cases this was the first time the teachers had presented at a conference. The Atlantic Coast Business, Marketing and Information Technology conference also exposed them to other teacher educators in the field.
   f. Creating & Applying: The use of the virtual environment classroom setting provided the pre-service teachers with a new technology that

they were able to share with their colleagues. Many of the pre-service teachers began looking at ways they could incorporate their lessons for use within the virtual environment.

Future Implementation

The success of the program is based on utilizing the 3D virtual environment to engage students through presentations, simulations, interactive games, live video events, and peer collaborations. The 3D virtual platform captures the interest of today's multi-tasking, social networking students with the technology tools implemented by the professor to encourage a community of learners. The purpose of Second Life® at ECU is to create a true virtual learning community that is designed for and by the students, following the constructivist theory. Simulations through Second Life® can provide a technology-rich world in which to learn.

Future Potential and Implications

As institutions of higher education continue to struggle with budget cuts, virtual environments provide a method of teaching and learning that does not require a physical structure or place. Programs can grow and be developed for a fraction of the cost of a traditional interactive classroom. As summarized

FIGURE 5.3 The desks shown in the image were used during the classroom design simulation. The students were provided a scenario in which they had to teach a particular style of class. When they clicked on each style, the desks and items in the room would automatically move so that students could determine the best layout for the type of instruction.

in Brown and Green's (2010) chapter for the *Educational Media and Technology Yearbook*, online learning will continue to grow and thrive during difficult economic times as it provides instructional delivery without the additional cost of travel. Furthermore, the technology enhances an innovative approach by adding an opportunity for students to have a more collaborative space in which to learn. The Second Life® virtual environment offers students the benefit of receiving course work that they are currently unable to obtain because of location, space limitations, and other constraints faced in a face-to-face class and even in distance education courses because of the lack of communication. The virtual environment supersedes discussion groups normally held in a course through a course management system. The students are able to get immediate feedback from either the faculty member or other students.

Second Life® offers the opportunity to access a vast store of knowledge and information 24/7. The University of Texas is one of numerous universities that recognized the possibilities of virtual environments and recently purchased 60 virtual islands to create a learning community allowing the connection of students, faculty, researchers, and administrators (Bloom's Taxonomy, 2010). Texas A&M offers STEM (Science, Technology, Engineering, and Mathematics) related courses that could serve as possible resources, thereby extending the community reach. According to Linden Lab (2010, p. 1), there are hundreds of colleges, universities, and organizations in Second Life®, creating immersive learning spaces and communities. Another list from Peter Miller (2010) shows 384 institutions currently in Second Life®. These universities and colleges are linked together by a community mailing list, supporting each other and sharing ideas, making a true open-source community.

As a catalyst for change, the program promises an innovative, technology sound, answer to advancing theory, methods, measurements, development, and application to a wide array of educational opportunities. The opportunities include a community of proportion never known before to educators. From science, math, history, theater, to teacher education, the possibilities are truly endless with a rich environment where students can learn, share, and develop their knowledge.

References

Bielaczyc, K., & Collins, A. (1999). Learning communities in classrooms: A reconceptualization of educational practice. In C. M. Reigeluth (Ed.), *Instructional-design theories and models: A new paradigm of instructional theory* (pp. 269–292). Mahwah NJ: Erlbaum.

Brooks, J., & Brooks, M. (2001). *In search of understanding: The case for constructivist classrooms* (2nd ed.). Retrieved June 15, 2011, from Funderstanding: http://www.funderstanding.com/content/constructivism

Brown, J. S., & Adler, R. P. (2008, January/February). Minds on fire: Open education, the long tail, and learning 2.0. *EDUCAUSE Review, 43*(1), 16–32.

Brown, A., & Green, T. (2010). Issues and trends in instructional technology: Growth and maturation of web-based tools in a challenging climate; social networks gain educators' attention.

In M. Orey, S. A. Jones, & R. M. Branch (Eds.). *Educational Media and Technology Yearbook, 35,* 29–44.

Concept to Classroom. (2004). ThirteenEd online workshop series website. Retrieved from http://www.thirteen.org/edonline/concept2class/constructivism/index.html

Dede, C. J. (1992). The future of multimedia: Bridging to virtual worlds. *Educational Technology, 32*(5), 54–60.

Dede, C. (1995, September). The evolution of constructivist learning environments: Immersion in distributed, virtual worlds. *Educational Technology, 35*(5), 46–52.

Dede, C., (2009, January). Immersive Interfaces for Engagement and Learning. Science *Magazine, 323,* 66-69).

Dede, C., Salzman, M., Loftin, R. B., & Ash, K., (2000). *Innovations in science and mathematics education: Advanced designs for technologies of learning.* Mahwah, NJ: Erlbaum.

Girvan, C., & Savage, T. (2010). Identifying an appropriate pedagogy for virtual worlds: A communal constructivism case study. *Computers & Education, 55,* 342–349.

Hodge, E., Collins, S., & Giordano, T. (2011). *The virtual worlds handbook: how to use Second Life® and other 3D virtual environments.* Sudbury, ME: Jones and Bartlett.

Kay, K., & Honey, M. (2005). *Beyond technology competency: A vision of ICT literacy to prepare students for the 21st century. The Institute for the Advancement of Emerging Technologies in Education.* Charleston, WV: Evantia. Retrieved December 18, 2011, from Critical Issues: Using Technology to Improve Student Achievement: http://www.ncrel.org/sdrs/areas/issues/methods/technlgy/te800.htm

Lave, J., & Wenger, W. (1991). *Situated learning: Legitimate peripheral participation.* Cambridge, UK: Cambridge University Press.

Lessiter, J., Freeman, J., Keogh, E., & Davidoff, J. (2001): *A cross-media presence questionnaire: The ITC-sense of presence inventory.* In *Presence: Teleoperators and Virtual Environments, 10*(3), 282–297.

Linden Lab. (2010). *Second Life® education/get started.* Retrieved June 16, 2011, from Wiki Second Life®: http://wiki.secondlife.com/wiki/Second_Life_Education_-_Get_Started

Miller, P. (2010). *SL educationa institutions c2010.* Retrieved June 16, 2011, from GoogleDocs, https://spreadsheets.google.com/spreadsheet/ccc?key=0Am1Q98bSWCCSdHB5TTE0N2p yVmRQYjZsaFREN0tMMWc&hl=en_GB&authkey=CPuEtKAC#gid=0

Perraton, H. (1988). A theory for distance education. In D. Sewart, D., Keegan, & B. Holmberg (Eds.), *Distance education: International perspectives* (pp. 95–113). New York: Routledge.

Schuman, L. (1996). Perspectives on instruction. Retrieved February 26, 2010, from http://edweb.sdsu.edu/courses/edtec540/Perspectives/Perspectives.html

Swan, K., & Shea, P. (2005). *The development of virtual learning communities.* In. S. R. Hiltz & R. Goldman (Eds.), *Learning together online: Research on asynchronous learning network,* (pp. 239–260). Mahwah, NJ: Erlbaum.

6

DEVELOPING A WIKI FOR PROBLEM-BASED ONLINE INSTRUCTION AND WEB 2.0 EXPLORATION

Teresa Franklin and Briju Thankachan

Introduction

The use of social networks such as Facebook, MySpace, LinkedIn, wikis and blogs bring a new and engaging social aspect to teacher preparation as these tools continue to evolve and challenge each new generation of classroom teachers. Social networking is a favorite pastime of many of our present teachers, teacher education students, and the students that will be or are presently are in classrooms. The use of these social networks crosses all boundaries of teaching and learning and appears even within virtual 3-D worlds such as Second Life (Wheeler & Whitton, 2007).

Wikis can foster interaction, collaboration, contribution, and problem solving by engaging large groups of people in the discussion of the problem at hand. An essential feature of a wiki is user generated content enabling sharing, creating, editing, and construction of knowledge. This knowledge reflects the collective intelligence of the users and supports a constructivist environment for teaching and learning (Sua & Beaumont, 2010).

Online courses pose an interesting problem when teachers are asked to engage in discussion, present work and ideas in cyberspaces that are often not the *norm* for their beliefs on what constitutes a classroom. Often, teachers have difficulty collaborating with individuals who arc not a personal friend or contact when online. The use of social networking can help bridge the needs of the online classroom by bringing groups of people together across a distance and helping multiple collaborators to create and present new ideas in a dynamic and interactive space (Parker & Chao, 2007).

A Wiki as a Collaborative Tool

In the 21st century, studies have investigated the potentials of participatory learning (Cunningham, 2009; Warhurst, 2006). In the digital world, traditionally passive learners have become active participants with connectivity and the social rapport. Social software has created a participatory culture and learning environment for all to engage in sharing their expertise (McLoughlin & Lee, 2007). A wiki allows students to interact and participate beyond the classroom and in collaborative projects (Leuf & Cunningham, 2001). According to Solomon and Schrum (2010), "Wikis are webpages that students can use to write, edit, and add elements, such as images and video, to create collaborative projects" (p. 135). The advantages of using a wiki in the classroom are its ability to support transparent writing and editing, teamwork, and continuous feedback (Greenhow, 2006).

Wiki in Higher Education

Several studies have investigated the use of wiki in higher education (Karasavvidis, 2010b; Wheeler, Yeomans, & Wheeler, 2008). Karasavvidis (2010a) identified two main problems in the implementation of wiki in the higher education; first student resistance, and second is the mode of work. Students' resistance suggests they may welcome the wiki but not always as a means of completing assignments. Mode of work is the complexity in shared editing, lack of synchronization and constructive criticisms and inappropriate contributions often found in assignments involving a wiki. The success of implementing wiki in the classroom depends on the perspective and participation of students (Karasavvidis, 2010a) and adequate support to teachers who are new to the wiki technology (Witney & Smallbone, 2011).

Problem-Based Learning

Problem-based learning (PBL) as a concept was originally formed by John Dewey (1916), who proposed the idea that learning through social interaction created an environment in which students acquire new knowledge related to the problem and application or development of new problem solving skills (Barrows & Tamblyn, 1980).

PBL creates an authenticity and ownership among students by, "Honoring the importance of authenticity, ownership, and relevance of the learning experience of students in relation to the content to be learned and the process by which it is learned" (Nelson, 1999, p. 245). In problem-based learning, the organization of knowledge allows for open-ended situations or problems, and the facilitator acts as the enabler of opportunities for learning (Savery & Duffy, 1995).

In an online environment, problem-based learning has different advantages. When PBL is used in an online environment, students can enjoy the wider resources, innovative problems, and instant communication that are afforded by the Web (Savin-Baden, & Wilkie, 2006). The challenge implementing PBL online is that "students can be overloaded with information and the problem scenarios may be all at the same level, with gradients being seen in terms of complexity of information management rather than the development of criticality" (Savin-Baden, & Major, 2004, p. 168). Using a wiki to help organize thoughts and discussions may help to manage this complexity and improve the adoption of technology use in teaching and learning (Savin-Baden, 2000).

The Concerns-Based Adoption Model (CBAM)

Hall, Wallace, and Dossett (1973) first proposed the conceptual framework of CBAM in 1970 at the University of Texas Research and Development Center for Teacher Education. Hall and Hord (1987) hypothesized that "there was a set of developmental stages and levels teachers and others moved through as they became increasingly sophisticated and skilled in using new programs and procedures" (p. 7). Anderson (1997) elaborates,

> The model is concerned with measuring, describing, and explaining the process of change experienced by teachers involved in attempts to implement new curriculum materials and instructional practices, and with how that process is affected by interventions from persons acting in change-facilitating roles.
>
> (p. 331)

The CBAM system represents two-systems, a resource system and a user system. The change facilitator such as a school administrator may determine the implementation process of the innovation. The resource system represents any innovation or idea; the user system represents innovation adaptors usually teachers (Hall & Hord, 2011).

Diagnostic Dimensions of CBAM

To measure change in an individual, the CBAM model has three diagnostic dimensions: Stages of Concern, Levels of Use, and Innovation Configurations. The diagnostic dimension used in this study was Levels of Use as a means of identifying the graduate student's level of comfort in using the wiki and open source applications. The main concern was that the open source software and the wiki needed to be perceived as useful within a classroom setting by educators if adoption of these tools were to occur. In the past, the researchers had identified that teachers were reluctant to change the software or methods used in the classroom to teach. Research by Parker and Chao (2007) concerning online learning suggests that the use of a wiki can be met with resistance by teachers.

CBAM Levels of Use

Hall and Hord (2011) identified eight different Levels of Use in the adoption of a new innovation. According to the model, the initial level is the *nonuse* state in which the teacher has little or no knowledge of the innovation, no involvement with the innovation, and is doing nothing toward becoming involved. The final level is the *renewal* state in which the teacher re-evaluates the quality of use of the innovation and believes the innovation is necessary for teaching and learning.

The Level of Use framework was used to examine teachers' behavioral patterns and level of comfort when they prepare to implement a classroom change and begin to use technology. The progressions in the level of use are:

- Level 0—Nonuse
- Level 1—Orientation
- Level 2—Preparation
- Level 3—Mechanical
- Level 4a—Routine
- Level 4b—Refinement
- Level 5—Integration
- Level 6—Renewal

As teachers perceive their use of the innovation (in this study the wiki and open source software) to be helpful in their work, and, as they become more comfortable with the technology, and move through the Levels of Use over time to the renewal stage. Hall and Hord (1987) determined in their research that "there must be appropriate and promising practices and procedures (i.e., innovations) that they [teachers] develop or adopt and, when necessary, adapt" (p. 4). According to Anderson (1997), CBAM is, "the most robust and empirically grounded theoretical model for the implementation of educational innovations" (p. 331). Levels of Use information can be used to help districts to identify the adoption of technology tools by teachers.

The Development of the Wiki PBL Course

As with many universities, graduate level courses are provided online to support the working schedules and needs of educators returning to the university to improve their classroom teaching practice. In 2009, a review of the Technology Applications in Education course was undertaken to determine its viability as an online course. The course evaluations for the past two years were reviewed for concepts, activities, or issues that had been identified as valuable or not valuable by students. The first theme in the evaluations was how graduate students were changed by the instruction concerning the integration of software for teaching and learning. They noted that software incorporated in the course, the models for integration, and examples of use changed their perceptions of not only their personal use but their classroom use of technology as well. A second theme included statements and questions such as, "how will I be able to do this in class since we do not have the money for this software" or "we are not allowed access to the Internet by our principal so we can't do many of these great activities." The third theme suggested a personal and social benefit to the course with many graduates providing comments similar to, "it is great to be with other educators and share ideas, thoughts about classrooms, the technology used, etc. I would never have time to come up with all of this on my own" (Graduate Evaluations – Educational Studies, 2008–2010). It became evident from these themes that a social network and Web 2.0 software might support the three themes found in past evaluations. Comments concerning discussion boards and collaboration from the teacher evaluations also pointed to a need to move teachers online to collaborate so that they would understand the changing field in education as face-to-face classrooms become virtual learning environments.

In order to transition the course, the faculty decided to use a wiki as a virtual learning environment in which graduate students would collaborate as teams, discussions would be held and open source software would be examined. After reviewing several wiki products, the faculty identified the open source wiki, Wikispaces, as the wiki to be used in the course. Wikispaces was chosen because it had tutorials to help in creating a team wiki, contained templates to allow the teams to individualize the site (which can increase ownership of work; Parker & Chao, 2007), allowed for privacy settings, formatting followed typical word processing practices, contained email capabilities for the users, the user could upload and attach files and pictures to the site and, most importantly, it was free to educators and therefore did not increase class costs. The faculty believed this would be a valuable site for teachers to use after leaving the course as well. For the instructional model, the faculty created a problem-based scenario by presenting a school district problem in which the graduate students would be challenged to find a district solution to a software budget crisis.

[Note: The problem presented to the graduate students is a real school district problem that was identified as a need during a regional school superintendents meeting. The superintendents asked the researchers to help in identifying open source software to use in their districts.]

Problem Background

Before the real world problem was presented to the students, the following activities occurred within the Learning Management System used at this university:

- online chats;
- course readings;
- discussions on the use of technology in schools;
- research on technology's impact on student achievement;
- the role of the school administration, technology coordinator, and teachers in software selection;
- the use of open source software.

This provided graduate students with the background knowledge supporting the problem and possible solutions. By moving to the wiki during the problem-solving phase of the course, graduate students shifted into their own space for collaboration and role-playing.

The Instructional Problem Presented to the Graduate Students

Students were presented with the following problem and explanation as part of the Technology Applications in Education course at the first class meeting.

> Budgets for technology in schools continue to shrink and the latest esti-mate of a 10% decrease in funding by state agencies further challenges school districts in the area of technology integration. As funds decrease, school districts must make difficult decisions on the purchase of hardware and software for the classroom. Web 2.0 tools and applications known as Open Source Software (OSS) may be able to help districts meet their software needs as free, Internet-based software. Upon reviewing the local school district budget, a superintendent from the local school district has asked the following questions:
>
> - Can Open Source Software (OSS) save the district money as a replacement for purchased software?
> - Can the open source software deliver the same educational value?
> - Can the software support higher-order thinking skills and activities in the classroom?
>
> The superintendent noted that he has no real knowledge of Open Source Software and will submit a report to the school board and parents of the district in solicit their support for the change to open source software if it is found to be a viable solution. Members of the course are being asked to help the school district in finding a solution for providing software in the district that is affordable and supports the activities of the classroom for teaching and learning. The following list is suggested for use in helping you organize thoughts and find a solution.

1. Identify possible open source software that could be used to replace the software being used in the classroom(s).

2. As software is located and reviewed, create a wiki in Wikispaces of your exploration of the possible software choices. Concerns, issues identified, problems, reviews from other educators, etc., are to be kept in the wiki. Critically examine the suggestions. Peer-review of the comments from the course team wikis is expected each week and a response by the team to the peer-review is also expected.
3. What are the critical software questions that need to be discussed in your school district?
4. Review all wikis, then comment, critique, and share information that will help district personnel in solving this problem.

Finding a Solution

Identifying Roles. Each pair of graduate students was asked to role-play a person in the school [Roles: Classroom Teacher (RT) and Technology Coordinator (RTC)]. One graduate student role-played the district technology coordinator and a partner graduate student role-played the classroom teacher. The researchers (faculty and teaching assistant) played the role of school superintendent and school principal. Blackboard was used to connect all of the wikis such that each wiki could be viewed by all members of the course and cross-team comments could be made within the wikis.

Identifying Critical Questions. The paired teams worked with all the other district technology coordinator/teacher paired teams to identify a common group of critical questions such that decisions could be made consistently across all the reviews of the OSS software. From the common set of questions, the analysis, evaluation, and selection of a district's software was to be completed by each team and presented on the final day of the class at a face-to-face meeting.

Identifying School Demographics. The teams next establish demographics for their school using the state funding agency website to obtain demographic data. Many of the graduate students in this class were already school teachers, technology coordinators, or within a school structure in their work environment and sought to solve the problem using his/her own school district as the location for the implementation of open source software and decisions.

The Study

While the nature of the course was to research, evaluate, and solve a real problem facing schools concerning budgets and software purchases, the researchers sought to understand the use of a wiki for providing the needed social space in an online environment. This assignment had in the past positively impacted teacher's adoption of technology beliefs about software purchases, budgeting and the impact of administration on technology use in schools; the researchers were concerned that the change of delivery method might impact the desired. The level of use and the adoption of the technologies encountered in the course were a concern as students had identified that these were two areas in which they had experienced a positive personal change in perceptions of technology.

The research questions of the study included:

RQ1: To what extent does a wiki provide the social networking support for graduate students to collaborate in identifying software, organizing discussions, and evaluating open source software?

RQ2: To what extent does a graduate student's identity with his/her program major impact discussion of open source software?

RQ3: To what extent do the graduate students indicate levels of innovation/change through use of the wiki and open source software?

This research and classroom practice used a single case study approach in which the graduate course was the single case. The case consisted of 36 graduate students enrolled in either the Masters in Computer Education and Technology Program (CET; n = 21) or the Adolescent to Young Adult Teacher Education Program (AYA; n = 15). The CET students were in their first and second years of the program, while the AYA students were in their first year of their program. Sixty percent of the graduate students were from 21 to 29 years of age. There were 19 females and 16 males in the case. Sixty-seven percent of the graduate students were in their first year of study in graduate school. Eighty-three percent were teachers in the United States and 6% were teachers internationally All but the 4 international students were teachers or technology coordinators. Fifteen pairs and two groups of three students were formed to study the presented school district-based problem.

Through the application of qualitative research principles of grounded theory, the study examined the problem posed by a school. The data were comprised of graduate student wikis, peer-reviews, discussions and the final presentation of the team's solution to the district software problem. Data were coded and categorized by each researcher independently on a weekly basis. Coded themes were then placed in memo format to help articulate emerging ideas and patterns observed in the data. When all data had been coded, categorized, and placed in memo format, the researchers compared their results and identified discrepancies in interpretation and came to consensus on the emerging themes and categories across all data collected.

The Procedure

Graduate students were presented with the problem of a school district in the area being in need of software and posted their wiki and invited others to review their work and identify concerns, ask questions about the software chosen, and similarities and differences in the choices of open source software across members of the teams. At the final presentation of their solutions to the budget crisis problem, the graduate students presented an overview and implementation plan. The recommended list of open source software was compiled from all teams. In the final class meeting which was face-to-face, the teams reached a consensus on the software selections and the final list and discussion were presented to the superintendent for consideration. The faculty and graduate students completed a peer-review of each presentation and discussion of strengths and weaknesses of the wiki and its use.

Findings

Wiki Collaboration in Selection of Open Source Software

RQ1: *To what extent does a wiki provide the social networking support for graduate students to collaborate in identifying software, organizing discussions, and evaluating open source software?* It was easy to identify that within the first week after the problem introduction, the teams had come to agreement on the criteria for the selection of the open source software. These criteria included: (a) educational use within the classrooms (ease of use by students; easy for the teacher to learn; ease of reaching/obtaining the software on/from the web), (b) cost and registration issues, (c) content area and added value of the software to instruction, and (d) use of higher order thinking skills when working with the software.

The teams began by organizing all discussions around these four aspects and wrote extensively with respect to these criteria. The wiki criteria evolved over the weeks to include more specialized discussions depending on school demographics. The wiki provided an interesting picture and exhaustive discussion of progression through software selection not typically available in the face-to-face classroom setting. The wiki supported the extensive comments on the software, descriptions of its use and critiques/questions by other teams.

Over time, many teams reorganized their sites to identify specific content areas to be given preference and then software that would serve the general population of the district. Teams identified software that would support creative endeavors or general needs of students and then utility needs by the teacher. Twelve of the seventeen teams followed this reorganization: (a) content specific software, (b) general software, and (c) creative software while still maintaining the criteria for each evaluation originally determined. An examination of the *history* of the wiki, allowed the researchers to identify this decision in weeks 5 and 6 of the course. Figure 6.1 is an example of what many of the wiki sites provided in the early two weeks of the discussions.

The discussion by Team 12 provides an example of examining open source software that could be used as teacher utility software.

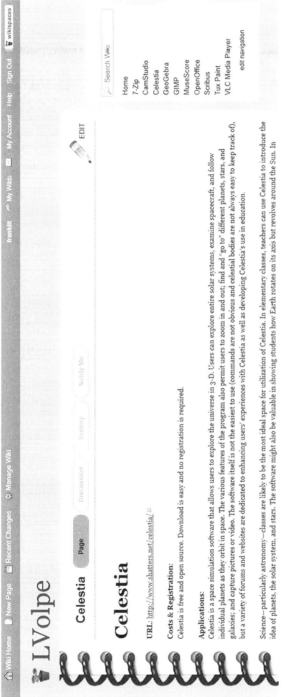

FIGURE 6.1 Sample of wiki from Technology Applications in Education.

[Team 12-RT] I enjoyed playing around with this software as it was quite easy to create crossword puzzles. This provides a fun alternative to traditional learning for the classroom. Although at first glance it did look somewhat intimidating, within minutes I was on my way to creating my first crossword puzzle with definitions. This program can be adapted to the classroom as assignments or in the home as a way to reinforce what has been learned at school. The biggest drawback of the program I found to be in actually creating the puzzle that is given to your students. It would be much more useful if the puzzle were to print as one document rather than having to print each individual aspect of the puzzle. I would also like the capability to be able to save the puzzles that I make; instead users only have the option to print their puzzles.

[Team 12-RTC] This program definitely lacks the bells and whistles that many times help the more novice users successfully navigate through and utilize the features of the software. Because crossword puzzles require the correct spelling of words in order to successfully complete, this may be problematic for some students.

[Team 12-RT] Yes, it may not be as pressing of an issue for a Geography teacher if a student misspells Mississippi on an assignment. By using the crossword puzzle the student's learning may actually be impeded because by misspelling one word in the puzzle, it is almost impossible to correctly answer any of the other words in the puzzle.

[Team 12-RTC] The fact that some teachers may not even make it past the first step automatically lowers the rating of this software. This particular title may be of better use for more technologically experienced teachers.

Most of the teams exhibited this form of give and take in their discussions with each presenting the software and then noting positives and negatives of its use.

In five of the teams, those playing the role of Classroom Teacher (CT) expressed their frustration with their school district and the implementation of software similar to the following:

[Team 4-RT] I have found some great resources in the open source software but when I spoke to my technology coordinator and principal it was very depressing. The technology coordinator seemed to believe that only viruses were associated with open source software and the principal just "backed-up" the technology coordinator. While I know the whole virus thing is not true, it annoys me that neither person was interested in finding out the facts. The answer was "no" when I started asking the question.

The partner of this teacher who was a technology coordinator responded:

> [Team 4-RTC] It is unfortunate that you had this experience. Many of those in school technology coordinator positions are actually from the more "hard core" technology side of computing and not very familiar with education and how the needs of teachers when working with student and computers are different than working with other "computer geeks." Teachers have different expectations and tend to be more constructivist in nature and expect exploration by students. You may want to explore how a technology committee could be formed by teachers and the technology coordinator and administration to discuss changing needs for technology and 21st century skills. This has worked well at my district.

In the wiki environment, this discussion quickly moved across all the wikis with the consensus being that the school districts need to remove the restrictions to Internet use and allow more flexibility for use in the classroom.

Most team conversations were around the criteria and how it would be used in the classroom suggesting a strong desire by all members to select the best software for the school district of their study. Team-3 provides a sample of these conversations.

> [Team 3-RTC] I can't believe the strength of OpenOffice as a tool to replace Office [Microsoft Office] in our school. We have the oldest version of Office, 2000 I think, and it is so difficult to use and we cannot purchase an upgrade. Wow! OpenOffice does everything and more—it seems just like Office and opens all my files and saves in a compatible format—which I was skeptical about! I have looked at Google Docs too. The only drawback with Google Docs is the need to have Internet access. Both pieces of software would provide the word processing, presentation, and spreadsheet we need but OpenOffice can be downloaded for free and put on every computer.

> [Team 3-RT] Students could be taught how (they probably already know how to do this) to download and have it on their home computer to use and bring work to class on their USB. They would not need to be connected to the Internet which can be a problem in our community due to the cost of Internet access and many only have dial-up at slow speeds.

> [Team 3-RTC] With a little PD, I think this could easily become our main software in the classroom and our offices with the only cost being the time to put on the machines—which we have to do anyway each year.

The use of Google Docs versus OpenOffice discussion continued throughout the quarter as more and more teams examined the software. The final statement from the teams was, "both Google Docs and OpenOffice are fairly equivalent pieces of productivity software, and the issue is really the flexibility of the school district in allowing access to the Internet to use Google Docs."

The graduate students had difficulty thinking about the higher order thinking skills that might be addressed when using a particular piece of open source software. While the teams would attempt to talk about the higher order thinking skills, typically the answer was more of a "yes" or "no" as to whether or not higher order thinking skills could be enhanced or challenged by use of the software. This is an area in which more discussion and possibly a rubric should be developed to help focus on supporting higher order thinking skills with the integration of software use in the classroom.

Viewing Collaboration through the Identity of a Student's Major

RQ2: *To what extent does a graduate student's identity with his/her program major impact discussion of open source software?* In examining the paired comments for impact of discussions and posting with relationship to their program major at the university, the technology coordinators provided much more detail in the explanation of the review of the software in the wiki than the teachers. Their comments took on a more holistic view of the district, the time to install as a cost, possible extension of the software to home computers (6 teams contained graduate students who were already technology coordinators in their present school environment). Over the 10-week quarter, most pairs averaged 8 to 15 entries per week with a final total of 2189 entries during the course.

While the technology coordinator often provided more detail in the comments or asked very technology support situated questions, there was very little difference in the length or number of words used in writing the comments by major (CET vs. AYA; teacher vs. technology coordinator). All team members worked diligently and provided extensive comments, questions and critiques in support of the other teams and their software selections. Comments when critiquing other wiki comments were of the following nature:

> [Team 15-RTC] It seems you have found a piece of software [Gimp 2] that allows for a great deal of creativity by the student. Do you think the software is more difficult or easier than Photoshop Elements? Students love to use Photoshop, which is fairly inexpensive to purchase. Do you think this is a better value? I agree that "free" can be good, but sometimes the purchased version is really better at teaching a particular artistic technique or in developing artwork that the students like as much by using the free version.

Technology coordinators focused on the value of the software being free versus purchased more often than the teacher. The teacher nearly always focused on the need for free software in the classroom which could be used at home as well.

Examining Innovation and Change

RQ3: *To what extent do the graduate students indicate levels of innovation/change through use of the wiki and open source software?* The CBAM model was used to examine the perceived level of use and level of adoption and comfort by the graduate students in using open source software in their own classrooms or school district in the case of technology coordinators. Past graduate students had indicated a change in the perceptions of their own personal adoption and comfort level concerning the use of technology for teaching and learning. Faculty sought to identify if this perception was maintained in the online course and if the students suggested that the wiki or software encountered in the course supported this change.

A survey was constructed using the CBAM definitions which asked the graduate students to rank their perceived level of use of open source software (identified innovation) at the end of the course. The CBAM scale for use of an innovation ranges from *nonuse* (Level 0) in which the user has little or no knowledge of the innovation, no involvement with the innovation, and is doing nothing toward being involved, to the *renewal* (Level 6) in which the user re-evaluates the quality of use of the innovation, seeks major modifications of or alternatives to present innovation to achieve increased impact on students, examines new developments in the field, and explores new goals for self and the system (Hall & Hord, 2011). The full range of the scale and the percentage of graduate students identifying with a level are found in Table 6.1.

A chi-square test of independence was performed to examine the relationships between level of adoption and major (CET; AYA), year in their program of study (Year1; Year 2) and gender. The lack of significance suggested that major, year in the program of study and gender did not impact the graduate student's level of adoption of open source software. Table 6.2 provides a summary of the chi-square test results between the level of use and the major, year in the program and gender.

The outcomes of the chi-square data and CBAM survey data suggest graduate students had started to use the open source software that would help them in their work either in the classroom, personally, or in the district as was the case with OpenOffice, which was widely identified as a useful software replacement for Microsoft Office. Comments included: "I found most of the software to be easy to use and I had no idea there were so many free pieces of software that I could use" or "I had not used a wiki and now I am using it in class. My students love it."

From the 2,189 discussions/comments in the team wikis, the following applications were identified as meeting the criteria developed in class for educational settings and were part of presentation discussions at the end of the quarter. The graduate students noted that there were many different and interesting open source software choices for the classroom, but this list met the criteria and performed well in the classroom. The final team presentations provided to the

TABLE 6.1 *Graduate Student's Use of Open Source in CBAM's Diagnostic Dimension — Level of Use*

Level	Use Statements	Percentage
Level 0: Non-use	I have little or no knowledge of Open Source technology use in education, no involvement with it, and I am doing nothing toward becoming involved.	0%
Level 1: Orientation	I am seeking or acquiring information about Open Source technology in education.	11%
Level 2: Preparation	I am preparing for the first use of Open Source technology in education.	17%
Level 3: Mechanical Use	I focus most effort on the short-term, day-to-day use of Open Source technology with little time for reflection. My effort is primarily directed toward mastering tasks required to use the Open Source	9%
Level 4 A: Routine	I feel comfortable using Open Source technology in education. However, I am putting forth little effort and thought to improve Open Source technology use in education or its consequences.	26%
Level 4 B: Refinement	I vary the use of Open Source technology in education to increase the expected benefits within the classroom. I am working on using Open Source technology to maximize the effects with my students.	20%
Level 5: Integration	I am combining my own efforts with related activities of other teachers and colleagues to achieve impact in the classroom of Open Source technology use.	9%
Level 6: Renewal	I can re-evaluate the quality of use of Open Source technology in education, seek major modifications of, or alternatives to, present innovation to achieve increased impact, examine new developments in the field, and explore new goals for myself and my school or district.	9%

TABLE 6.2 *Summary of the Chi-Square Test Results between the Level of Adoption and the Program, Year, and Gender*

Variable	Test	Value	df	Asymp. Sig. (2-sided)
Program	Pearson Chi-Square	19.950	12	.068
Year in the Program	Pearson Chi-Square	7.875	6	.247
Gender	Pearson Chi-Square	4.362	6	0.63

school administrator a list of the software selected for use in the schools and the cost of the software and any registration issues. An artifact was created to by each team to demonstrate the higher order thinking skills addressed by the software and the possible uses of the software in the classroom.The list below was presented to the superintendent as the solution to the problem of addressing open source software to be used in the K-12 school district.

1. OpenOffice (word processing, presentation, spreadsheet)
2. Gimp (Adobe Photoshop-picture enhancement software)
3. Google Earth (provides various views of the)
4. Celestia (presents views of the solar system)
5. Tux Paint (outstanding paint program)
6. CamStudio or Audacity (free recording software for podcasts)
7. Freemind (concept mapping software)
8. Gcompris (game-based software)
9. Blender (advanced model drawing software)
10. Moodle (content management software)

This list was presented to the real world district superintendents who had posed the original question to the faculty member teaching the course. The list contains software for almost all content areas and deals with the needs for the district as a whole with OpenOffice and Moodle while attending to specific content areas through the remaining software.

Conclusion

The development of the wiki as a support for a problem-based online course supported more discussion than the researchers had seen in previous face-to-face courses. None of the students in the course had used a wiki to the extent of this class to support their work, discussions, presentations, and data collection. Comments concerning the use of the wiki were very positive. Reflections similar to the following were found in many of the final postings,

> [Team 7-RT] I had no idea a wiki would support pictures, files, and could be such an interesting way to journal. Upon reflection of the course, the use of the wiki really made me think about how my own students could use the wiki to keep journals and collaborate on stories.

The role-playing aspect as well as the real world problem provided to the class required collaboration in finding a solution.

Witney and Smallbone (2011) suggest that having a real problem and structured framework encourages collaboration in an online wiki environment. In our online environment, the wiki supported the graduate students remarkably well with one student noting,

[Team 3-RT] I have talked to my team member more this quarter than I normally do in f2f classes … The discussion was so interesting that I could not wait to read what my team member had written and to comment. I did not want to be seen as the one not participating or doing my share of the work. I felt an obligation to do my best and not embarrass my team with poorly researched answers.

Findings indicate that the level of knowledge concerning open source software was very limited and even those with extensive technology experience noted in comments that they had not had time to explore the possibility of using free open source software in the classroom and had generally been opposed before taking the course. Team 8-Role Technology Coordinator wrote, "I am impressed. I thought a wiki was pretty much useless. I was very wrong." The comment speaks to the need to have time to explore the software found on the web that can support collaboration and technological innovation of our educators and their students.

References

Anderson, S. E. (1997). Understanding teacher change: Revisiting the concerns based adoption model. *Curriculum Inquiry, 27*(3), 331–367. doi:10.1111/0362-6784.00057

Barrows, H. S., & Tamblyn, R. M. (1980). *Problem-based learning: An approach to medical education.* New York: Springer.

Cunningham, C. A. (2009). Transforming schooling through technology: Twenty-first-century approaches to participatory learning. *Education and Culture, 25*(2). Retrieved from http://rave.ohiolink.edu/databases/login/eric/EJ912434

Dewey, J. (1916). *Democracy and education: An introduction to the philosophy of education.* New York: The Macmillan Company.

Greenhow, C. M. (2006). *From blackboard to browser: An empirical study of how teachers' beliefs and practices influence their use of the Internet and are influenced by the Internet's affordances.* Doctoral dissertation, Harvard University, Cambridge, MA. Retrieved January 30, 2011, from Dissertations & Theses: A&I. (Publication No. AAT 3221595).

Hall, G. E., Wallace, R. C., & Dossett, W. F. (1973). *A developmental conceptualization of the adoption process within educational institutions.* Texas University Research and Development Center for Teacher Education. Retrieved from http://www.eric.ed.gov/ERICWebPortal/contentdelivery/servlet/ERICServlet?accno=ED095126

Hall, G. E., & Hord, S. M. (1987). *Change in schools facilitating the process.* SUNY series in educational leadership. Albany: State University of New York Press.

Hall, G., & Hord, S. M. (2011). *Implementing change : Patterns, principles, and potholes* (3rd ed.). Boston: Pearson.

Karasavvidis, I. (2010a). Wiki uses in higher education: exploring barriers to successful implementation. *Interactive Learning Environments, 18*(3), 219–231. doi:10.1080/10494820.2010.500514

Karasavvidis, I. (2010b). Wikibooks as tools for promoting constructivist learning in higher education: Findings from a case study. In K. Elleithy, T. Sobh, M. Iskander, V. Kapila, M. A. Karim, & A. Mahmood (Eds.), *Technological developments in networking, education and automation* (pp. 133–138). Dordrecht, The Netherlands: Springer. Retrieved from http://www.springerlink.com/content/q232r635n5675n3q/

Leuf, B., & Cunningham, W. (2001). *The wiki way: Quick collaboration on the web.* Boston: Addison-Wesley.

McLoughlin, C., & Lee, M. J. (2007, December). Social software and participatory learning: Pedagogical choices with technology affordances in the Web 2.0 era. ICT: Providing choices for learners and learning. Paper presented at Proceedings Ascilite, Singapore.

Nelson, M. L. (1999). Collaborative problem solving. In C. M. Reigeluth, & I. NetLibrary (Eds.), *Instructional-design theories and models* (pp. 241–268). Hillsdale, NJ: Erlbaum.

Parker, K. R., & Chao, J. (2007). Wiki as a teaching tool. *Learning. 3*(1), 57–72.

Savery, J. R., & Duffy, T. M. (1995). Problem based learning: An instructional model and its constructivist framework. *Educational Technology, 35*(5), 1–31.

Savin-Baden, M. (2000). *Problem-based Learning in higher education: Untold stories*. Buckingham, UK: The Society for Research into Higher Education & Open University Press.

Savin-Baden, M., & Major, C. H. (2004). *Foundations of problem-based learning.* Maidenhead, UK: Society for Research into Higher Education & Open University Press.

Solomon, G., & Schrum, L. (2010). *Web 2.0 how-to for educators.* Eugene, OR: International Society for Technology in Education.

Sua, F., & Beaumont, C. (2010, November). Evaluating the use of a wiki for collaborative learning. *Innovations in Education and Teaching International, 47*(4), 417–431.

Warhurst, R. P. (2006). "We really felt part of something": Participatory learning among peers within a university teaching-development community of practice. *International Journal for Academic Development, 11*(2), 111–122.

Wheeler, S., & Whitton, N. (Eds.). (2007, September). *Beyond control: Social software for the network generation.* Research proceedings of the Association for Learning Technology Conference (ALT-C 2007), University of Nottingham, England.

Wheeler, S., Yeomans, P., & Wheeler, D. (2008). The good, the bad and the wiki: Evaluating student-generated content for collaborative learning. *British Journal of Educational Technology, 39*(6), 987–995. doi:10.1111/j.1467-8535.2007.00799.x

Witney, D., & Smallbone, T. (2011). Wiki work: Can using wikis enhance student collaboration for group assignment tasks? *Innovations in Education and Teaching International, 48*(1), 101–110.

7

LEARNING AND TEACHING AS COMMUNICATIVE ACTIONS

Social Media as Educational Tool

Scott J. Warren and Jenny S. Wakefield

Introduction

Teachers today need a strong understanding of how instructional technologies can best be used and blended into the course content; however, they also need to be able to nurture this kind of aptitude in learners to accommodate adjustment (Moore et al., 2002). Computer-mediated communications (CMC) tools provide educators with venues to monitor and participate in student meaning-making processes; further, understandings gained from such communication and discourse provide an initial point for future instructional design (Paulus, Payne, & Jahns, 2009). For many instructors, course design is a continuous process in which components or modules are revised or redesigned as each seeks and implements new methods for improving their courses. Some instructors now build entire courses around authentic activities as a means of improving student participation, engagement, and understanding (Reeves, Herrington, & Oliver, 2002). These students are no longer passive learners simply reading, listening, and repeating; instead, they interact actively with faculty and respond to the learning content as participants in the pedagogical process. In addition, today's learning occurs in many places and in many ways outside of the brick and mortar institutions.

How then do educational experiences take place? Brown (2001) remarked that "[l]earning is a remarkably social process, one very much influenced by the social groups that provide the resources to learn and the identity of the learner, who develops as he or she assimilates knowledge and information" (p.21). In this conceptualization, learning is collaborative and has roots in social constructivist learning methods (Duffy & Cunningham, 1996). From this epistemic view, knowledge is a shared, social product rather than something individually created (Prawat & Floden, 1994).

As instructional methods and technologies advance, learning no longer takes place only in face-to-face settings; instead, it increasingly occurs in computer-mediated environments. It has been noted that when learning moves from face-to-face to online, the intimacy and rapport that normally transfers some of the learning dimension is reduced, particularly if the medium lacks visuals (Jones, Warren, & Robertson, 2009). In these instances, appearance of physical distance between and among learners and instructor becomes more obvious as non-verbal cues, such as body language and eye contact, are removed. For example, using video when talking over Skype™ may provide more social presence than texting over Skype™ as video provides facial cues. However, as Short, Williams, and Christie (1976) put it, if the speaker chooses to take a distant approach to the conversation, there is less likely to be a perception of social presence.

The concept of social presence is traced to Short, et al.'s book *The Social Psychology of Telecommunication* (1979). These authors define social presence as a "quality of the communications medium itself" (p. 65) and state that this quality becomes evident in the "degree of salience of [one] person in [an] interaction and the consequent salience of the interpersonal relationships" that takes place over the medium (p. 65). The concept of social presence has been positively correlated with *perceived learning* (Lowenthal, 2009; Richardson & Swan, 2003) as well as *course satisfaction* (Gunawardena & Zittle, 1997; Lowenthal, 2009; Richardson & Swan, 2003). Further, Gunawardena (1995) states that *perceived interaction* is a contributing factor to social presence. However, we suggest that interactivity in a CMC is also a *choice actors take*. Such actions may result in social connections. Some learners may realize actions may generate connections, while some may remain oblivious to the fact that action has the potential to generate a sense of *being there together* with the other community members in an environment. Further, some learners may opt not to participate without understanding how this impacts their involvement in the learning community, some may feel uncomfortable with the communication, and others may understand but transgress against established norms for personal reasons. "Transgression and failure to participate limits the effectiveness of communicative actions taken by learners" (Wakefield, Warren, & Alsobrook, 2011, p. 567). The idea of social presence today revises the concept of *being* to one in which we are community members, participants within intact, identifiable groups. Concepts of *existence*, *being*, and *social presence* have taken on new dimensions with social networking and a media culture that has enraptured students and faculty alike over the last several years.

Lev Vygotsky (1978) suggested powerful links among speech, social experience, scaffolding, learning, and teaching. Leveraging such interactions, a higher education instructor sought to develop a new learning landscape for his students and decided to harness on many of the above-mentioned discoveries to innovate in their courses. He also turned the lens on himself to examine how the incorporation of blogging and social media technologies can create a rapid, responsive, peer and instructor-scaffolded environment for both learning and teaching by employing specific types of communicative actions. In two post-secondary courses, he sought to transform a formal classroom learning environment embedded in a learning management system (LMS) and classroom meetings into something more informal. In keeping with Clark's (1983, 1994) view that media tools cannot *directly* influence learning, the transformation focused instead on improving *communication via social media tools*. These technologies provided channels for different types of communicative actions including normative and strategic direction, critique and guidance, as well as emancipatory discourse, continuous dialogue, and dramaturgical expressions of student understanding of learned content. By incorporating social media as channels for engaging in and encouraging particular communications, the instructor aimed to amplify regular classroom discussion and also increase interactivity and connectedness to extend student discourse.

Using social media as this vehicle, the two courses were redesigned to further combine and extend classroom discourse to providing students with additional materials and quick updates. The instructor also sought to allow students avenues to construct their own knowledge contributions needed to make sense of covered material rather than to provide only his own understandings. He felt that expanding on the materials covered in the classroom through blogging and Twitter allowed succinct expression of his points and critiques of established knowledge (Warren, 2011). Students could further share their understanding of the material covered in class and engage in commentary and critique as a means of allowing for constative communication—discourse. Combining his and students' contributions—a collaborative transcript of truth claims and rejections emerged that allowed the development of a new conceptual knowledge map; it is such a map in which human communication and discourse are recognized as the primary vehicle for successful learning and teaching in the 21st century.

Learning and Teaching as Communicative Actions Theory

Warren and colleagues outlined the nascent concepts of the Theory of Learning and Teaching as Communicative Actions (LTCA), a theory that seeks to improve human communication towards instructional and learning goals (Warren, Bohannon, & Alajmi, 2010; Warren & Stein, 2008). LTCA theory builds on Jürgen Habermas' *Theory of Communicative Action* (1981/1984, 1981/1987)—a pragmatic theory that seeks to understand human communication as a universal means to comprehend the social world (Habermas, 1998). We claim that this communication and related academic principles are the core of social research and educational theory. Building on *teleological action,* the central point of the philosophical theory of action since Aristotle, Habermas merged teleological actions with *strategic action*. He also identified three additional actions: *normative*, *communicative* (a term he later revised to constative), and *dramaturgical* (1981/1984). In LTCA theory, each of these actions underpins how teaching and learning are constructed. Further, they govern the transmission, reception, critique, and construction of communicated knowledge (Warren et al., 2010). To better understand how these speech acts work in concert in the educational settings and help learners reach objectives, we provide the following definitions and examples.

Normative communicative actions preface learning activities and are commonly established through printed rules such as lists or verbally expressed by the professor in class. Norms not explicitly stated by instructors or other authority, often convey personal views of correct action. These are commonly passed among students outside of class (e.g., Professor Smith thinks students should use pens instead of pencils). Such norms are often revisited and may be changed in response to discourse among stakeholders. In postsecondary courses, norms often include statements about what students should do. They are commonly placed in the syllabus and provide students with guidelines for appropriate behavior. They include how students should act in order to receive a certain grade, implications of plagiarism, etc. Such norms stem from societal expectations of fairness and legal rules.

In classrooms, *communicative actions* (strategic or teleological) usually follow the establishment of general norms. These are speech acts used to direct the learner to engage in a particular activity such as to complete a particular assignment (Warren & Stein, 2008). They are the most commonly used learning actions in today's educational settings and are phrased so that learners have only dichotomous options: either (a) to accept or (b) to reject the presented direction, which is most commonly phrased in the imperative. In an educational setting, this may require a learner to use Twitter, a real-time information network service in order to receive direction from the instructor. For instance, students could be asked to follow the instructor's account and read weekly articles he posts links to thereafter tweet three major things they learned from this reading to be shared with the larger community of Twitterers and open to their critique. If the learner accepts this strategic speech act, then she completes the assignment as specified. It is expected from the instructor's truth claim that the knowledge and learning shared through the reading assignment is useful and thus is accepted as valid by the student; if they do not consent to the truth claim, they do not complete the reading, thus rejecting the inherent truth of the claim. In a classroom, such strategic claims commonly express reified knowledge such as textbook information.

Constative communicative actions are conversations or arguments in which one participant makes a claim to truth, which often leads to rejection, negotiation, and/or counter-claims between one or more interlocutors—the speakers engaged in the conversation. Warren and Stein (2008) suggest that constative speech acts, with their interactive component, allow for development of "critique [of] the theoretical understandings of speaker and hearer" (p. 276) towards agreements between or among participants in this conversation. Here, both learners and instructor should challenge the validity of truth claims by any class member. Disputation comes from presentation of evidence, critique of evidence and examples, or through claims that emerge counter to the original truth claim. Negotiation through discourse, leads to the social construction of new knowledge or the acceptance of a different set of truth claims.

Instructor claims are intended to incite *constative discourses*. These may spur critique and discussion by student participants. In educational landscapes, constative conversations take place as an instructor makes the validity claim on, for instance, a blog that the poor design of a vehicle was the factor that led to a recall of 65,000 Mazda vehicles (Woodyard, 2011). Prior to engaging students in a communicative learning activity tied to this validity claim, the instructor expresses guidelines for communicative actions within and among student groups in the classroom.

After normative guidelines are negotiated and re-established, the instructor should ask students to read, research, and reflect on whether they either accept or challenge his claims about the poorly designed vehicle. Students then provide additional details about the recall, the cause of the recall, or other relevant evidence used to support the original claim and they may either further bolster it or undermine it. Further, challenges to a truth claim may come from research findings or even from within their "*Lifeworld*" (italics added) experiences that Habermas (1981/1984, p. 13) explains are those that take place outside of institutional systems of communication, such as through their own subjective lived experiences and knowledge. In the blog, students and the instructor(s) then post comments and it is through these *constative* conversations that new meanings and knowledge are constructed. These help explain how the recall came about, allowing for multiple perspectives where design, human factors (e.g., decision processes), and biological evidence each contribute to a bigger picture. This complex view is then used to challenge the original truth claim that the recall was purely a design problem. As new consensus about truth is constructed through these communications, they foster student predictions about design approaches and precautions to emerge. Through these, the instructor asks learners to express thoughts in individual blog reflections, through digital stories, or visual design in dramaturgical actions.

Finally, *dramaturgical communicative actions* are expressions of understanding that function as a snapshot of internal Lifeworld or identity expressed to the outside world. Dramaturgical communicative actions often take shape through individual artistic creations, including means such as poetry, thoughtful blog reflections, painting, graphic design, or other means of expression (Warren & Stein, 2008). In the context of Benjamin Bloom's (1968) taxonomy, dramaturgical actions correspond to application of learned material and time spent on task.

Approach to Development

Learning and Teaching as a Communicative Actions theory was linked to ideas from situated cognition in which the teachers act as facilitator (Brown, Collins, & Duguid, 1989). As such, the instructor redesigned his formal, hybrid classroom and LMS-driven learning environment. One major change was the inclusion of informal activities for students to participate in a continuous dialogue outside of class starting with blogs.

Prior to the redesign, the instructor had largely used blogs for professional communication and reflections. These posts were meditations on both large- and small-scale (local) problems conveyed to the public, and also served as attempts to expand on the instructor's ideas to promote both student thinking processes and to challenge his own thinking (Warren, 2011). They also serve as logs for future contextualization in research work within his field and a reflexive means for improving personal teaching and instructional design methods. In all courses, the instructor provides the direction for students to keep blogs and to make weekly posts. Through these postings and reflective entries, students are expected to benefit from exposure to work in the field while opening up their own work to critique in an authentic, public space. Further, it simultaneously serves as a record of their academic progress—a living electronic portfolio and expression of Lifeworld—while allowing for future change through reflection and discussion with peers.

Building on reading assignments and discussion in class, the instructor expanded on the classroom topics in "Through Stories," his blog where he captured class-related ideas and stories related to and of the covered topics. Here, students could review and expand on their individual knowledge as conceptualized in class discussions. Having access to different types of information online allowed the instructor to easily link and share additional readings with students for thoughtful consideration and future classroom discussion. Other media such as the instructor's reflective videos, helped maximize the effect of the past lesson by lending his perspective. Students were encouraged to post comments, suggestions, questions, thereby challenging the instructor's claims to truth, providing counter claims, and continuing the dialogue throughout the week.

Wanting to further student learning discourses, the instructor added Twitter to his professional social interaction repertoire. Twitter allows users to post rapid updates, exchange short messages, repost interesting tweets from other users, comment on tweets, and share pictures, video, and website links using a maximum of 140 characters. Realizing that some of the students were on Facebook, he set Twitter to repost there, providing students with *a choice of technological channel*, as choice is one of several important components of student success

(McCombs, 2001; Zimmerman, 1994). His preference of Twitter stemmed from the succinct status updates the tool made possible and the broader educational community it connects with.

Using Twitter, the instructor was able to reach, follow, and share information with and from a wide group of experts in the field of their interest and also share job opportunities with students. Using mobile phone applications, he managed both tweets and the LMS—Schoology, a tool with Facebook-like functionality and appearance. Students were not required to follow the instructor on Twitter or Facebook and participation was not graded; instead, the information shared over these channels was implemented to add value for students *choosing to commit*.

Method

Participants, Setting, and Data Collection

Study participants included 12 of 16 students in two courses: one the instructor's doctoral and the second his Masters course. These students attended a higher education institution in the southwestern United States in spring 2011. Data was collected from student reflective blogs on prompted questions and student survey responses. These reflective questions focused on student experiences with hybrid courses, use of Twitter, blogging tools, and perceived connection with peers and the instructor throughout the semester. A constant-comparative analytic process was used when examining the data in which the researchers sought similarities and differences (Corbin & Strauss, 2008).

Findings

In hybrid courses, communication must be upheld between students and instructor as well as among students between face-to-face sessions. Blogs and micro-blogging encourages conversational actions/interactions—free-flowing, real-life communication in which participants outside the class community may help shape the learning, making it more authentic. Twitter provides rapid communication in which replies arrive almost in real-time and from a pragmatic perspective, these tools both allow for an exchange of viewpoints, collaboration, clarifications, and communications regarding course content, and for the sharing of resources and experiences with the public as well as within a field of study. A crossover between the two forms of blogging allows bloggers to share their postings over Twitter, thus making the Twitter world aware of the blog posts. It allows learners to be part of a 21st-century community that uses technology for learning *together* and remaining interconnected. We found both positive and negative lessons learned from implementation of these technology tools in the courses and share five lessons for instructors and designers.

Learning Management Systems for Strategic Communicative Actions

At the beginning of the semester, strategic communicative actions were provided to students through the Schoology LMS. This online expedient allowed for course communication, assignments, directions, and materials to be shared. The instructor chose this LMS as he perceived it to be a better choice for communicating directions and supporting students than Blackboard™. While working on group projects between class sessions, students could use whatever means they preferred to connect with the instructor and peers.

While the instructor intended the LMS to be a means of delivering strategic communications and as communicative support among students, when asked what technology tools students had chosen to use for their group work, Skype™ was the most commonly mentioned, followed closely by email. Skype allowed students private or group synchronous connection using either voice or text chat. Group work encouraged students to make truth claims about the subject matter, challenge one another's claims, and construct knowledge in conjunction with evidence they uncovered to support their positions. GoogleDocs, Twitter, or Facebook were the next choice as tools for helping students connect with peers and the instructor. Schoology was thereafter tied with Adobe Connect™. This last tool was used for synchronous class-sessions between the face-to-face sessions.

George and Frederick felt Twitter had negatively impacted their life. George stated that "I have used [Twitter] extensively before, and it was one of those technologies that started to intrude too much into other things" while Frederick noted possible positive outcomes of Twitter, while having a similar concern:

> Twitter has a lot of potential as a communication tool and I appreciate the opportunity to use it in support of [class] this semester. I struggle with finding time to check my Twitter feed and I feel that if I don't check it regularly I'm missing out. Frankly, I hate the pressure. It's a very conflicted part of my life.

Lesson 1—Give students technology tool choices in their interactive learning

Feeling Connected in a Networked World

A feeling of being connected is something perceived by individuals; it depends on an individual's ability to have a sense of "being there" together with others to foster a community (Jones et al., 2009). Social presence does not presuppose or require co-presence. However, there is an implication that there must be "participation in an activity system about which participants share understandings concerning what they are doing and what that means in their lives and for their communities" (Lave & Wenger, 1991, p. 98).

From our participants' experience, this feeling of "being there" is fostered by instructors in a CMC environment in a number of ways:

- By choosing an appropriate tool to support participant communicative acts;
- By ensuring that both legitimate peripheral and core participation is prominent, apparent, and properly cultured especially through normative, constative, and dramaturgical communicative actions, and;
- By providing participants with interactive experiences in which they can imagine themselves being with others in the networked environment by encouraging the same forms of communicative action (normative, constative), they would encounter in face-to-face learning environments.

We find that intimacy can be transferred through what Landow (1994) calls *network textuality*. Depending on the placement and elucidation of the words the reader can sense or imagine intimacy in a message shared over a network. Landow noted that with our ability to write on the Web our "comments [transform] from private notes, such as one takes in margins of one's own copy of a text, into public statements ..." (p. 14). With social networking tools such as Twitter, Facebook, and blogs, we see participants are able to rapidly provide responses to such subjective messages. When shared in social media, texts take the place of the spoken language, allowing communication to be perceived as immediate if the CMC textual response is imagined by participants to be real-time discourse.

Balancing Power for Meaningful Communication and Group Connectedness

Frederick shared his thoughts on power relationships and how these contributed to intimacy:

> The in-class pair-and-share activity and the small group activity where we explored one another's theories and frameworks for implementing technology were particularly helpful. These allowed us a low-risk environment to question our assumptions and get honest feedback on our thoughts.

In this instance, Frederick indicated not only intimacy, but also *how* the activities supported small group constative communicative actions. While he notes that the learning activities were geared towards theory building, the class group concurrently engaged in normative discourse towards developing guidelines for behavior that encouraged sharing and a fair critique of ideas.

Further, students felt connected both during in-class sessions and while working from a distance in their groups. Student's sense of feeling connected tended to stem from mutually meaningful communicative interactions among peers and instructor. As Betsy commented, these included constative and normative speech acts in which students engaged in "[s]haring the ideas and stories, common ground and differences." There were several instances in which instructor facilitated discussions and assignments required students interact synchronously face-to-face in groups, or using student-selected online communication tools. This allowed them to keep up with group work from a distance. Amanda noted that group discourse, not the tools, were most important:

> There is not one particular activity [that helped me feel connected] but what has always made me feel well connected is regular communication and interaction with the group - whether it's online discussions, commenting on each other's blogs, working on a group project or coming together at a designate time and place (even online) for a lecture and discussion. One activity that was especially helpful was how [the instructor] would provide real-time notes on the digital version of our instructional design paper.... It really helped to be able to focus on presenting, listening and responding to feedback. The fact that at the end of our presentation we were given our document back with his notes in the margin was EXTREMELY useful and efficient.

Amanda's reference to "real-time notes" refers to a session using the Adobe Connect™ tool in which the instructor synchronously gave feedback on students' instructional design documents and allowed students to comment on one another's work. Learners make truth claims in their design documents; peers and instructor challenge them through their feedback. However, this discourse is not one-sided; instead, it is a theory-building dialogue among learners towards a goal of constructing, as Habermas suggests, "empirical-theoretical knowledge" (1998, p. 171). In keeping with LTCA theory, this was a specific form of constative speech act that the instructor sought to foster through synchronous discourse in order to support learning.

Twitter Connections: Local and Global

By suggesting Twitter-using scholars for students to "follow," the instructor provided students with the opportunity to connect with professionals in the technology field. Through these connections, students immersed themselves in course related topics, learning from professionals and academics all over the world that are heavily engaged with the topics of instructional design and systems implementation respectively, as well as normative communicative actions about *how things should be done* (italics added) that these experts express. Students either witnessed or took part in discourse regarding these norms about instructional design or systems implementation that are considered best practices by those working in the field. This is a form of enculturation that decontextualized, LMS-driven courses failed to include previously. It yields opportunities to encounter both shared topical resources and for students to gain personal impressions of these scholars through their tweeted voices. Students learned from them and brought dialogue back to the next classroom session to further the constative discourse among participants towards establishing intersubjective understandings. As Jean stated:

> I feel I stayed connected with [the instructor] over Twitter. He has been quick answering my tweets.... Twitter can be a chatty social tool but I feel it is less so than Facebook, which is why I like it. I realize it depends on who you follow as well and who you allow to follow you. I use Twitter as an avenue to share my educational thoughts and resources I come across so follow those who think-a-like.... The feeling of being connected comes from having a common interest. That is when communication becomes meaningful.

Not everyone felt that CMC helped students feel positively connected. Josef noted, "Skyping and virtual communication still lacks a certain...'human' interpersonal touch to the experience...."

Lesson 2—Support students' efforts to stay connected and achieve social presence

The Hybrid Classroom: Effects on Learning

The fact that participants sensed their peers as *being there together with them* was correlated with learning for many students. They felt having met each other in person was important to this sense of presence, even though group work was later conducted virtually. Amanda noted that, in terms of learning and experience, "it helps emphasize what we all bring to the table." Brian added that he "feel[s] peers are important reinforcement to learning and the fact that they are there, it needs to be fully taken advantage of." Being able to see and learn from a more skilled peer was also mentioned as contributing to raising the performance bar. Jean typifies the group's thoughts on the influence of sensing peers as *being there* on learning stating:

> nothing happens in a vacuum [*sic*] and when we share resources, ideas, and have discourse we are able to influence each other and awaken new thoughts that allows us to grow. If we don't feel we have peers around us that care and are there learning the same materials, the learning can easily become meaningless. An open dialogue about the learning materials helps foster knowledge building and understanding.

Jean obliquely refers here to the development of intersubjective meaning among participants through discursive acts. As students make validity claims about the topic, these claims are tested and contested by peers and professor. They are examined in terms of three factors as Habermas (1981/1984) notes: truthfulness of the claim itself, rightness or correctness, and comprehensibility.

It is through this dialogue that learning becomes meaningful and this is at the heart of the conception of LTCA theory. Ideas are not merely accepted or rejected on their face based on individual's purely subjective understanding, instead, they are proposed by a speaker and then critiqued by the hearer or hearers based on claims and supporting reasons. Support is generally taken from the resources provided by instructor or learners. It is through this process in which discussant's subjective Lifeworld understandings are brought to bear on the claims that intersubjective understanding among all participating members is established. From this process, shared knowledge is constructed akin to the process of meaning making and knowledge construction posited in social constructivist theory as outlined by Duffy and Cunningham (1996). Twitter allowed for dialogues to occur *between* class sessions that helped students build this intersubjectivity that may have been a missed opportunity if such communications had been unavailable.

Josef added to Jean's thoughts in the context of the primarily online Masters program:

> Personally, I have had many courses were I never met the real people I was involved with in the class. This created a surreal learning environment where you never really felt connected to the other people and so conversations on discussion boards, etc., were more like talking to yourself than really sharing meaningful thoughts with one another.

The hybrid format worked well for students in the two courses. As many students were dispersed across a wide geographical area, face-to-face meetings were opportunities to connect and provided students with motivation to stay engaged with course materials. Robert sums up what the students felt were important characteristics of an effective hybrid course: "Regular communication between instructor and students and between students and F2F meetings spaced out frequently through the course."

Lesson 3—Make the most of the face-to-face time in hybrid classrooms

Lesson 4—Foster meaningful learning through peer influence and group communications

Twitter for Freely Flowing Communications

After the instructor introduced his Twitter name in class, students started following his feed with its many posts and reposts of relevant ideas and information. Each included all four forms of communicative actions over the course of the semester ranging from strategic speech acts reminding students to complete learning activities and turn them in by certain dates to constative acts including truth claims regarding the course materials. These were both theoretical and

FIGURE 7.1 Introducing Twitter

practical and geared towards a goal of directly engaging either students or the larger Twitter community in discourse intended to test or contest these ideas.

As the course progressed, individual students saw other students in class post questions and comments to the instructor, whereby they began following each other. An online community of student Twitterers developed as they became aware of one another's presence. Jean noted on the supportive, social aspect of Twitter: "It's fun to share short messages of encouragement and help and receive the same." Students engaged in different forms of communicative acts through Twitter-supported discourse as modeled by the instructor. The instructor maintained this voluntary community, towards a goal of fostering a community of learning practice. By posting meaningful tweets every day, a sense of immediacy developed and social presence built contributing to what Dunlap and Lowenthal's (2009) call "free-flowing, just-in-time communication." Brian noted about Twitter: "It (…) almost has the rapid response time of a text message" and this rapid online discourse helped the instructor to interactively continue the face-to-face, classroom dialogue with the students even after it had ended. Students sent the instructor quick questions and received timely, short replies along with clarifications that increased their assignment completion workflow.

George noted, "I did feel a little more involved in the day to day activities" and Amy felt "[i]t kept me up to date with everything that everyone was doing as I was touching base with everyone on a daily and up to the minute basis." Frederick, being part of this voluntary online class community without posting much himself said, "I learned more about the personal lives of my classmates that I wouldn't have otherwise known and I've learned of events/activities/resources that I found useful and/or entertaining." This exposure to peer Lifeworld expressions was valued by many of the students as providing a way to gain context. However, this was not limited to student Lifeworld expressions. Jean, who had been using Twitter for a few years started tweeting more and was able to connect more broadly through the help of the instructor's shared resources and profiles of experts within the field. Throughout the semester, students and instructor shared their Lifeworld activities, in addition to resources for getting assignments done, places to shop, restaurants to visit, films to watch, and personal frustrations with Twitter, other tools, and learning. Betsy noted that she "would not have (learned) of many things had I not been looking" at Twitter.

Lesson 5—Use Twitter to allow students to connect in a social space for add–value

Conclusion

Covey (1989) has said that "communication is the most important skill in life" and being able to express oneself and to argue briefly is to a person's advantage. This can be a challenge for many when using Twitter; however, Twitter allows for extended tweets though certain services and sometimes the limitation is also part of the learning opportunity as expressing oneself concisely can be positive and add to their professional networking experience. Amanda noted, "[Twitter] opens up for other people to perhaps join in the conversation, providing a richer experience." She went on to write about her own experience with various technology tools through-out the semester "in particular, Twitter has been especially helpful in expanding my personal (professional? I can't decide) learning network of educators."

Communication, discourse, and human interactions provide the vehicles for successful learning and teaching in the 21st century. The four types of communicative actions framed here in LTCA theory, and used to design and develop the two courses, engendered increased computer-mediated communication in support of learning. Such discourse elicited challenges and revisions to student theories through interactions with peers and the Twitter academic community at large. By establishing informal discursive practices to support all forms communicative actions in these courses, the instructor supported students between formal class meetings and encouraged them to interact with one another using the social media tools.

The instructor also developed norms by modeling appropriate knowledge critique practices and helped acculturate a sense of social presence and a community of learning practice in which students felt connected to one another, something that is an increasing challenge for instructors who mainly interact with students asynchronously online. This personal rapport, the sense of being in sync, interaction, trust, and responsiveness, was uncommon for many students in their past course experiences, and many of them met for the first time, learning about one another's interests outside of class. We found in the implementation of hybrid formats computer-mediated courses that the communication among all learning participants was enhanced by the face-to-face sessions and contributed to a sense of community and social presence. We have also found that by ensuring that encouraging all four types of communicative actions can provide educational experiences that ensure student discourse results in learning.

As we move forward with our design and research, we will seek additional tools and a better balance of power among students and instructor to encourage additional dialogues to support student learning. The instructor reflected, "LTCA Theory [is] finally enunciated [here] as clearly as the Habermasian roots allow. If it is too clear, I'll go back & add Wittgenstein." Perhaps including humor will be the next lesson.

References

Bloom, B. (1968). Learning for Mastery. *Instruction and Curriculum*. Number 1.ED053419. Retrieved from http://www.eric.gov

Brown, J. S. (2001). Learning in the digital age. Forum for the future of higher education (Archives). *Educause*. Short version. pp. 20–23. Retrieved from http://www.educause.edu/ir/library/pdf/ffp0203s.pdf

Brown, J. S., Collins, A., & Duguid, P. (1989). Situated cognition and the culture of learning. *Educational Researcher, 18*(1), 32–42.

Clark, R. E. (1983). Reconsidering research on learning from media. *Review of Educational Research, 53*(4), 445–459.

Clark, R. E. (1994). Media will never influence learning. *Educational Technology Research & Development, 42*(2), 21–29.

Corbin, J. M., & Strauss, A. L. (2008). *Basics of qualitative research: techniques and procedures for developing grounded theory.* Thousand Oaks, CA: Sage.

Covey, S. (1989). *7 habits of highly effective people.* New York, NY: Free Press.

Duffy, T. M., & Cunningham, D. J. (1996). Constructivism: Implications for the design and delivery of instruction. In D. H. Jonassen (Ed.), *Handbook of research for educational communications and technology* (pp. 170-199). New York, NY: Macmillan.

Dunlap, J., & Lowenthal, P. R. (2009). Instructional uses of Twitter. In P. R. Lowenthal, D. Thomas, A. Thai, & B. Yuhnke (Eds.), *The CU online handbook. Teach differently: Create and collaborate* (pp. 46–52). Raleigh, NC: Lulu Enterprises.

Gunawardena, C. N. (1995). Social presence theory and implications for interaction in and collaborative learning in computer conferences. *International Journal of Educational Telecommunications 1*(2/3), 147–166.

Gunawardena, C. N., & Zittle, F. (1997). Social presence as a predictor of satisfaction within a computer-mediated conferencing environment. *The American Journal of Distance Education, 11*(3), 1997.

Habermas, J. (1984). *The theory of communicative action. Volume 1. Reason and the rationalization of society* (T. McCarthy, Trans.). Boston, MA: Beacon Press. (Original work published 1981 in German)

Habermas, J. (1987). *The theory of communicative action: Lifeworld and system* (T. McCarthy, Trans. Vol. 2). Boston, MA: Beacon Press. (Original work published 1981 in German)

Habermas, J. (1998). *On the pragmatics of communication* (M. Cooke, Trans.). Cambridge, MA: The MIT Press.

Jones, J., Warren, S. J., & Robertson, M. (2009). Increasing student discourse to support rapport building in web and blended courses using a 3D online learning environment. *Journal of Interactive Learning Research, 20*(3), 269–294.

Landow, G. P. (1994). What's a critic to do? Critical theory in the age of hypertext. In G. Landow (Ed.), *Hyper/text/theory* (pp. 1-48). Baltimore, MA: The John Hopkins University Press.

Lave, J., & Wenger, E. (1991). *Situated learning: Legitimate peripheral participation.* Cambridge, UK: Cambridge University Press.

Lowenthal, P. R. (2009). Social presence. In P. Rogers, G. Berg, J. Boettcher, C. Howard, L. Justice, & K. Schenk (Eds.), *Encyclopedia of distance and online learning* (2nd ed., pp. 1900–1906). Hershey, PA: IGI Global.

McCombs, B. (2001). Self-regulated learning and academic achievement: A phenomenological view. In B. J. Zimmerman & D. H. Schunk. *Self-regulated learning and academic achievement. Theoretical perspectives* (pp. 67–123). Mahwah, NJ: Routledge.

Moore, K. M., Alibrandi, M., Beal, C., Grable, L. L., Spires, H., & Wibe, E. N. (2002, March). *Direction, magnitude, and constructive chaos: Identifying the vectors of technological chance in a college of education.* Panel presented at the 13th International Conference of the Society for Information Technology & Teacher Education, Nashville, Tennessee.

Paulus, T. M., Payne, R. L., & Jahns, L. (2009). "Am I making sense here?: What blogging reveals about undergraduate student understanding. *Journal of Interactive Online Learning, 8*(1), 1-22. .

Prawat, R. S., & Floden, R. E. (1994). Philosophical perspectives on constructivist views of learning. *Educational Psychology, 29*(1), 37–48.

Reeves, T. C., Herrington, J., & Oliver, R. (2002, April). Authentic activity as a model for web-based learning. Paper presented at the annual meeting of the American Educational Research Association, New Orleans. Retrieved from http://bit.ly/f3QDdV

Richardson, J. C., & Swan, K. P. (2003). An examination of social presence in online courses in relation to students' perceived learning and satisfaction. *Journal of Asynchronous Learning, 7*(1), 68-88.

Short, J., Williams, E., & Christie, B. (1976). *The social psychology of telecommunications.* London: New York, NY: Wiley.

Vygotsky, L. S. (1978). *Mind in society. The development of higher psychological processes.* Cambridge, MA: Harvard University Press.

Wakefield, J. S., Warren, S. J, & Alsobrook, M. (2011). Learning and teaching as communicative actions: A mixed-methods Twitter study. *Knowledge Management & E-Learning,3*(4), 563–584.

Warren, S. J. (2011, June 23). A reason to blog. [Web log message]. Retrieved from http://bit.ly/ikLUGC

Warren, S. J., Bohannon, R., & Alajmi, M. (2010, April). *Learning and teaching as Communicative actions: An experimental course design.* Paper presented at the American Educational Research Association Annual Meeting.

Warren, S. J., & Stein, R. A. (2008). Simulating teaching experience with role-play. In D. Gibson & Y. Baek (Eds.), *Digital simulations for improving education. Learning through artificial teaching environments* (pp. 273-288). Hershey, PA: Information Science Reference.

Woodyard, C. (2011, March). Spider infestation leads to recall of 65,000 Mazda cars. *USA Today.* Retrieved from http://usat.ly/fyqZIG

Zimmerman, B. J, (1994). Dimensions of academic self-regulation: A conceptual framework for education. In D. H. Schunk & B. J. Zimmerman (Eds.), *Self-regulation of learning and performance: Issues and educational applications* (pp. 3–21). Hillsdale, NJ: Erlbaum.

UNIT III

Teaching Successfully with Social Media

8

EVERYONE'S ALL A-TWITTER ABOUT TWITTER

Three Operational Perspectives on Using Twitter in the Classroom

Matthew Krüger-Ross, Richard D. Waters, and Tricia M. Farwell

Introduction

Based on recent research from the Pew Internet & American Life Project, Twitter use is on the rise (Fox, Zickuhr, & Smith, 2009). In November, 2010, 8% of online adults reported using Twitter. That number has increased to 13% by May, 2011. More than half of Twitter users (54%) are mobile while tweeting. The fastest growing group of Twitter users continues to come from 18- to 24-year-olds (Smith, 2011a). Yet, college instructors are still reluctant to implement the technology into their courses.

To assist teachers in determining whether Twitter is right for their classes, this chapter builds on the existing literature to present three cases reflecting on the integration of Twitter into higher education. The chapter discusses whether instructors should encourage students to participate in real-time tweeting during class from the perspectives of a teacher just starting to implement the platform, a student who has used Twitter extensively in coursework, and a teacher who is experienced in encouraging real-time tweeting in classes. The chapter concludes with suggestions for best practices for faculty to consider.

Literature Review

Twitter Outside the Classroom

Twitter is a free, real-time micro-blogging service where users are identified by an @ plus a username of their choosing, such as @BarackObama for the President of the United States (as of January, 2012). At first, it prompted users to respond in 140 characters to the question, "What's happening now?" ("About,"

2011). To answer this question, people using Twitter, sometimes called Tweeps, Tweeple, Tweeters, and the disparagingly used Twits, can either post a new comment (tweeting) or repost something that someone else has said (retweeting). The purpose of the platform is not just to share information about work and interests, but to foster conversation and community. Hashtags are often used to track conversations. Hashtags, such as #edtech, focus around keywords with a community that allow others to search for the conversation and join. Honeycutt and Herring (2009) provide a more detailed overview of Twitter.

While using Twitter sounds simple, tweeting can have far reaching and sometimes adverse consequences. Some infamous missteps on Twitter include James Andrews (@keyinfluencer) formerly of Ketchum public relations, Skittles (@Skittles), and former Congressman Anthony Weiner (@RepWeiner). These examples point toward the underestimated power of the public group conversation. In Andrews' case, the expression of his personal feelings that led to his downfall. On January 14, 2009, he flew to Memphis to pitch a campaign to FedEx. During the trip, he tweeted, "True confession but I'm in one of those towns where I scratch my head and say 'I would die if I had to live here!'" (Marks, 2009). A FedEx employee saw the tweet and notified management at Ketchum's corporate offices that they were not amused. Shortly thereafter, Andrews was terminated from Ketchum.

Skittles misunderstood how Twitter was used when the company changed their web page to a live streaming-feed containing any post that mentioned Skittles in March, 2009. The resulting effect was mixed. Some loved the integration, while others despised it. Many thought it was a cheap publicity stunt (AgencyToolbox, 2009), while those who hated the idea of stealing the conversation posted negative things about the product/company so they would show up on their website. The company still experiments with how to incorporate Twitter into their website.

Finally, former Congressman Anthony Weiner (D-NY) made the mistake of publicly posting a message to Twitter instead of using the private messaging feature. After Weiner sent revealing pictures to a female follower through Twitter's public channel, bloggers and mainstream media caught wind of the social media misstep. The claim that his Twitter account was hacked was quickly found to be false when women around the country shared the pictures they received from him. Due to the scandal, Weiner resigned from Congress and ended an anticipated New York City mayoral run. He has not tweeted since the scandal.

While these examples show how individuals and organizations may make social media mistakes, there are numerous success stories. Organizations, such as Starbucks and Comcast, have connected with their audiences via Twitter to build stronger relationships. For continued detractors, Evan Williams' TED Talk discusses the global benefits of Twitter, including assisting in disaster relief fundraising and communication, spreading messages of democratic reform around the globe, and disseminating important updates to increase awareness of neglected social causes (Williams, 2009). These messages help to solidify Twitter's reputation for being a beneficial network that allows individuals throughout the world to connect with a variety of networks.

Twitter is used widely among current and future generations of students who have grown up in the age of ubiquitous technologies (Badge, Moseley, Johnson, & Cann, 2011). While Facebook is the preferred outlet for connections with family and friends, Twitter is increasingly being used to build professional networks (Java, Song, Finin, & Tseng, 2007). Whether at home, work, or traveling between the two, today's students are connected to these social networks at greater rates than ever before due to the widespread adoption of smartphone technologies. Fifty-eight percent of 25- to 34-year-olds use smartphones as do 49% of 18- to 24-year-olds (Smith, 2011b). Given the prominence of mobile technologies in students' lives, it is not surprising that discussions about social media in the classroom are beginning in faculty meetings.

Twitter Inside the Classroom

Conversations about Twitter's role in academia are starting to develop globally (Badge et al., 2011). While some insist that a tweet's 140-character limit cannot be useful in the classroom, others encourage the use of the micro-blogging platform to promote discussion ("Props," 2010), connect students outside the formal classroom (Stieger & Burger, 2010), assess on-going course assignments (Aspden & Thorpe, 2009), facilitate collaboration ("BETT," 2010) and encourage continued informal learning outside of the classroom (Ebner, Lienhardt, Rohs, & Meyer, 2010). Libraries are even including Twitter as part of their resources (Kroski, 2008).

Mainstream media has recently included examples of K-12 teachers who are using Twitter in their classrooms (Gabriel, 2011; Simon, 2011). These educators encourage discussions in their classrooms and engage students using technology that they already know. Twitter's real-time feed has been seen as an asset to classroom discussions ("BETT," 2010). Teachers can ask questions and get immediate responses from students via Twitter; this approach is especially helpful for hearing previously silent voices—students who may not be eager to participate by speaking up in class but feel comfortable responding anonymously via Twitter. These conversations essentially run behind the conversations in the classroom as a "backchannel."

With younger students, teachers may feel a need to protect them from such open conversations. To maintain privacy for younger students, teachers in elementary education have used their own accounts to tweet students' questions, thus protecting minors from having online interactions with strangers. Using this method, students discuss the tweets and responses in class, not online. However, they still have the benefit of online interaction through an adult moderator ("BETT," 2010). This conversation, moderated via the teacher's account, protected the students from privacy issues while maintaining the discussion and social feel of Twitter.

Teachers have adopted Twitter in the classroom to serve many different purposes. Ritchie (2009) suggests that the key to successful implementation in the classroom is not to teach Twitter as a technique, but to figure how to use it to facilitate learning. This can include improving discussion, presenting course material, and assisting with collaborative work. Ritchie (2009) presents options, such as privatizing tweets, using Twitter-like services devoted to education, and keeping separate personal and professional accounts, to bypass privacy concerns that many have. However, these "work-around" solutions detract from the public nature of Twitter and can be viewed as antithetical to the social media culture that focuses on open sharing.

While it seems that teachers in elementary and high schools have embraced Twitter, postsecondary faculty are slower to join the service. Gabriel (2011) found that while only 2% of college professors have used the platform in class, more than 50% of those surveyed feared Twitter would have a negative impact in the classroom. Others have argued that by having students use social media as a running class commentary would keep them more focused on course content and less focused on distractions (Ritchie, 2009).

Twitter has been used effectively for assignments completed outside of the classroom. Farwell and Waters (2011) designed an assignment using Twitter to facilitate cross-university collaboration. This assignment introduced students from two universities over Twitter and subsequently held conversations to define industry concepts and identify best practices relating to those concepts. While there was some resistance at the project's start, many students acknowledged they recognized the value and importance of Twitter when it ended. This feedback is common when introducing emerging technologies into the classroom and should be expected.

Discussion Questions

Incorporating Twitter in the classroom is not a simple decision. Therefore, this chapter discusses implementing Twitter into the classroom by presenting three case studies reflecting diverse educational perspectives. As Yin (2009) notes, the case study is a valid research method which "allows investigators to retain the holistic and meaningful characteristics of real-life events" (p. 4) while investigating specific research questions. The first case offers reflections from a professor who has never been involved with real-time in-class tweeting. The second provides a graduate student's perspective based on using Twitter in multiple classes. Finally, a case focusing on a professor who has in-depth experience with students using real-time tweets concludes the case studies. Through their various viewpoints, these research questions are addressed:

1. What are the users' experiences with Twitter in the classroom?
2. What best practices can be suggested for interested faculty?

Courses Involved

To put the case studies in perspective, it is necessary to describe the courses that each of the authors will be using or have used real-time tweeting. The courses range from advertising and public relations to educational multimedia and web design for educators. While each course was structured and taught independently from the others, real-time Twitter use remained consistent throughout them.

An Advertising and Social Media course was selected to introduce real-time tweeting for the first time. The professor had taught the class before and included discussions of Twitter, but did not incorporate real-time tweeting for class discussion. The course focused on both the theory and professional practice regarding social media and advertising, and it is the only course in the school that focuses completely on social media. It is taught in a computer lab providing easy access to computers during class time for tweeting. In previous class sections, students' experience with Twitter prior to the course was mixed with a handful being frequent users and most having never used the platform.

Two education technology courses were utilized to present the students' perspective. The first course focused on teaching videography and required independent projects alongside regularly scheduled live-Tweet-chats. The content of the Tweet-chats were required readings that prompted the instructor's open-ended questions to begin Twitter conversations. The second course taught web design and web-based technologies for educators. Twitter was incorporated as a tertiary tool to provide students with another avenue to continue optional class-related discussions online.

The final perspective was from the instructor who had live tweeted in several public relations courses, specifically ones on campaign strategy and non-profit communication. These courses brought theory and practice together to inform the students about the skills needed to be a successful practitioner. Students received an introduction to Twitter and the concept of live-tweeting on the first day of class and were encouraged to tweet questions and comments regardless of the daily activities (e.g., discussion, guest speakers/panels).

Reflections on Twitter Implementation

Case: A Beginning Real-Time Tweeter

Earlier this year, a student referred to me as a Twitter expert. The statement made me cringe. Not just because the comment was on my Twitter feed when people were questioning how knowledgeable some "experts" really were, but also because I was not using the platform to its fullest. I mentioned Twitter in class and showcased how it can be used, but had never taken advantage of real-time tweeting. Instead, my students turned technology off so they could focus on class. It seemed like privacy concerns, maintaining (virtual) class discussions, and workload issues outweighed Twitter's benefits. In the next semester, I am changing my previous policy of no technology in the classroom to try in-class tweeting. But before that happens, here is one last summation of my previous thoughts.

Impact on Privacy. While people are increasingly conducting their lives in the public sphere, there are still areas where privacy is expected. For many, the classroom is one of those remaining private spheres. Concern for student privacy is built into the educational system, and professors are constantly reminded about the Family Educational Rights and Privacy Act.

It is fair for students to expect some protection from what they may consider appearing inexperienced to outsiders while learning. Off-point or misunderstood comments frequently occur in the classroom and are forgotten by the next session. However, when the comment is made on Twitter, it exposes the student to potential mockery from a global audience. While this illustrates an extreme hypothetical example, it is real. More likely, students would post a tweet and someone would attempt to make the situation clearer, which aids in student learning. Having outside professionals join the conversation helps reiterate that advertising classes are similar to the real world.

One other significant privacy concern focuses on opting out of Twitter. In a previous class, students were asked to work together on an assignment using a Facebook group. Facebook was selected because students spend significant time on the site and groups could be made private. However, one group complained because a student was refusing to use Facebook. We found a solution using Google Docs, but what about Twitter. If a student refuses to use Twitter for a legitimate reason, where does that leave the class? Does the student miss out on a valuable experience by opting out?

Additionally, concern about the nature of the professor-student relationship because of social media interaction becomes an issue. Many of my students are friends with me on Facebook and follow me on Twitter. Those who have connected with me via social media think of me more as a friend than as an educator. The boundaries are blurred. These students see posts about work situations and pictures of walking my cat on a leash. Sharing my private life has taken me from being just a professor to an actual human being. This can be a blessing and a curse. It can make it more difficult to impose an authoritative order in the classroom since students may feel more comfortable negotiating assignment terms or cutting class because their friend/professor will understand. However, socially mediated relationships make it easier for students to trust class content and make it easier for them to ask questions and voice concerns. They relate to their professor better and, they assume, their professor can relate to them.

Impact on Class Discussion.   Another significant concern centers on the quality of classroom discussions. If a robust discussion among students and others online can be maintained, then the negative impact of social media is less of a concern. However, I still question how to use the platform to promote discussions effectively.

CNN profiled Enrique Legaspi's use of Twitter in an eighth-grade classroom (Simon, 2011). Legaspi worked in front of the computer with real-time tweets streaming behind him as he asked questions. Students responded by tweeting the answer, not raising their hands. The teacher provided feedback on the content of tweets and shared techniques for using Twitter properly. His goal was to encourage students to participate in discussions more and seemed to be achieved. Yet, I wonder what class participation is like when CNN's cameras are gone and whether the participation is a result of his teaching style and not the use of Twitter.

I am afraid of asking a question and having silence in the classroom and on Twitter. Prompting in-class comments can be difficult enough, but how can I get others to use Twitter for discussions without requiring a minimum number of tweets per class session? To use the platform properly and have a free-flowing conversation, students have to participate without being forced.

An additional concern regarding real-time tweeting impacting discussion is how to stop off-point discussions. It is easy to see real-time tweeting turning into the modern version of passing notes in class. Tweets marked with the class hashtag and harsh comments, such as "Prof just stumbled over words. Talk much?" or "How many slides are in this PowerPoint?" might appear. Realistically, these tweets should not bother me as they may be valid reactions to the classroom environment. Without Twitter, off-topic thoughts still exist, but at least they remain private. With Twitter, everyone would have access to these off-topic thoughts. I try to imagine how I would react to the situation. Do I address it, or do I ignore it and continue with the lecture?

Lastly, I want to make sure my voice is heard online during the conversation. Students will be tweeting regarding things I am saying and doing. But for me to join in the real-time online conversation, I would have to stop what I am doing and respond to their tweets. That seems awkward. Yet, if that does not happen, then how does the rest of the world hear my response? While students are turning to Twitter for real-time discussion, the teacher, it seems, is still relatively bound to the classroom.

Impact on Workload.   My final concern is a practical one for my workload. Educators are already stretched thin with teaching, research, and service requirements. These are difficult to keep in check with a reasonable work-life balance, but how will real-time tweeting impact that. Considering discussions can continue after class has ended, will students expect me to monitor the conversation and keep it going after class? I envision using the service more often as a result of the real-time tweeting implementation, but I cannot let it surpass other work obligations.

It is easy to see that Twitter can impact my workload inside the classroom as well. As mentioned earlier, it becomes difficult for one to join the online conversation without awkward pauses. Monitoring tweets can be an additional classroom obligation. While the hashtag can be used to stream real-time tweets, how does that impact the flow of conversation in the classroom? There are also technical aspects that have to be considered, such as the use of Powerpoint and other software while having an Internet window up and running throughout the discussion. It seems that there may be a trade-off or that the educator has to constantly switch between multiple programs.

My last concern regarding impact on the workload concerns grading; specifically, figuring out how students should be graded on their tweets. Should it count as classroom participation because Twitter will be aiding classroom discussions? Should more points be awarded for those that share links and information from outside sources? Should students earn extra points if they can engage industry professionals in the conversation?

I am sure there are other issues that will arise once I implement real-time tweeting in my advertising class, but these are the ones that are most pressing on my mind. I anticipate running into issues that never crossed my mind. In the end, I am hoping that the benefits to my teaching, my classroom and my students will outweigh whatever Twitter-related obstacles come my way.

Case: A Graduate Student Perspective

I discovered Twitter in late 2007 at a conference where up-and-coming technologies were discussed in the educational context. Twitter was explained as a tool where people simply answered the question "What are you doing?" After the conference, I quickly created a Twitter account when I returned home. My account sat dormant for almost two years before I logged back in and started using it when I began my graduate studies in 2009.

In one course, Twitter was used as a tool to structure synchronous "live chats" between students on course topics, such as the use of video and other media in classroom settings. There were four scheduled hour-long Twitter chats throughout the semester. To collate the tweets, we were required to use an instructor-assigned hashtag for tweets related to the discussion. The course had 25 students enrolled, and the chats were scheduled on back-to-back evenings so that half of the course would participate on the first day while the other half participated on the second day with similar structure and content of the earlier chat. The instructor joined us on Twitter at the appropriate time and facilitated the discussion by leading with questions that had been shared via email at the beginning of that week's chat.

Most recently, I served as teaching assistant for a course on web design for educators, and I required students to maintain a Twitter account for the course. Students were asked to share resources, lesson plans, and videos via their Twitter accounts and include the course hashtag throughout the semester. Students were asked to follow their peers and instructors as well as regularly check the course hashtag and the specific course account. The course account sent due dates and reminders for assignments as well as relevant course information. These activities were done in hopes of sharing information with students and building a community online. Within both courses, I had concerns and challenges within the areas of privacy, class discussion and workload.

Impact on Privacy.   In the videography course, being required to tweet publicly was at first a tenuous activity—almost as if you were sharing a comment in a face-to-face course that was being broadcast for the entire world to see. For many of my peers, this fear served as a factor in their inability to fully embrace the functionality of the tool. Yet, the public nature inherent to Twitter is at the core of social media technologies. Several students who followed me on Twitter but were not engaged in the conversation told me that they enjoyed watching the conversation evolve. Knowing that others were reading my tweets made me pause more than once considering my posts were directly tied to my identity. While this intimidated some of my peers, I learned to embrace purposefully thinking through my tweets.

People who were not enrolled in the class even jumped into the discussion and that caused me to wonder how many people were reading my tweets. While it brought unexpected insights and critical voices, it also gave me moments where I waited before submitting tweets to make sure the tweet reflected how I wanted to be portrayed on Twitter. I felt confident that this was the ultimate goal of using Twitter in the classroom: to understand the how-to's of the platform, but more importantly to think about it critically to begin developing a professional persona so that it did not matter who was reading my tweets.

Impact on Discussion.   As an experienced Twitter user, I enjoyed the live chat experiences. Based on the expectations of the assignment, I knew that I needed an additional, external tool to assist in sorting and processing my colleagues' many tweets. I chose TweetDeck as my Twitter interface because of its level of customization. Prior to the chat, I warned my non–classmate followers that an onslaught of class-related tweets would be made during the upcoming chats. Many were grateful for the warning and temporarily unfollowed my account, but oftentimes followers not taking the course would express their opinions or answer questions posed by the instructor.

Many of my peers in the videography course were new to Twitter, and this affected their ability to fully embrace the tool and interact with others. In preparation for the live chats, the instructor provided students with a guiding list of questions that would be used to structure the hour-long dialogue. Also included were a number of guidelines to encourage participation, including reminders about the 140-character limit and using the @mention-function to engage others directly in conversation. Given this support, it was surprising that only half of my peers were truly engaged in the chat while the others participated more sparingly. I believe this came from a lack of conceptualization of what Twitter is, what Twitter is not, and what Twitter is capable of doing.

Impact on Workload.   A common theme throughout my courses was a marked complaint about the time required to use Twitter. Many students complained about having to login daily to check for class updates. Given that I wanted to help others learn the platform, this concern left me puzzled. The nature of social media technologies is one of streamlining and creating a simpler, more organized life. Yet the challenge of finding time to learn a new technology tool and then incorporate that tool into their daily lives must be acknowledged.

When I was a teaching assistant for the web design course, I noticed that several students complained about the little return they were receiving for the amount of time that they putting into Twitter. I saw that using Twitter in a manner that was not bound to a specific timeframe allowed students to put off their Twitter usage until the deadline. This was noticeably frustrating for those students who planned to complete assignments before the deadline, and their complaints were targeted toward the platform rather than the procrastinating students. Making sure Twitter activities are time specific and not open-ended is something that instructors need to consider to avoid two rounds of frustration: one from those who cannot finish the activity early and one from those who fail to start the activity until it is almost due.

Case: A Proficient In-Class Tweeter

Following the pattern of the two previous perspectives, I have thoughts to share on my classes' use of Twitter in line with privacy, class discussions, and workload. I, too, was a bit apprehensive when I first started requiring students to tweet in 2008 but my concerns quickly disappeared after seeing the positive reactions from my students.

Impact on Privacy.   I learned about Twitter in response to a hashtag take-over attempt at a professional conference I attended. Organizers had created a hashtag for a nonprofit management conference, but outsiders started using the hashtag to disrupt the conference's Twitter feed with obscene and disparaging messages. This was my biggest concern with using Twitter in the classroom. I had to use hashtags to keep discussions organized for myself and the students, and I feared that others might attempt to takeover the class-designated hashtag. To my surprise, outsiders used the hashtag—but as a means of communicating with the class and providing words of encouragement. In the three years I have used Twitter in the classroom, I have never had any negative experiences related to hashtags.

Another privacy concern that I still grapple with focuses on giving non-students the opportunity to see what we are doing in the classroom. In particular, I was concerned about tenured faculty members discovering that junior faculty encouraged real-time tweeting in class. The traditional image of the university classroom has the professor pontificating behind a lectern rather than an academic environment where students use netbooks, tablets, or mobile phones to communicate with each other. I worried that tenured faculty may think the students are distracted, bored, or not sufficiently engaged with the topic for effective learning under the latter scenario. Thinking that students are playing with technology for entertainment rather than learning can be detrimental for future tenure decisions even if the students were actually using technology for class activities.

Additionally, other faculty members would be able to track class discussions online. The open availability of Twitter comments provides an outlet to demonstrate teaching ability and student interest. It also could show that what a professor is doing reaches beyond the classroom. This level of transparency can also backfire if comments become too casual and those voting on my tenure case feel that the academic environment is too relaxed. However, most of my colleagues have been supportive of my classroom social media endeavors because of the networking that has been stimulated with the professional community.

Impact on Discussion.   Initially, I was skeptical that students' use of Twitter would reach out to the industry practitioners; however, a few out-going students sought professional input on classroom topics, and soon after our classroom conversations reached out to public relations practitioners around the country. I was surprised at the response from professionals. Not only did participants represent every corner of the country, they also represented every aspect of the professional continuum. We had entry-level practitioners commenting on class discussions as well as mid-level managers and well-known chief executive officers. In-class tweeting became one of my favorite dimensions of the class because students were engaged in conversations in ways that I could not produce confined to the physical classroom environment.

I would be lying to say that classroom discussions were an instant success. It took time for students to become comfortable with tweeting, and many students complained that they could not express their thoughts with only 140 characters. With practice and time, the complaints lessened. I never required students post a predetermined number of tweets, but I encouraged them to contribute as they saw fit. While this did limit the initial number of tweets, students began sharing more as they saw how tweets were woven into in-class conversations and lectures. Students even had side conversations during and after class that took classroom discussions further than I had anticipated. There is some risk involved with having the Twitter backchannel become a series of off-topic conversations. However, teachers have been dealing with these class-room distractions as notes, texts, and conversations, and we must be prepared to address them in the social media realm as well.

Impact on Workload. For Twitter to be used effectively, I knew that there had to be a separate component of the class with a grade that was derived from Twitter usage. I felt that grouping Twitter into class participation would result in students relying on in-class performance for their grade and only casually experiment with Twitter. To this day, I continue to make 10% of the overall class grade come directly from Twitter. Having Twitter activity represent one full letter grade on the 100-point scale gives students the incentive to partici-pate but is a small enough portion that their grade is not harmed if they are reluctant to use the platform. However, having a standalone grade required creating rubrics to let students know how their contributions would be graded.

Because I use Twitter to help students reach out to professional networks, I require students to act professionally online. This means using proper spelling, grammar, and punctuation as well as eliminating Internet and text message slang from their posts. Additionally, I encourage students to share information and links to outside resources to expand the scope of the class. I do not require students to contact Twitter users who are not enrolled in the course, but I reward professional behavior when students engage with working practitio-ners. Ultimately, these criteria require me to evaluate students' performance on Twitter. Fortunately, my classes have been relatively small (e.g., less than 35), so I can search the class hashtag each week and grade those tweets in a single session. I evaluate each student's overall performance weekly as grading them on a tweet by tweet basis could become overwhelming. Weekly grades help students understand where they stand grade-wise and ultimately boosts their participation, but I will not lie that it does not add a significant amount to the instructor's workload.

Suggestions for Implementing Twitter in the Classroom

Given the experiences from the three cases presented, the authors tried to answer the question: Should teachers promote the use of real-time tweeting to facilitate classroom discussion? The question cannot be answered quickly with a simple "yes" or "no" answer. For the chapter's authors, the answer was a resounding yes. Despite our different perspectives, we all see the value of encouraging backchannel conversations and developing deeper interactions with students. However, we also acknowledge the privacy, interaction, and workload issues that each teacher must assess for themselves to decide if Twitter is appropriate for their classrooms. Implementing live-tweeting, or any Twit-ter activity, needs to be carefully developed so that everything is clear in the instructor's mind prior to the start of class.

For those wavering on Twitter adoption, we hope that teachers will take time to read additional resources on Twitter, have conversations with other educators to gauge their thoughts about using the platform in the classroom, and, most importantly, ask current and former students about their thoughts and concerns with using Twitter as a classroom supplement. For those who are ready to use Twitter in their classrooms, we have listed some best practices for Twitter-usage based on social media literature and our own experiences.

1. Be sensitive to privacy issues. Social media makes it easy for boundaries to blur and relationships to change. While this can add to classroom interactions, it can also detract as students see the teacher-student relationship as being more informal. Create guidelines for yourself and for your students and clearly communicate these to students.

2. Be sensitive to students' fluency with technology. Students need a working knowledge of Twitter, its functions, and its basic etiquette prior to participating in a real-time discussion. Take time to explain the platform and answer student questions before beginning. It may be good to have them brainstorm ways Twitter can be used in class as an introduction to it. Finally, prepare an alternate assignment for those reluctant to use Twitter for valid reasons.

3. Encourage students to find ways to use Twitter beyond the classroom. Encourage students to tweet with their cell phones when they are on the go. The more the students are connected with the platform, the more comfortable they will feel tweeting in real-time. This comfort level will translate to class activities that require students to connect with each other and course content.

4. Be prepared to recommend and demonstrate supplemental software that may help students manage their Twitter accounts. Some of the more popular programs are TweetDeck, Seismic Desktop, the official Twitter application for Apple's iOS devices, and Plume for Android-based devices. These services not only allow users to post and monitor tweets, but also allow them to search specific hashtags. This last feature will enable students to monitor class discussion inside and outside of the classroom.

5. Make your expectations for Twitter usage clear. For example, tell students to check Twitter three times daily or have students tweet five original things and retweet another 10. Have them follow 10 people in one evening and then unfollow half of them after one week. This familiarizes students with the platform and encourages them to interact with others.

6. Issue a 4-6 character hashtag with a name that is relevant to the class. Using shorter hashtags gives students enough remaining characters to tweet comments with interesting content. Keeping the hashtag linked to the course topic makes it easier to remember. Most importantly, require students to use this hashtag whenever they are tweeting for the class.

7. Have students draft tweets using a word processing program prior to posting. This make it easier to edit their words down to 140 characters while being able to check for spelling and grammar. This writing exercise forces students to work within limits to communicate accurately and concisely. Drafting prior to posting also helps reinforce the importance of editing to all forms of writing.

8. Serve as a Twitter role model by demonstrating etiquette through acknowledging retweets and @ mentions. Recognizing others contextualizes Twitter in relation to the larger, social media picture of sharing and connecting. It is essential to help students grasp the reality of these tools so that they feel empowered rather than overwhelmed and fearful.

9. Provide students with a private space to reflect on their Twitter experiences. Given the publicly accessible nature of Twitter, creating an opportunity for students to engage critically with their own thoughts about their tweets, followers, and those that they follow may strengthen students' understandings of the technology. If students share their reflections (e.g., required course or activity reflection), this may also serve as a sounding board for their impressions of the course, their peers, as well as Twitter.

10. Be prepared for a different dynamic with your students. Use this increased interaction to foster conversations and learning on deeper levels. Remember that a primary benefit to incorporating real-time tweeting in classes is that learning can happen outside of the classroom. Interactions beyond the classroom walls can challenge students' traditional conceptualizations of information and knowledge and may require your attention.

Final Thoughts

Incorporating these practices into your classes' Twitter-related activities will result in a better Twitter experience for everyone. People will always resist something new. Colleagues not using Twitter may question its effectiveness and speculate as to whether the class is more focused on playing with technology than learning. Students unfamiliar with the platform may complain about having to do something that strays from traditional classroom expectations while those familiar with Twitter may complain about their lagging colleagues. Parents may even challenge the use of Twitter as being irrelevant and a risk of exposing their children to outsiders. As our parting words of advice, be prepared for these views and others designed to discourage the using Twitter in academia, but do not let the naysayers win. Embrace technology and search for innovative ways to enhance student learning whether that happens within the physical confines of a classroom or happens virtually using social media.

References

About Twitter. (2011). Retrieved from http://twitter.com/about

AgencyToolbox, (2009), Interweb the rainbow? The Skittle's [sic] twitter feed site re-design. Retrieved from http://www.agencytool.com/blog/interweb-the-rainbow-the-skittles-twitter-feed-site-re-design

Aspden, E. J., & Thorpe, L. P. (2009). Where do you learn?: Tweeting to inform learning space development. *EDUCAUSE Quarterly, 32*(1). Retrieved online April 11, 2012, from http://www.educause.edu/EDUCAUSE+Quarterly/EDUCAUSEQuarterlyMagazineVo>lum/WhereDoYouLearnTweetingtoInfor/163852

Badge, J., Moseley, A., Johnson, S., & Cann, A. (2011). Observing emerging student networks on a microblogging service. *Journal of Online Learning and Teaching, 7*(1), 90-98.

BETT 2010 (2010). Twit to woo: How to harness social media. *Times Educational Supplement.* Retrieved from http://www.tes.co.uk/article.aspx?storycode=6032750

Ebner, M., Lienhardt, C., Rohs, M., Meyer, I. (2010). Microblogs in higher education – A chance to facilitate informal and process-oriented learning? *Computers & Education, 55*(1), 92-100.

Farwell, T. & Waters, R. D. (2011). Introducing students to micro-blogging through collaborative work: Using Twitter to promote cross-university relationships and discussions. In C. Wankel (Eds.), *Teaching arts and sciences with the new social media* (pp. 297-320). Bingley, UK: Emerald Publishing Group.

Fox, S., Zickuhr, K., & Smith, A. (2009, October 21). Twitter and status updating, Fall 2009. Retrieved from http://www.pewinternet.org/Reports/2009/17-Twitter-and-Status-Updating-Fall-2009.aspx

Gabriel, T (2011, May 12). Speaking up in class, silently, using social media. *The New York Times.* Retrieved from http://www.nytimes.com/2011/05/13/education/ 13social.html?_r=1&scp =1&sq=twitter+in+the+classroom&st=nyt

Honeycutt, C., & Herring, S. C. (2009, January). Beyond microblogging: Conversation and collaboration on Twitter. Paper presented at the proceedings of the 42nd Hawaii International Conference on System Sciences, Waikoloa Village, Hawaii.

Java, A., Song, X., Finin, T., & Tseng, B. (2007, August). Why we Twitter: Understanding microblogging usage and communities. Paper presented at the Joint 9th WEBKDD and 1st SNA-KDD Workshop, San Jose, California.

Kroski, E. (2008). All a Twitter. *School Library Journal, 54*(7), 31-35.

Marks, O. (2009, January 17). Online diplomacy: The famous FedEx Twitter/email exchange. Retrieved from http://www.zdnet.com/blog/collaboration/online-diplomacy-the-famous-fedex-twitteremail-exchange/189

Props for Twitter. (2010). *School Library Journal, 56*(1), 12.

Ritchie, M. (2009, April 24). Chirping about Twitter. *Times Educational Supplement.* Retrieved from http://www.tes.co.uk/article.aspx?storycode=6012335

Simon, D. (2011, June). Twitter has place in classroom. Retrieved from http://www.cnn.com/video/?/video/tech/2011/06/09/simon.twitter.classroom.cnn

Smith, A. (2011a, June). Twitter update 2011. Retrieved from http://www.pewinternet.org/Reports/2011/Twitter-Update-2011.aspx.

Smith, A. (2011b, July). Smartphone adoption and usage. Retrieved from http://pewinternet.org/Reports/2011/Smartphones/Summary.aspx

Stieger, S., & Burger, C. (2010). Implicit and explicit self-esteem in the context of Internet addiction. *Cyberpsychology, Behavior, and Social Networking, 13*(6), 681-688.

Williams, E. (2009, June). Evan Williams on listening to Twitter users. Retrieved from http://www.ted.com/talks/lang/eng/evan_williams_on_listening_to_twitter_users.html

Yin, R. K. (2009). *Case study research: Design and methods* (4th ed.). Thousand Oaks, CA: Sage.

9

ONLINE VIDEOS IN THE CLASSROOM

Exploring the Opportunities and Barriers to the Use of YouTube in Teaching Introductory Sociology

Nick Pearce and Elaine Tan

Introduction

This chapter will discuss the use of online videos in teaching. There is a long history of using video content for educational purposes, but the transition from hard copy formats (such as cine film, VHS and DVD) to online video has brought about a number of dramatic changes in the nature of this material which may impact their pedagogical value (Snelson & Perkins, 2009). There is an overwhelming amount of video content available, and it is as freely available to students as it is to staff. This has implications for those wishing to use video content in their class.

The project which this chapter is based on was funded by C-SAP a Higher Education Academy (UK) network which exists to support and share best practice in learning and teaching in Sociology, Anthropology and Politics. The project centred around the use of YouTube videos in learning and teaching at a 10-week introductory sociology course at the Foundation Centre at Durham University. The centre prepares mature and international students for their undergraduate degree. This course was taught across two campuses to three classes of students once a week, with 75 students in total. The Foundation Centre at Durham teaches a range of subjects to its students, with specific courses relating to the degree programme that they are registered for. The nature of the centre means that there is a diverse student body in terms of age, nationality and subject specialism. This has an impact on the design of the course, which is intended to be a stimulating introduction to a wide variety of sociological topics such as class, gender, crime and media.

During the course of this programme, online education videos had been integrated into the classroom practice of the lecturer. Online videos were used within class in a number of ways, to promote discussion, to illustrate new ideas, to allow key sociologists to discuss their work directly and so on. These videos were also made available through the institutional VLE, based on Blackboard. In addition to this a YouTube playlist was established and made available to students in the associated online environment. A key initial intention of the project was to publicise this playlist amongst the community of sociology teachers at C-SAP to create a shared resource.

A series of focus groups were carried out to explore a range of issues with the students. The research questions focussed on evaluating student perceptions of this teaching approach and investigating independent use of the created playlist. The use of focus groups, which were carried out by somebody external to the course, allowed for the emergence of unexpected themes and these will be discussed in the course of this chapter. This chapter finishes with a tentative model for best practice in using video in class, based on the results of this project.

Literature Review

Since 2005 YouTube has emerged as a major host of online video content and is now the third most popular website behind Google and Facebook (Alexa, n.d.). The site hosts an enormous range of material and is popular for sports clips and music videos but has also been used within higher education as a way to communicate with current and potential students and disseminate research and teaching based material (Wilkes & Pearce, 2011). As of September 2009 there were 102 university YouTube channels in the UK, and at the time of writing this report over 400 university channels worldwide (Azyan, 2009).

There is a creative tension within YouTube as a platform for mainstream broadcasters (including Universities) and a community of individual content creators who see the site as a social network, which has resulted in a wide range of content and uses/users which has been widely studied in the social sciences (Burgess & Green, 2009; Lange, 2007; Snickars & Vonderau, 2009).

The site offers a wealth of multimedia content that could potentially be used for sociology teaching. This includes material specifically developed with sociology in mind such as interviews with leading theorists and teacher-created content as well as more general content that may be useful in illustrating key concepts and theories.

Talking about the use of technology more generally, Weigel argues that it has the potential to improve both the quality and access ("richness" and "reach") of teaching, that is the level of engagement with learners and the numbers of learners engaged. In practice institutions tend to focus on the reach potential of the internet (Weigel, 2002; Wilkes & Pearce, 2011). In the context of YouTube, this is shown by the number of institutions hosting content on their YouTube channels for promotional purposes, using YouTube as a channel to reach a global audience. However, Weigel argues that new technologies can enhance the richness of the learning environment through combining 'bricks and clicks': where online video resources can "enrich and extend the students' exploration of new territory" (Weigel, 2002, p. xiii). This would include the use of online videos to enhance a student's learning.

The potential impact of YouTube on teaching has begun to be explored in the academic literature. A recently published literature review examined 188 peer reviewed journal articles and conference papers with 'YouTube' in the title (Snelson, 2011). The recent arrival of YouTube and length of time typically involved in peer review, as well as the review's narrow focus, would suggest that 188 peer reviewed scholarly artefacts represents an under-estimate of the academic interest in the use of online video. Whilst the review considered a wide range of articles of interest to this project, there were a subset of 13 articles that included instructional strategies and general tips for incorporating YouTube videos in the classroom. Many of these were from fields with limited application to sociology (e.g., medical education, where videos could be used to demonstrate complex procedures).

Of particular relevance for this project is an article about the incorporation of multimedia content in a sociology course in the United States (Miller, 2009). Here the author incorporates multimedia content (audio as well as video) content into their introductory sociology course and states:

> [The] most critical function in terms of cognitive learning appears to lie in their capacity to serve as representational applications for key ideas. Whether in the form of a news story, movie clip, interview or documentary, information and illustrations afforded by media are particularly valuable in helping students acquire the initial mental imagery essential for conceptual understanding.
>
> (p. 396)

This quite clearly relates to Weigel's idea of the Internet enhancing the richness of the educational experience. In addition to this use of multimedia a variety of other uses are suggested, including as an icebreaker for initiating classes. This is similar to another US sociologist who uses topically relevant songs to start his sessions (Palmer, 2011). The Miller (2009) article provides a good list of some of the potential issues and problems that may arise from employing online media, and these include student resistance (possibly as a result of technological limitations) and technical issues such as broken links, poor image quality and classroom technical problems, although he concludes that "multimedia integration is not a daunting task" (Miller, 2009, p. 404).

John Seely Brown (2000) discusses a case study where video materials were viewed by groups of students who were unable to access more traditional lectures. They viewed the videos as a group, in a social setting. Viewed in this way, students collaboratively constructed their own meaning of the material, and went on to outperform the students who had only attended lectures. This is an important point, this project does not just propose incorporating videos as a replacement for lecture material, or as a way of 'flipping the classroom' where information transmission takes place outside the class allowing for activities (which might usually be set as homework) but as a means of supporting and enhancing learning within the traditional classroom environment.

Using videos in the classroom can be the starting point for class discussions where students use the multimedia potential of YouTube to engage with new and diverse topics and apply their knowledge and understanding of new topics within and beyond the classroom. This specifically social consumption of online video in class has yet to be fully explored in the literature that has been surveyed and is the basis of this study, which will examine the role of online video in students' learning both within the classroom and outside of it.

Methodology

The first activity carried out as part of this project was the collation of videos from YouTube and the creation of an online playlist (available at http://tinyurl. com/76owdoq), which at the time of writing contains 32 videos. This playlist covers a range of topic matter and is from a wide variety of sources. As an indication it includes a feature length documentary about Pierre Bourdieu (in 7 parts), a 10-minute animation video produced by a Further Education (FE) lecturer about Weber's Protestant Work Ethic and the Spirit of Capitalism, a comedy sketch from John Cleese, Ronnie Barker and Ronnie Corbett illustrating social class in Britain and many others. Some of these have been produced specifically for a sociological audience, others have not, but they have all been selected by the lecturer as a useful resource for students taking an introductory sociology class.

The initial intention was to publicise the playlist via the C-SAP community and encourage contributions from others sociology teachers. This achieved a certain degree of success although not the impact hoped for. The playlist was embedded within the VLE and promoted to students. The playlist was viewed 290 times in approximately nine months (as of 20th June 2011) but there is no further data on unique viewers or their location. This figure may seem relatively disappointing but only relates to users who accessed the playlist, rather than aggregating users who viewed the individual videos within it, which were linked to separately in course materials.

The next stage of the project was incorporating the videos into the course. Not all of the videos were used in class (e.g., the Bourdieu film) but many were incorporated into the class sessions, which were 3 hours long. It is also important to note that whilst there was a focus on YouTube, other sources of video were used in the course such as Vimeo and TED talks, and some videos which were on DVD and not available online. For the latter, where a hardcopy was required, there was limited scope for students to follow up the video in their own time, but is worth noting that despite this the resources were used and useful.

Some videos were used to introduce key sociologists to the group, others illustrated key points or data in an engaging way and others provided some entertainment while still reinforcing key concepts. These videos were included as links or embedded within the PowerPoint slides which were available in the VLE alongside the separately embedded playlist. Questions were displayed whilst the videos were being viewed by the students to stimulate discussion, encourage critical analysis and promote deeper learning on the part of the students.

In the ninth week of the course, a series of three focus groups (24 students in total) were held across both campuses with representation from international, mature and domestic students. The focus groups were promoted in class and through an e-mail list. They were conducted by an experienced co-ordinator who was not linked with the course in any way; this was to ensure that the students could be open about their views of the use of video in class and confident in being critical if need be. These sessions were recorded, and the notes were anonymised before being analysed.

Results

The results uncovered a range of issues surrounding the use of videos as part of classroom teaching and a number of themes can be identified from the results.

In-Class Use of Videos: Supporting Learning

During the focus groups, the students were first asked broad questions about their perceptions of watching the videos in class and whether they believed that this was a valid and effective way of supporting and enhancing their learning. The results suggested broad support for this practice with most students stating that they felt it was effective for a variety of reasons. One student mentioned how they felt video helped them to "to understand more, visually" and referred to their preferred learning style. The same student expanded on this statement to say, "I learn visually so things with diagrams, I know it sounds silly but bite size, stupid little cartoons. That clicks somehow, where text and where someone telling you doesn't."

There were negative comments about the use of video in class that contrasted with the majority of student responses, one student stated that they "were not really for the use of videos in class. You can watch it at home" and another questioning the need to come into campus at all and suggested that "if you're saying that the best way to learn this is to watch horizon (a UK television programme), email me and I'll watch it at home." These comments were, however, in the minority and many valued the opportunity to engage with these materials in class time as "we've got to understand that not everyone has that time at home to watch these things. People are not just students, they have jobs, they have kids. In class they actually get the time to watch the video."

The students made repeated reference to "enjoyment" of watching the videos, and from these it can be seen they are seen as both supporting the interactive nature of lessons and presenting information to students in an accessible way, one student stating that, "it can portray some serious points in an interesting way. So something that isn't normally going to hold your attention will be got across, without your realising it really."

The students also made a number of subject specific comments as to how they believed videos had supported their learning within their social science course and explored how they had come to appreciate the subjective nature of the subject stating that, "it means that you're able to think about it from different angles and you're actually able to make up your own mind about things." Several students stated that they valued the representation of alternative stances on contentious issues and how these supported their learning, one student phrasing this as: "I think it's desperately important to get the opinion of others than the lecturer. That's where ideas come from, you get discussions going and you bounce back ideas and this leads to something new doesn't it? If you only just had one opinion you wouldn't learn anything."

Acceptable Use

As one of the main focuses of the project was to explore student reception of open education resources, the students were asked about how they perceived these to be of value, not only financially but also educationally. As to the first question, concerns surrounding how these resources represented value for money in the context of being fee paying students were dismissed "I think it is value for money. I'm an international student, and it's not that different to what we would do at home." They were clear that what they were paying for was the facilitation, by the lecturer and not the content and repeatedly stated that they were dependent upon the lecturer to source, evaluate and explain the material.

When the groups explored the second issue of how these videos could be used educationally the students seem to have developed arbitrary criteria for what they considered to be acceptable use. These criteria were fairly sophisticated with one stating it as succinctly as "it depends on the video, the content of the video and what it's trying to get across, and the lesson." The length of the video proved to be an area where there was a range of responses, some students feeling that the maximum acceptable length was "a couple of 5 to 10 minute clips built into the class." When discussing video that had been longer than this some said that they were "a little bit suspicious if they go on a little long" stating that "'I'd start to feel you know, there's no effort gone in" (when referring to the activity of the tutor) but others reporting an incident when longer clips had been used "they were quite long, but there was no way he could have got that level of information across to us without the use of video."

Facilitated Value

We have touched upon the facilitator's role in the previous section and this is an area in which there was the strongest student opinion. The questions posed in this section sought to find out what the added value of tutor engagement and input was so that a video's perceived value was increased. All groups agreed that the key to the value of the videos is "the tutor explain[ing] the video afterwards" and that for the videos to be integrated properly with the rest of the session there "needs to be some evaluation and commentary on the video."

The students were then asked whether they perceive any difference between self-directed use of these materials in comparison to the facilitated use in the classroom. This is a shift in focus from asking how videos can enhance the lecture to how the lecture can change and enhance their engagement with these resources (cf. Brown, 2000).

One student spoke of how he felt that the facilitated value of watching a video altered their understanding and analysis of the footage, stating that: "If you watch things at home, I've watched things and just thought 'ah that's pretty' but to watch it in a lecture situation, you analyse it and the lecturer's saying this is because of this [...] and you read so much more into it because you're watching it with someone who knows what they're talking about they're explaining it to you."

The participants in the focus group were largely in agreement with this statement as a way of enhancing the videos and being able enhance their own interpretation of these in light of the concepts covered in class. One student simply stated that, "if you watched it on your own the Simpsons would just be a cartoon, you wouldn't get the underlying meaning."

Enhancing the Education Experience

A number of the students commented that the use of videos improved the lecture by making it more interesting and "break[ing] the lecture up." Another aspect that was frequently mentioned was the role of videos not as a means of illustrating concepts but for the role they played in the classroom dynamics, as a means of promoting discussion as an activity in the sessions, enhancing their engagement and overall learning experience.

These discussions were highly valued by the students as way of supporting their learning and one student stating that the videos played an essential role "as a starting point" for discussion; the same student who stated this, continued "I think using it as a starting point is more valuable than the video itself." This suggests that there is much benefit of watching the videos in class, as a group, as discussed by Brown (2000). The discursive aspect of the session was also explored by another student who honed in on the value of discussions in supporting their learning stating that "you get discussions going and you can bounce ideas and this leads to something new."

Recommended Viewing

The second aspect of this inquiry was to evaluate the use of the playlist and to ask students to comment on their independent use of online videos. The students were asked about how they engaged with and evaluated materials online, their general practice when watching educational videos and if the use of the playlist provided had influenced their independent assessment of the quality of materials.

The first question, of individual practice highlighted a number of concerns on the part of the student and a general confusion as to what was deemed as appropriate and acceptable for academic purposes. One student commented, "I do worry though. We're told not to go onto Wikipedia, and with YouTube it's exactly the same" and this illustrates the conflicting messages that are being presented to students by lecturers who might ban them from citing Wikipedia in assessments but integrate Youtube videos into their teaching. The similarity between the two was noted by the student who remarked that, "it's just people uploading things as well'. This posed the question about how to evaluate online resources, and the students presented a number of strategies that they employed, such as "looking at the sources, for instance if it's from the BBC", "how many stars there are on it" and "if they use academic language, you think they're more likely to know what they're talking about."

Students were also asked about how they valued the playlist of videos compiled by the lecturer, and how they interacted with these materials. What became apparent from this was the materials selected by the lecturer were seen to hold a higher value than those the students were self selecting. This was explicitly stated one student as, "I hold this as better than anything I could find myself. I could Google sociology and YouTube it, but you just don't know what you are going to get, but if you use something that's been recommended it seems more relevant to me." By providing this online playlist of relevant videos, the tutor was seen to have taken on the role of an online guide to finding resources and the students "need the tutor, someone who's more versed in the subject to tell you what is good and bad."

Perceptions of This the Practice of Online Playlist Provision

The students made a number of comments surrounding the provision of a playlist itself as an additional education resource for learning support. The comments the students made showed that they were in favour of this practice and viewed it as simply an extension of existing academic practice. They compared the playlist to the traditional reading list provision as "the modern version" and as such was met with little resistance. To the students it seemed an appropriate way of giving information to students, as one participant observed:

> It's a way of passing on information in this day and age. If we want to pass on information about what is happening, we need to do it in this format and it seems like we should learn in this kind of context really.

Discussion

Role of the Teacher: Retention of Imparter of Knowledge

The results of this research highlight a number of factors surrounding the use of videos in education. Firstly, the role of discussion is highly prized by the students, and the video's role in stimulating this was frequently mentioned. Secondly, the students valued the teacher's input into these discussions and appreciated the additional commentary provided whilst watching the videos in class. The results indicate that the students felt that the combination of being able to ask questions, offer opinions as well as benefit from the additional expertise of the lecturer meant that the video's quality was added to. It would seem that even though students had access to and were given exactly the same resources, they still felt that there was added value when these were viewed collectively and the role of the teacher in this process was important.

Establishing a Benchmark

The students in this group, when asked about how they evaluate the quality of video online, stated that they referred to the videos provided by the lecturer as a way of judging the value of a video that they had found themselves. The students appreciated the presentation of differing opinions within the classroom, although they seemed to require an evaluative framework when presented with the choice of selecting their own additional learning material. It was mentioned by several of the students that they saw this material provided by lecturer input as having been 'validated'. This is interesting as it contradicts the assumptions that students are happy to find their own material online and calls into question the extent to which they use this as a mechanism to support their own learning, preferring more traditional approaches of lecture handouts and textbooks to sourcing their own material. It seems that the students on this course were overwhelmed by the variety of learning resources available and as such welcomed a seemingly 'validated' resource as a way of creating a comparative framework and a means of charting a course through other self-located material.

Diversity and Democracy

One aspect to come out of the research surrounded the use of videos in the course to highlight the subjective nature of social science. The students recalled incidents where the lecturer had used videos that opposed information he had just outlined to them as a way of representing other views and described these incidents positively, stating that this had helped them make up their own minds. Being able to analyse different arguments and weigh the merit of these is a process involved in deep learning, where a learner has to actively engage with material and will make value judgements based on their own opinion. In this use of video, there is evidence to suggest that by providing these other opinions and opposing arguments, the students were critically analysing information that they were presented with and synthesising their own conclusions. This is a fundamental feature of deep learning and would indicate that the facilitated use of video can be escalated on Bloom's taxonomy to reach higher order thinking skills and not simply the lower order of understanding and remembering. The students spoke about 'humility' on the part of the lecturer to allow for other oppositional arguments be shown and as such felt "freer to express [their] own opinions in class discussions."

Social and Sharing

The students used the videos almost as a social currency between members of the class and as a way of fostering bonds in social networking sites. They spoke of how they would post videos (not always education related) onto their friend's walls, and use this as a way of starting conversation that would sometimes lead to conversations about work. The students also had positive feelings, and were actively seeking to share materials with other members of their class. In the focus group, the students asked about the possibility of sharing videos that they found online with a wider audience than just friends on Facebook. When asked about what format they thought that this could take and what could be done with it, they suggested it could be given to the next year's cohort as a way of finding some of the resources that they had found useful during the time on their course.

A Model for Teachers

By building on the discussions of the previous section and interactions and discussions with staff and a workshop, which was held to discuss the findings of this project, we have developed a simple model for best practice in using video in class. This is a descriptive model which helps to delineate the different stages which a teacher may go through in selecting and using a video, and hopefully will help guard against the all too easy practice of just including a video as a time filler or break.

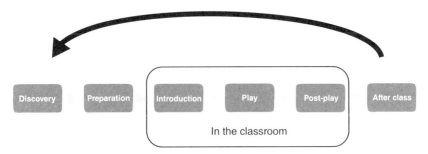

FIGURE 9.1 A model of video use in the classroom.

Stage 1: Discovery

This stage takes place before the class and involves the initial search for video content. It is important at this stage to use a variety of sources (e.g., YouTube, Vimeo, TED, etc. as well as subject specific sources) as good content can be spread across different sources. Our evidence suggests that it is worthwhile encouraging student participation at this stage by giving them the opportunity to suggest materials for revision or future week's topics.

Some tips for this stage are to:

- Ensure that you watch the video in entirety, as there may be some quality or unexpected issues.
- Think about how you would use the video in the classroom and its role in the session; discussion starter, illustration or plenary activity?
- Investigate the source of the material: who produced it and why- you will need to explore these with the students to give the video context and meaning.

Stage 2: Preparation (Before Class)

This stage is undertaken when you are preparing for your class. This will involve creation of your own learning materials and integration of the found video resources.

Some tips for this stage are to:

- Place the video (link or embed) somewhere accessible to your students (playlist, VLE, blog, wiki), this will prevent unnecessary distractions such as advertisements from disrupting class activity;
- Ensure that the video is still available. A drawback of using online materials in the classroom is that they can be taken down if breaching copyright legislation;
- Check the technology first, and every time (in particular Internet connection and sound)!

Stage 3: Introduction (in Class, Before 'Play')

This stage will occur in the classroom and is essential for contextualising the video. Asking your students to think about a video, by posing a number of questions or interpreting the video in light of a specific concept, will alter how they engage with this material and provide part of the facilitation mentioned in this chapter.

Some tips for this stage are to:

* Open up discussion as to why the material is important and how it supports students' learning and understanding of a particular topic.
* Explain where you got the video from and the context in which it was produced. If the producers have an agenda for producing the video, make your students aware of this.
* Provide an outline of the video, and pose the questions that you want the students to keep in mind whilst watching the footage. This will direct their engagement with the material and ask that they engage with it on a more than superficial level.

Stage 4: Play (In Class)

During this stage, the video will be playing; however you will also be monitoring the technology and, where appropriate, stepping in to highlight more subtle features or points that will enhance the students' viewing of the material.

Some tips for this stage are to:

* Don't be afraid to pause the video to make a point;
* Keep the video fairly short, longer ones can be broken up for discussion at key points.

Stage 5: Post-Play (In Class)

This is the stage where the video and concept meet. It is important that you ask your students to critically analyse what they have just seen, so that the reasons for the content selection and your learning objectives align. This is your opportunity to evaluate the first reaction of your student to the video and assess whether it was beneficial in supporting their understanding.

Some tips for this stage are to:

* Always lead discussion on video—your students may have questions about the footage that they need an opportunity to pose, again we refer to the facilitation of the videos that the students considered necessary for them not only to be acceptable but also useful.
* Refer back to your reasons for selecting the video in Stage 3 and link these reasons to the concepts of your overall session.
* Revisit the questions that you posed to your students in Stage 3 and use their responses to check for understanding and how they have interpreted the material.

Stage 6: After Class
This stage is comprised of two separate activities—a reflective component based upon your own teaching activity and a secondary feed-forward activity undertaken by the student. Having used the video, the reactions and responses of the students will be known. This reflection will be an opportunity to evaluate the efficacy of the video in supporting your student learning.

Some questions you may want to think about at this stage:

- Did the students find the video interesting and engaging?
- Were the students able to make the connections between the video material and the concepts to be conveyed in the session?

Feedforward Activity

The students have now seen an example video in the classroom and how this illustrates a concept that they were trying to learn. They will now be in a position where they will be able to source supplementary material. Encourage your students to examine and explore additional videos that support their learning in this area. These videos can be shared amongst the students and tutor and included in future sessions if appropriate.

Conclusions

The focus groups discovered a wide range of complex issues surrounding the use of online videos in learning and teaching. These included the extent to which video was already incorporated into some of their learning, the willingness to collaborate and contribute to a communal resource and the strategies that students used to assess the quality of videos that they discovered and are actively establishing their own mechanisms for quality assurance and benchmarking. Some of these strategies will be effective, but there is a danger of being exposed to misleading or incorrect material, in particular about potentially contentious and political issues such as gender and race, where the majority of material may not be produced with a sociology class in mind.

As an example of this, the lecturer in this project was sent a link to a video by a student which was a satirical description of feminists by a right- wing American group, presented as if created by a feminist group. To a student unfamiliar with these kinds of debates, it was taken as an entertaining look at a complex issue, despite the educational content being negligible, but in fact the video was a crude parody, which was missed by the student in question. This might suggest that in the future some form of video literacy could be included within key skills provision to encourage the kinds of critical thinking that students are already being encouraged to develop with text based resources.

The results of this research would indicate that the students interviewed felt that the use of videos was an effective way of supporting their learning. They offer a number of explanations for this, providing alternative views and opinions on subjects, providing variety in delivery mechanisms, and using every day examples to illustrate points. The students overall did not feel that the use of videos represented poor value for money and felt that the facilitated use of these teaching materials surpassed any autonomous use of these as they valued the additional explanations and discussion that accompanied them.

What can be determined by the results of this research is that the students interviewed had a traditional assumption of the role and authority of the teacher and that the views are not easily displaced by the introduction of video resources. What can be seen is that the aspect students valued most was the discussions surrounding the resources. This is an interesting outcome as it supports a constructivist approach to teaching and learning that, whilst including content is an important element, the focus should be on the discussions that surround this. This may be of particular relevance to teaching in the social sciences;,perhaps future research could investigate whether this is true for other subjects such as the natural sciences.

The results of this research confirm that the use of video in education can be an effective way of engaging students and supporting their understanding. Video production can be a costly and time consuming activity, in both staff time and, if done to a high quality, equipment. The results show that the use of openly available video resources is not viewed by students as a poor alternative to these home grown resources and, as long as they are properly facilitated and integrated into the lesson, then the perceptions of students of this material does not diminish the perceived effectiveness of this method.

In a climate where resources are scarce this has significant implications as the use of such free content can allow staff to focus on the ways in which to facilitate the delivery of these open access educational resources instead of being concerned with generation of new content, encouraging deeper learning and in the case of this research potentially improving the student learning experience by supporting communication, increased interaction and a wider view of their chosen subject. The use of freely available online videos in class can enhance students' learning if it is not used as a substitute for class discussion, but as a way to stimulate it.

References

Alexa. (n.d.). Alexa the web information company Retrieved April 7, 2011, from http://www.alexa.com/

Azyan, L. (2009). UK universities on YouTube. http://www.lizazyan.com/uk-universities-on-youtube

Brown, J. S. (2000). Growing up digital: How the web changes work, education, and the ways people learn. *Change* (March/April), 10–20.

Burgess, J., & Green, J. (2009). *YouTube: Online video and participatory culture.* Cambridge, UK: Polity Press.

Lange, P. (2007). Publicly private and privately public: Social networking on YouTube. *Journal of Computer-Mediated Communication, 13*(1), 361–380.

Miller, M. (2009). Integrating online multimedia into college courses and classroom: With application to the social sciences. *MERLOT Journal of Online Learning and Teaching, 5*(2), 395–423..

Palmer, N. (2011, 10th April). iTeach with iTunes how about you? Sociology Source : Resources & Ideas for Teaching sociology http://www.sociologysource.com/home/2011/4/4/iteach-with-itunes-how-about-you.html

Snelson, C. (2011). YouTube across the disciplines: A review of the literature. *MERLOT Journal of Online Learning and Teaching, 7*(1), 159–169.

Snelson, C., & Perkins, R. (2009). From silent film to YouTube: Tracing the historical roots of motion picture technologies in education. *Journal of Visual Literacy, 28*(1), 1–27.

Snickars, P., & Vonderau, P. (2009). *The YouTube reader.* Stockholm: National Library of Sweden.

Weigel, V. B. (2002). *Deep learning for a digital age: Technology's untapped potential to enrich higher education.* San Francisco: Jossey-Bass.

Wilkes, L., & Pearce, N. (2011). Fostering an ecology of openness: The role of social media in public engagement at the Open University. In C. Wankel (Ed.), *Teaching arts and science with the new social media* (pp. 241–264). Bingley, UK: Emerald.

10

A FRAMEWORK TO ENRICH STUDENT INTERACTION VIA CROSS-INSTITUTIONAL MICROBLOGGING

Suku Sinnappan and Samar Zutshi

Introduction

The use of microblogging has become very popular. However, until recently, its usage in higher education has been largely limited to informal, social interaction (Faculty Focus, 2010). This chapter presents findings from Sinnappan and Zutshi (2011a, b) that suggests that microblogging can facilitate all aspects of a Community of Inquiry (CoI). Encouraged by the findings and based on our reflection, we propose a framework to facilitate CoI in higher education by facilitating learning activities that require students to interact with their peers as well as other student cohorts. Here we present some key findings from our trial use of microblogging to facilitate a CoI and also presents our initial framework for further usage of microblogging in higher education.

From a number of perspectives, including in particular the social constructivist one, interaction and community can be considered fundamental to the learning experience. This position can be seen in the educational literature as far back as in the work of Dewey, who maintained that both the psychological and sociological aspects of the educational process were equally important (Dewey, 1959 cited by Garrison, Anderson, & Archer, 2000). Taking such a position leads to the notion that, rather than conventional conception of a class as a group of students enrolled in a unit being taught by a teacher, it is desirable to conceive of a community of learners who are engaged in the purposeful, mutual construction of knowledge facilitated by staff member(s) (Ebner, Lienhardt, Rohs, & Meyer, 2010). A widely used model to describe this kind of learning community is the Community of Inquiry (CoI) model developed by Garrison et al. (2000).

The study was motivated by anecdotal evidence and observation that students were spending less time interacting with each other outside of class. This meant that student interaction could be limited to the class time during their specific tutorial groups. Possible explanations for this phenomenon could include changing lifestyles, increased pressure to work and long commutes to and from campus. While the learning management system (LMS) based discussion forums were available to the students to allow them to interact outside of class hours, these forums were hardly used at all. The LMS is a website that requires students log in to see whether there has been any activity (as opposed to "pushing" information out to them). Further, the design of the LMS precludes students from interacting with other students not enrolled in the same unit through it. We consider both of these facts subtle but significant barriers to their widespread use for the kind of informal, spontaneous interaction we considered was missing.

Social Media and Community of Inquiry

In this section, we provide a brief background regarding the use of microblogging for education. We also introduce the CoI framework and discuss our rationale for adopting microblogging as a tool to facilitate CoI.

Microblogging and Twitter

A microblogging platform allows users to post brief messages for public view. The messages appear in reverse chronological order. Microblogging combines aspects of blogging and social networking and as such is considered one of the "social media". Users can "follow" other microbloggers so that they have access to a "feed" of posts with recent posts appearing at the top. Microblogging has become very popular since the inception of Twitter in 2007. Despite several other microblogging platforms now available, Twitter remains the most popular, and in the literature reference is often made directly to the use of Twitter for education rather than to the use of microblogging (e.g., Dunlap & Lowenthal, 2009a,b; Junco, Heiberger & Loken, 2010; Ling, 2007; Rodens, 2011). Although the microblogging platform used in this study was Twitter, it is worth noting that other platforms can also be used depending on student/instructor familiarity, linguistic and cultural preferences, and availability.

The key features of microblogging are the ability to publish posts that are very brief (up to 140 characters in the case of Twitter), the ability to include abbreviated hypertext links, and the ease and mobility with which such posts can be made. Twitter, for instance, allows posting via Short Messaging Service (SMS); mobile computing devices such as mobile phones and tablets; instant messaging (IM) services, email amongst others. These are all in addition to a conventional web-based interface and custom application software.

The pragmatic implication of the multiple channels of accessibility is that the flexibility thus afforded may be well suited to any scenario where a diverse group of people with differing levels of technological equipment and ability can all interact in a common forum. This flexibility can be particularly powerful, we argue, in online and blended education, where in our view the ideal is to have the technology be adaptable to the needs of the learner rather than vice versa.

The preliminary studies in the education literature on the use of micro-blogging in education suggest that it has significant potential, despite some drawbacks. For example, a report describing the use of Twitter to complement a traditional LMS found that it encouraged free-flowing, just-in-time social interactions between students and staff (Dunlap & Lowenthal, 2009a). Ebner et al. (2010) studied the use of Twitter by Masters' students at an Austrian University. They concluded that there was great potential for microblogging as a tool to support informal learning and collaboration by students. It also allowed for the staff to provide feedback to students and get a feel for the overall "learning climate." Badge, Johnson, Moseley, and Cann (2011) studied the networks that emerged between students using Twitter and concluded that there were a number of potential applications for it as an educational tool, such as a peer-to-peer support tool, an administrative tool (e.g., to broadcast announcements), and adding an "extra dimension" (p. 97) to time and location sensitive events.

However, educators have recognised some drawbacks in the use of Twitter, such as the possibility of it being distracting and addictive (Grosseck & Holotescu, 2008, cited by Dunlap & Lowenthal, 2009a). This may be related to findings around Twitter usage generally (i.e., outside the tertiary education context) such as Java, Song, Finin, and Tseng (2007) and Krishnamurthy, Gill, and Arlitt (2008), which emphasised the social aspects of Twitter usage. The latter claimed that the frequency of updates correlates directly to the number of followers, if the followers were also friends. However, most of these studies report the social presence within Twitter. Other studies, such as Honeycutt and Herring (2009), focused on content analysis of the "@" reply/mention function in Twitter, which lead to categorisation of tweets. Similarly, Naaman, Boase, and Lai (2010) analysed a random sample of 3,379 tweets and produced nine message categories by extending work done by Java et al. (2007) to evaluate message content. The categories were: information sharing (IS), self-promotion (SP), opinions/complaints (OP), statements and random thoughts (RT), me now (ME), question to followers (QF), presence maintenance (PM), anecdote me (AM), and anecdote other (AO). The study found that typically there are two types of Twitter users. The first group, which is made up of 80% of the users, are engrossed in disseminating messages about themselves while the second group of 20% are far more informative, conversational, and more involved with their followers. The latter proved to be more interesting and thus attracted more followers, given the benefits of information sharing, chance of discussion, and chance of being heard by a larger crowd. These findings suggest that most tweets are non-factual. Educators acknowledge the possibility that Twitter usage could potentially suffer from such drawbacks, however in general their findings suggest that the potential benefits outweigh the drawbacks, e.g., Dunlap and Lowenthal (2009a,b) and Junco et al. (2010) report improved student engagement and a positive effect on grades from Twitter usage in conjunction with an LMS.

An interesting aspect of using microblogging to complement a traditional LMS is the fact that students can take the discussion beyond the barriers of the traditional classroom. Most LMSs allow access to the discussion only to fellow students in the course. For many discussions, this is perfectly appropriate. However, topical discussions and debates can benefit from more open discussion, e.g., with students from other courses and institutions or by tapping into discussions and debates in the wider society. Being able to participate in such discussion may also be a possible contemporary alternative to the kind of social, free-flowing, informal interaction that used to take place between students on-campus outside of formal classes. Such interaction may be limited due to altered student lifestyles, as students often have more demands on their time, meaning they spend less time on campus outside of class (Dunlap & Lowenthal, 2009a,b; Ebner et al., 2010).

The Community of Inquiry Model

The Community of Inquiry (CoI) model proposed by Garrison et al. (2000) provides a conceptual framework for characterising the overall higher education experience in terms of the interaction between three elements: cognitive presence, social presence, and teaching presence (see Figure 10.1). CoI has been used extensively in research about Computer-Mediated Communication (CMC) in education (Garrison, Anderson & Archer 2009).

The CoI model proposes that learning occurs through the interaction of three elements: cognitive presence, social presence, and teaching presence. Cognitive presence refers to the extent to which the participants in the community are able to construct meaning through their communication. Social presence is the extent to which participants in the CoI project their personal characteristics to the community. This goes beyond a simple notion of a sense of belonging that previous work had focused on (Garrison et al., 2009). The teaching presence refers to the dual functions of educational experience design and facilitation. While the educational experience design is largely within the purview of the staff in the higher education context, the facilitation function can be shared by the staff and students.

In principle, social media applications, such as microblogging, could be leveraged to enhance all three types of presence in an educational setting. Cognitive presence can be enhanced through social media based on students' ability to build meaning through ongoing communication involving individual and

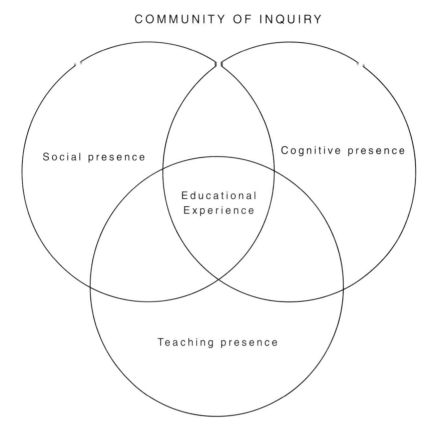

FIGURE 10.1 Elements of the educational experience (Garrison et al., 2000).

social exploration of ideas to develop understanding of a particular issue. Social presence is significantly enriched based on students' capability to present their ideas and identity while developing valuable links with the community for socio-emotional support for learning. Finally, teaching presence, involving the design and facilitation of the educational experience, can be facilitated to allow natural, informal, and personal expression by staff and students. Further, it is desirable that students can also exhibit teaching presence for instance by guiding and advising others in their cohort.

CoI and Microblogging

Garrison et al. (2000) originally proposed the CoI framework in the context of ensuring that the critical components of higher education identified were in fact carried over to distance and online courses using CMC, primarily in the form of asynchronous discussion boards. However, the framework of the higher education experience is fundamentally independent of the mode(s) of communication employed. Furthermore, subsequent work has adapted the framework for use in "blended learning," i.e., courses where a significant degree of CMC complements face-to-face communication in the community of learners and teacher. For example, a report describing the use of Twitter to complement a traditional LMS found that it encouraged free-flowing, just-in-time social interactions between students and staff, thus enhancing the social presence aspect of the CoI (Dunlap & Lowenthal, 2009a). Microblogging, while having what is sometimes referred to as a "real-time" characteristic, i.e., a user received updates almost at the same time as they are posted and are often responded to very shortly afterward, still remains asynchronous and thus is compatible with the original CoI principles. The fundamental differences from "classical" asynchronous interaction include much briefer messages and less explicit "thread" structures in most user interfaces used.

A Framework to implement CoI through Microblogging: MiCoI

Despite the uptake of Twitter as noted in Faculty Focus (2010), there have been few reported examples of microblogging usage in a CoI context in tertiary education. Therefore, based on our aforementioned case study, we propose a framework which offers guidelines for educators intending to broaden their students' horizons. This is achieved by having them interact with other students and possibly external experts and the wider online community in real time, thus enriching the student experience. Research has linked the importance of social presence to a range of critical factors such as student satisfaction and development of a community of peers (Dunlap & Lowenthal, 2009b).

The MiCoI framework is designed with the intention to suit any microblogging platform. The design is based upon the common features seen in microblogging platforms such as usage of limited characters (such as 140), the ability to follow and un-follow any users within the platform, ability to involve one or many users within a message, direct messaging and forming groups. The framework proceeds through three phases, a Planning phase (educator-educator interaction prior to teaching and learning activities), an Implementation phase (student-student and student-staff interaction, actual learning and teaching activities, and Monitoring phase (educators monitor exchange of information and encourage discussion among student). Each phase is discussed below.

Planning Phase

Topics, Duration. and Collaboration.   The planning phase requires an educator intending to use microblogging to identify possible topics that lend themselves particularly well to debate and discussion and in which students would benefit from exposure to a wide variety of opinions and in near-real time interaction.

Having identified a number of such topics, the next step is to find one or more educators (intra-institution or inter-institution) who would find such topics to be of interest to their students. The group of similar discipline educators would then identify possible overlaps in their semester times such that their respective students are able to engage in cross-cohort discussions. The educators would then collaboratively synchronise the key topics, and select appropriate in-class activities. The activities are then shared among the educators. It would also be possible for different educators to take the lead at different times as the group collaborates. This will ensure that the discussion load is distributed and facilitated well. Further, during this phase, educators need to collaboratively agree on procedures and protocols for microblogging usage. This is mainly due to the subtle differences each microblogging platform has.

Platform and Tools.   First is in the selection of the microblogging platform. There are several platforms such as Twitter, Jaiku, Pownce, Plurk,Tumblr, Laconica, amongst others. This is important as different applications have different features to suit the educator's requirements and familiarity to guide students through the collaboration. Further, accessing microblogging application within class would be free, but this would not be the same if students decide to access via their mobile devices as they will have to pay for the message sent.

Choosing the right platform would also help managing the microblog communication and information flow as the platform in itself has limited features. For example, the Twitter platform can be used via the default web interface. However, a free tool like TweetDeck provides more options to manage communication via Twitter. It allows longer messages with feature called long update. TweetDeck also allows users to track messages based on certain keywords and hashtags which is useful for engaging in concurrent discussions with many students at the same time. The custom tool itself may require other supporting software (e.g., TweetDeck requires Adobe AIR which allows web applications to operate as standalone client applications without the constraints of a browser). The educator is required to ensure that lab computers have the appropriate software, as student accounts typically have limited installation privileges. This might pose an obstacle to the introduction of a new technology in class. Should an instructor wish to deploy an installation of a microblogging platform at low cost, an open-source platform such as Yonkly or Jaiku may be considered.

Learning Activity Design.   To encourage usage and help familiarize the educator needs to plan simple, in-class learning activities allowing students to explore the software environment. For example, as part of the learning activity, students could be asked to research about the latest trends of green technology within Australia. Upon obtaining the information, they will be required to post their findings to be shared with others using pre-specified hashtags for example #greenIT and #unitcode. Students will be allowed to post as many messages as they want but are required to meet a minimum number of micro-blogs. Educators can further probe and extend students' findings to meet the objective of the learning activity.

Implementation Phase

As part of the implementation phase, students and educators engage in the planned in-class activities and post microblogs accordingly. The implementation phase runs for the period planned with inter-cohort collaboration around common topics of interest, which could be for several weeks.

A key aspect of the implementation phase is familiarisation with the micro-blogging platform preliminary socialisation with each other. Introduction in class supported by appropriate learning activities are crucial to build under-standing and the know-how approaching how to use microblogging for aca-demic discussion.

Initially, students are instructed on how to create an account with the plat-form chosen. This allows students with no pre-existing account to get started. It also allows students with pre-existing accounts to create a new one for edu-cational use alone, if they so wish. The students then notify the cohort of their user name. This will allow others in the class to follow them, including the educators. Students are then encouraged to communicate freely and use the features of the microblogging platform. This is an important stage especially for students who have never microblogged before.

Prior to commencing the collaboration between various cohorts under MiCoI, students need to be able to organise messages meaningfully, send and receive direct messages, and to follow dialogues. They should also be conversant with including peers in a dialogue (e.g., using the @mention in Twitter) and creating a group (e.g., using the list feature or creating unique hashtag). This will allow students to discuss relevant topics, share messages, share resources (through links), and form groups.

Within the implementation phase, the educators should also set up an infor-mation repository using LMS. The information repository acts as a back-up to all discussions in case a student cannot access the Internet. To do this, educators can require students to post all their microblogs into the LMS every week. A weekly record is envisaged to help continue the thought process and so that a disruption to Internet connection will not hamper the ongoing discussions (provided intranet functions).

Monitoring Phase

The third and final phase is the Monitoring phase and it is critical to ensure that the intention of the collaboration is achieved. Monitoring is actually concurrent with the implementation phase, while evaluation can occur at the end of an implementation phase. Here, educators need to be aware of what is being discussed and clarify student messages to align them as closely as possible to the objectives of the unit. Given the open nature of the Internet and the microblogging platform, it is common for students to go astray to discuss irrelevant topics as mentioned in (Grosseck & Holotescu, 2008). Here educators need to ensure that a healthy balance of CoI elements is present in their weekly discussion. This would mean that there are all three elements of CoI with a reasonable emphasis on the Cognitive elements (CRE, CTP, CIX, and CEX) as shown in Table 10.1.

To ensure this balance, the messages need to be informally analysed on a weekly basis. Educators also stand to benefit from this weekly exercise as they get to know how the class is progressing to meet the unit's requirement.

Case Study: A Trans-Pacific Experience

In this section, we present a study on the adoption and usage of the MiCoI framework using Twitter as the microblogging platform at our Australian university. We discuss in detail how this allowed us to engage with another tertiary institution from the United States on certain topics within the Information Systems discipline as part of an undergraduate unit. We describe the adoption of the MiCoI framework in this setting and discuss aspects deemed as best practice. In particular, how microblogging sparked dialogue and appealed to students to participate and engage with each other online through topic-based discussions via Twitter. We also content analyse tweets posted by students to assess how well a CoI was facilitated in this particular instance of MiCoI adoption by comparing the relative frequencies of tweets matching to indicators of various presences, in an approach similar to that of Garrison, Cleveland-Innes, Koole, and Kappelman (2006).

Methodology

The experimental setting was a second-year, undergraduate unit on eBusiness delivered primarily in a face-to-face mode with some online support (e.g., Blackboard LMS for materials availability). Twitter was used as the microblogging platform due to its popularity and the instructors' familiarity with the platform. The basic experiment involved setting up in-class tutorial activities that were suitable as the basis of students posting their thoughts and questions as tweets. They were encouraged by lecturers both in class and via Twitter to further their discussions and share information. The purpose of doing so was to encourage student interaction across the traditional tutorial-based boundaries. In-class activities included scaffolding in the use of Twitter and appropriately tagging tweets using "hashtags."Also, collaboration was undertaken with

TABLE 10.1 Coding Scheme Adopted, Based on Garrison et al. (2006)

Element	Category (Code)	Indicator	Brief Coding Guidelines	Example Tweet
Cognitive presence	Triggering event (CTP)	New topic introduced, Sense of puzzlement	Includes new resource and opinion or ask for comment	I found an article about WikiLeaks http://yhoo.it/hrJ6dN #cse2642
	Exploration (CEX)	Information exchange	Comments on previously raised resource, expresses an opinion on a previous tweet, expression of opinion with no linked resource	Some peoples in the government want to get WikiLeaks branded as a terrorist organization #cse2642
	Integration (CIN)	Connecting ideas	Draws connections from multiple tweets, multiple @s AND multiple URLs, multiple hashtags and multiple URLS	@Iserguy @VickyBlueWoody Do AUS parents need edu on how2censor??? http://tinyurl.com/25dd66w http://tinyurl.com/2g529bx #cse2642 #leb215
	Resolution (CRE)	Apply new ideas	Resolves an issue, brings a discussion to a close, uses ideas from learning material to settle an argument.	N/A
Social presence	Affective (SAF)	Expressing emotions	Emoticons, text-based expressions of humour eg LOL, LMAO, emotionally loaded words like ridiculous, includes emotionally laden value judgements e.g fantastic, brilliant	http://bit.ly/99BFZo This my not be ethical but I still LOL'ed so hard over the ignorance contained in this article #cse2642
	Open communication (SOC)	Risk-free expression	Bold statements, controversial statements (indicates a level of comfort making them), personal confessions	@dr_at_work the theory "never against a government" seems perfect in China. lol
	Group cohesion (SGC)	Encouraging collaboration	Replies with an opinion, or asks for clarification, e.g. RT with agreement, RT with disagreement, @ mention, multiple @ mentions, reply with URL	@Iserguy I think it does, it doesn't allow for every side to freely express themselves #cse2642 #leb215

Element	Category (Code)	Indicator	Brief Coding Guidelines	Example Tweet
Teaching presence	Design and organization (TDO)	Setting curriculum and methods	Communication on the units, methods, etc Typically staff-staff communication.	@stefaniemarkham saying hi from down under. looks like #cse2642 is going well. we #LEB215 will soon participate in your discussions.
	Facilitating discourse (TFD)	Sharing personal meaning	typically retweet or reply with extra/ counter resources, soliciting clatrification, asking for explanation	RT @Reeseandchips:@ Armein78 violent video gmes make children mre aggrssive #leb215 #cse2642 -what does this say. http://bit.ly/9IFcgW
	Direct instruction (TDI)	Focusing discussion	Provides guidelines on topic and/or format of discussion	@waacyweng can you retweet and add #leb215 in all ur tweets with #cse2642 students

a U.S. instructor running a similar unit to ensure that there were periods of overlap where both the Australian and the U.S. cohorts were covering similar topics in the curriculum. They were therefore able to interact with each other using microblogging in an ad-hoc, real-time manner. The purpose of doing so was to enrich the student learning through exploring a wider spectrum of perspectives than they would otherwise. It also harnessed the power of microblogging to take the discussion outside of the conventional "classroom" boundaries. The curriculum topics around which microblogging was encouraged included privacy, ethics, and censorship; these were topics common to the curricula of both cohorts.

The data set analysed for this study is the list of tweets tagged as being relevant to the curriculum-related discussions over a four-week period. The 4-week period corresponds to a 3-week overlap in teaching times when discussion activities were scheduled for both cohorts and one following week. This is because, while the learning activities were scheduled for three weeks, the discussions continued for an extra week. The tweets studied here are those posted by students and staff over the four-week period of interest that met at least one of two criteria. The first criterion is that the tweet was annotated with at least one of the hashtags "#leb215" and "#cse2642" (corresponding to the two unit codes). The second criterion is that the tweet included at least one of the participants' Twitter usernames with an @ mention. Satisfaction of either one of these criteria was deemed sufficient to identify the tweet as relevant to the experiment. The dataset includes tweets by both the American students and staff (referred to hereafter as Cohort 1) and the Australian students and staff

(Cohort 2). Note that this is a subset of tweets posted by the cohorts during this period; other discussion took place, which was tagged differently. Such discussion would not be related to the scheduled teaching activities and is therefore not included in the analysis here.

A content-analysis approach using a coding scheme adopted is adapted from Garrison et al. (2006) was used to analyse the tweets. The coding scheme used is shown in Table 10.1, which uses the elements and indicators from Garrison et al. (2006). Our adaptation of the coding scheme for the microblogging environment is illustrated via the examples and coding guidelines in Table 10.1.

In the initial attempt at coding, each tweet was to be assigned the single category into which it best fit. This would parallel the message level coding discussed in Garrison et al. (2006). To increase reliability of the results, two coders were used. The initial level of agreement between the coders was approximately 77%. As part of the negotiation process, both coders (two of the authors) decided that many of the tweets were rich enough to satisfy multiple categories. So, the two coders agreed to assign up to two categories to each tweet; a primary category, which seemed most applicable and, where necessary, a secondary category was also assigned. Not all tweets were assigned a secondary category. This form of categorization is comparable to other tweet analysis research, such as studies by Naaman et al. (2010) and Sinnappan, Farrell, and Stewart (2010). While Garrison et al. (2006) advise caution in using this approach, they acknowledge that the nature of the research and the purpose of the discourse may warrant its use. Given the exploratory nature of this study, in the breadth versus depth dilemma described by Garrison et al. (2006), we have chosen to focus on the depth of analysis with a view to gaining greater insight (Morse 1997, cited by Garrison et al. 2006). After negotiation and the use of secondary category, negotiated coder agreement was 98.5%.

Results

In this section we describe the results of the experiment while the detailed analysis and key findings are presented in the next section. Table 10.2 shows the general breakdown of tweets for both cohorts according to CoI elements. Given that this experiment was a non-assessable component, the response was considered encouraging from both cohorts as approximately 57% from Cohort 1 (20 from 35 students) and 60% from Cohort 2 (27 of 45 students) participated in the experiment. In total there were 324 tweets; 163 tweets made by local students (Cohort 2) and 161 tweets by U.S. students (Cohort 1). On average per person Cohort 1 has just over 8 tweets while Cohort 2 had 6 tweets for Category 1. For Category 2, Cohort 1 had more than 4 tweets while Cohort 2 had over 3 tweets.

As shown in Table 10.2, Cohort 1 had 161 tweets in Category 1 and 88 for Category 2, while Cohort 2 had 163 tweets for Category 1 and 98 for Category

TABLE 10.2 Breakdown of Tweets by CoI Element Code for Both Cohorts

Code	Cohort 1, n = 20(of 35)		Cohort 2, n = 27(of 45)		Total, n = 47(of 80)		Total (%)	
	Category 1	Category 2	Category 1	Category 2	Category 1	Category 2	Category 1	Category 2
CTP	78	2	4	0	82	2	25.3	1.1
CEX	72	1	122	2	194	3	59.9	1.6
CIN	3	0	0	0	3	0	0.9	0.0
CRE	0	0	0	0	0	0	0.0	0.0
SAF	1	2	3	2	4	4	1.2	2.2
SOC	0	1	1	2	1	3	0.3	1.6
SGC	4	82	4	92	8	174	2.5	93.5
TDO	3	0	5	0	8	0	2.5	0.0
TFD	0	0	22	0	22	0	6.8	0.0
TDI	0	0	2	0	2	0	0.6	0.0
Total Tweets	161	88	163	98	324	186	100.0	100.0
Average Tweets	8.05	4.40	6.04	3.63	6.89	3.96		

2. Thus on average each tweet represented 1.57 codes though Cohort 2 (1.6 codes) had marginally richer tweets than Cohort 1 (1.55 codes). On the whole, a significant proportion of the tweets were defined by codes such as CEX, SGC, CTP, and TDC. Other codes were not expressed and were found to be less significant as a consequent researchers decided not to report these. One such code in particular was CRE, which was not accounted due to fact that there were no arguments or conflict in information shared between the cohorts.

As mentioned above, certain tweets warranted a secondary category, which, while important, would not be a fair standalone characterization of the tweet. Consider, for example: "@abc123 I agree that people should know the real facts, not filtered information from censoring through the internet #cse2642 #leb215". Both coders agreed that the primary category (Category 1) for this tweet was CEX, as it clearly responds to a previous tweet but doesn't contain an additional linked resource. However, as it had an @mention, there is an element of the SGC category present too. The interpretation here is that this tweet is primarily taken as indicator that information exchange is taking place. However, the manner of the information exchange is such that collaboration is being encouraged. To reflect this phenomenon, we agreed that the secondary category (Category 2) should be weighted half that of the first. This would mean that two tweets of a certain code in Category 2 would equate to 1 tweet from Category 1. The weighted average thus calculated for both cohorts is presented in Table 10.2.

It can be seen that CEX was almost 50% of the total weighted average, which indicated the nature of the whole experiment which was to exchange information between two cohorts. For example: "@abc123 adults should be able to view any content. But when it comes to kids there should be some form of censorship #cse2642 #leb215." In this tweet a student is extending the discussion on censorship by including another student using the @ symbol to further the discussions. Further the student has directed the discussion to both cohorts by using the hashtag #cse2642#leb215. Both, @ mention and hashtag have been crucial in driving student discussion in this experiment. It is noted that both SGC and CTP had almost similar percentages at 23 and 20 respectively. This shows that 1 in every 5 tweets was seeking support and collaboration while also initiating a new dialogue either by posting a new resource, seeking opinions or asking for comment. For example "Should the ACMA blacklist be public? http://goo.gl/kbg0 #cse2642 #leb215." Here a student is asking a question directing it to both cohorts with regards to the Australian Communications and Media Authority's (ACMA) blacklist and whether it should be made public.

A small percentage of students were found to post comparatively more CTP coded tweets in attempt to initiate new topics of discussion. Though this is encouraged however this behaviour should be monitored as too many questions would initiate many threads of dialogue thus diluting depth of the discussion. It would be advisable for a student to have 20% CTP overall and this would be taken into consideration when this experiment is conducted next. Though this was not monitored in this experiment the exact ratio was reflected in Table 10.3 coincidentally. A typical example of SGC tweet would *be "How easy or difficult is piracy in Australia? #cse2642 #leb215.* Here a student is clearly asking a question about privacy in Australia to both cohorts without any other link to other information resource or citing a previous tweet. Similar SGC tweets were accounted for more than 93.5% on average in Category 2. It was also noticed that Cohort 1 had only 3 teaching related codes (TDO, TFD or TDI) as compared to Cohort 2 of 29 of which was mostly made up of TFD (22) aimed at facilitating the course. For example "RT @abc123: Would u create open srce sftware n why #cse2642 #leb215 yes & reason is tht the revenue means has changed, it's no more strategic." Here the instructor is answering a post from a student with regards to open source software linking it to revenue models. The instructor also cites the tweet in the process of answering by linking both cohorts using the hashtags #cse2642 and #leb215.

Analysis and Discussion

The key points to be drawn from the data are summarized in the following subsections.

Beyond Social Presence

The first finding we draw from the data is that the Twitter usage considered through the CoI lens strongly indicated a cognitive presence, over and above the social presence. This can be seen in the aggregates shown in Table 10.5, where cognitive components (67%) outweighed the social components (25%). This may seem to contradict the descriptive statistics from previous studies on Twitter messages, such as Java et al. (2007), Krishnamurthy et al. (2008), and Naaman et al. (2010), which emphasised the social aspects of Twitter usage. In particular, Naaman et al. (2010) concluded that 80% of the tweets were personal, random notes about the posters, while only 20% were genuine information sharing. These findings suggest that most tweets are non-factual. However, this was contrary to our findings in this experiment. Collected messages as shown in Table 10.3 clearly demonstrate the existence of not only social components (SAF, SOC, SGC) but more so cognitive components (CTP,CEX, CIN) and teaching components (TDO, TFD, TDI). This clearly shows that Twitter as a platform offers more than just social interaction. The primary reason our findings differ from that of Naaman et al. (2010) is that our dataset is drawn from a particular context, whereas that study looked at an arbitrary set of tweets which could have been from varying contexts. Our findings are consistent with previous work such as Sinnappan et al. (2010). While Dunlap & Lowenthal (2009a) largely focus on social presence in a tertiary education

TABLE 10.3 Weighted Average Tweets by CoI Element Code for Both Cohorts

Code	Weighted Aggregate (Cohort 1)	Weighted Aggregate (Cohort 2)	Weighted Aggregate (both cohorts)	(%)*
CTP	79	4	83	20
CEX	72.5	123	195.5	47
CIN	3	0	3	1
CRE	0	0	0	0
SAF	2	4	6	1
SOC	0.5	2	2.5	1
SGC	45	50	95	23
TDO	3	5	8	2
TFD	0	22	22	5
TDI	0	2	2	0
Total	205	212	417	100

* Percentages rounded to the nearest whole number

setting, they reflect on the potential of Twitter usage contributing to the cognitive and teaching presences. Our findings, although preliminary, support their reflection.

Despite the importance of deep discussion, which is often highlighted by the code CRE, it was found that the code was not expressed throughout this experiment from either cohort. This could be attributed to the short duration of time in which the experiment was conducted and also to the design of the learning activities. Both cohorts were more inclined to share information rather than argue factual details. In future, appropriate learning tasks could be designed with appropriate time to get students to discuss and engage in deeper discussions.

Encouraging Levels of Participation

On average, this experiment had almost 60% participation from both cohorts, and the findings demonstrate a healthy composition of CoI components across both cohorts. Though this was not an assessable component of their study, the number of tweets and the richness of each tweet suggest that students were keen to participate and contribute. Another factor supporting this is the fact that the discussion continued for a longer period than the duration of the assigned learning activities.

Limited Teaching Presence Exhibited by Students

Although there was 7.6% teaching presence as shown in Table 10.5, most of the tweets corresponding to teaching instructions were made by the instructors. This suggests that a low teaching presence from students was exhibited in the tweets. In a more mature CoI, we would expect that a larger number of participants could potentially contribute to the discussion in a manner that would indicate teaching presence. This could be facilitated in the future by designing learning activities that encourage selected students to take the lead in class discussions and activities for a stipulated time, and in duration of the sequence of activities, every student has the opportunity to participate in an instructor role.

Comparison Between Cohort Characteristics

From the results in Table 10.2, it could be noted that on average both Cohorts made a comparable number of tweets. However, on a per student basis, Cohort 2 was less prolific than Cohort 1 by two tweets. However, further analysis (Table 10.4) shows that on average the number of links introduced per tweet was equal across both cohorts. Cohort 2 used direct mentions using the @ symbol slightly more frequently than Cohort 1. These additional @ mentions are also reflected in the higher proportion of tweets labeled SGC in Table 10.2 for Cohort 2.

As the students were engaged with the same learning activities, we conjecture that the slight difference in the usage levels and patterns may be attributed to differing levels of comfort with Twitter prior to the start of the experiment. The instructors of both cohorts noted that only a handful of students had preexisting Twitter accounts, and those who had accounts had not necessarily engaged in academic use of Twitter. This was also evident in the style of tweets that were made by both cohorts at the start of the activity. The constraint of communicating in Twitter requires modification to normal sentences to embed more flesh in the message in one attempt. It is understood that familiar Twitter users converse and interact in a lingo specific to Twitter, unlike normal written sentences. Here, similar parallels could be drawn with the short messaging service (SMS) texts that are laden with abbreviations and emoticons. A polished Twitter post requires compromised spelling conventions, removal of vowels, violation of grammar, eschewing prepositions and heavy usage of Internet jargon and acronyms. Though Twitter has recently allowed users to post more

TABLE 10.4 Average Number Links and Direct Mentions

Measure of Richness	Cohort 1	Cohort 2
Average number of URLs per tweet	0.15	0.15
Average number of direct mentions per tweet	0.51	0.78

than 140 characters per message with the "long update" feature, most messages are still less than 140 characters. Further, to communicate efficiently, Twitter users need to be conversant in using symbols @ (to include and mention other users), re-tweeting (RT), sending a private message (D), and using hashtags and shortened URLs.

The scaffolding materials for the learning activities in the study did include methods of effective communicating using Twitter and using client-side software (e.g., TweetDeck) to manage tweets. If this is to be investigated more thoroughly, student levels of familiarity with and perceived ease of use of Twitter will need to be measured pre- and post-participation in the learning activity.

Limitations

There were several limitations to this experiment. First, we had a small sample size of 47 participants across both cohorts. This could have introduced some bias to the study, as more students could have resorted to more "noise" and non-class discussion eventuating in a different composition of CoI components. Second, though both cohorts were using Twitter independently throughout the semester, this experiment only ran for 4 weeks where they were asked to collaborate and exchange messages. A longer experiment would have yielded more representative data on both the cohorts and their progress throughout the semester.

Conclusion

This chapter presented a framework, MiCoI, that we propose for the use of microblogging for the creation and facilitation of a community of inquiry. We feel the work is especially of interest to educators who are considering the use of microblogging in their teaching practice. Our work supports and extends extant research (Dunlap & Lowenthal 2009a,b; Ebner et al., 2010; Junco et al., 2010) and suggests that mircoblogging has the potential for pedagogical use to enhance and complement all "presences" in CoI, i.e., it goes beyond merely the social presence.

TABLE 10.5 Aggregated Percentage of Tweets for Each CoI Element

CoI Element	Aggregate (%) Cohort 1	Aggregate (%) Cohort 2	Aggregate (%) Both cohorts
Cognitive Presence	37.05	30.46	67.51
Social Presence	11.39	13.43	24.82
Teaching Presence	0	6.95	7.67
Total	48.44	50.84	100

The chapter also reported on the outcomes of implementing the framework in a particular setting. Though the case study covered a comparatively small number of participants across only two institutions, the findings are encouraging and can help in extending the research done on microblogging within the tertiary education space, particularly since many tertiary institutions currently use microblogging only for social activities (Faculty Focus, 2010). Findings from the case study suggest that using the MiCoI framework can result in significant student participation and inter-cohort communication. In particular, students proactively shared opinions and resources with each other and engaged in discussion around them, as demonstrated by the high level of cognitive presence indicated. It is apparent that design of the learning activities that involve microblogging is critical; in particular, we will be revising some learning activities in order to facilitate deeper levels of discussion and to allow students to contribute more in terms of teaching presence.

This chapter reports on the first study (to our knowledge) that has used microblogging to facilitate a CoI between an Australian and U.S. tertiary institution. Though the cohorts were engaged in exchange of information and discussion only for 4 weeks, the study indicates that microblogging represents a feasible method for learning from peers from another institution and, in general, taking the learning outside the classroom.

In the future, the authors would like to extend the CoI to include other higher education institutions and to develop over a longer period of time. This can be used to further study the kind of learning that can occur based on the just-in-time interaction that microblogging allows and develop and refine the MiCoI framework.

References

Badge, J., Johnson, S., Moseley, A., & Cann, A. (2011). Observing emerging student networks on a microblogging service. *MERLOT Journal of Online Learning and Teaching, 7*(1), 91–98.

Dewey, J. (1959). My pedagogic creed. In J.Dewey (Ed.), *Dewey on education* (pp. 19–32). New York: Teachers College Columbia University. (Original work published 1897)

Dunlap, J. C., & Lowenthal, P .R. (2009a). Tweeting the night away: Using Twitter to enhance social presence. *Journal of Information Systems Education, 20*(2), 129-135..

Dunlap, J. C., & Lowenthal, P. R. (2009b). Horton hears a tweet. *Educause Quarterly, 32*(4). Retrievedfromhttp://www.educause.edu/EDUCAUSE+Quarterly/EDUCAUSEQuarterly MagazineVolum/HortonHearsaTweet/192955

Ebner, M., Lienhardt, C., Rohs, M., & Meyer, I. (2010). Microblogs in higher education — A chance to facilitate informal and process-oriented learning? *Computers & Education, 55,* 92–100.

Faculty Focus. (2010). Twitter in higher education 2010: Usage habits and trends of today's college faculty. Annual Survey on the Popular Microblogging Technology. Retrieved from http://www.facultyfocus.com/free-reports/twitter-in-higher-education-2010-usage-habits-and-trends-of-todays-college-faculty/

Garrison, D. R., Anderson, T., & Archer, W. (2000). Critical inquiry in a text-based environment: Computer conferencing in higher education." *The Internet and Higher Education, 2*(2-3), 87–105.

Garrison, D. R., Anderson, T., & Archer, W. (2009). The first decade of the community of inquiry framework: A retrospective. *Internet and Higher Education, 13,* 5–9.

Garrison, D .R., Cleveland-Innes, M., Koole, M., & Kappelman, J. (2006). Revisiting methodological issues in transcript analysis: Negotiating coding and reliability. *The Internet and Higher Education, 9,* 1–8.

Grosseck, G., & Holotescu, C. (2008, April). *Can we use twitter for educational activities?* Paper presented at the proceedings of the 4th International Scientific Conference, eLearning and Software for Education, Bucharest, Romania.

Honeycutt, C., & Herrıng, S. (2009, January). Beyond microblogging: Conversation and collaboration via twitter. In R. H. Sprague Jr. (Ed.), *Proceedings of the 42nd Annual Hawai'i International Conference on System Sciences* Waikoloa, Big Island, Hawaii. doi:10.1109/HICSS.2009.89

Java, A., Song, X., Finin, T., and Tseng, B. (2007, August). Why we twitter: understanding microblogging usage and communities. *In Proceedings of the 9th WebKDD and 1st SNA-KDD 2007 workshop on Web mining and social network analysis* (pp. 56-65). doi: 10.1145/1348549.1348556

Junco, R., Heiberger, G., & Loken, E. (2010). The effect of Twitter on college student engagement and grades. *Journal of Computer Assisted Learning,* Retrieved from http://doi: 10.1111/j.1365-2729.2010.00387.x

Krishnamurthy, B., Gill, P., & Arlitt, M. (2008, August). A few chirps about twitter. In *Proceedings of the first workshop on online social networks* (pp. 19-24). doi:10.1145/1397735.1397741

Ling, H. L. (2007), Community of inquiry in an online undergraduate information technology course. *Journal of Information Technology Education, 6,* 153–168.

Morse, J. M. (1997). Perfectly healthy but dead: The myth of inter-rater reliability. *Qualitative Health Research, 7*(4), 445–447.

Naaman, M., Boase, J., & Lai, C. (2010). Is it really about me? Message content in social awareness streams. In *Proceedings of the 2010 ACM Conference on computer supported cooperative work* (pp. 189–192). New York, NY: ACM. Retrieved from http://doi.acm.org/10.1145/1718918.1718953

Rodens, M. (2011). What the tweet? Twitter as a useful educational and professional development tool. *Communicating For Learners,* Spring, (2), 3.

Sinnappan, S., Farrell, C, & Stewart, E. (2010).*Priceless Tweets! A study on Twitter messages posted during crisis: Black Saturday.* Paper presented at the ACIS 2010 Proceedings. Retrieved from http://aisel.aisnet.org/acis2010/39

Sinnappan, S., & Zutshi, S. (2011a, November). *Towards increased student interaction across cohorts through microblogging.* Paper presented at the 22nd Australasian Conference on Information Systems (ACIS 2011), Sydney, New South Wales, Australia,

Sinnappan, S., & Zutshi, S. (2011b, December). *Using microblogging to facilitate community of inquiry: An Australian tertiary experience.* Paper presented at the ASCILITE 2011 proceedings, Hobart, Australia. Retrieved from http://www.ascilite.org.au/conferences/hobart11/downloads/papers/Sinnappan-full.pdf

Assessing Instructional Effectiveness with Social Media

11

DESIGNING ASSESSMENTS FOR DIFFERENTIATED INSTRUCTION USING SOCIAL MEDIA APPLICATIONS

Seung H. Kim and Ying Xie

Introduction

There is no one best way to meet all students' needs in teaching. Recognizing that students are different from one another, teachers should adjust curricula and create a variety of instructional pathways so as to provide varying opportunities to reach the intended learning goals based on students' differing abilities, strengths, and needs. Effective assessment is vital for differentiated instruction because high-quality differentiated instruction considers students' diverse needs and learning abilities while ensuring due student achievement. However, traditional assessments such as classroom observations, class discussions, homework and tests are limited for monitoring each student's learning process. Unlike traditional assessment tools, emerging technologies including social media provide great potential to monitor individual student learning process in differentiated instruction. Such technology-based assessments using various social media also offer great flexibility in terms of time, location, and format.

This chapter describes why differentiated instruction (DI) and social media are significant in today's classroom and explores some successful cases of assessing differentiated instruction with social media applications. The chapter mainly focuses on the social media tools that can be used to access students' achievements and how social media applications can facilitate assessment in differentiated instruction.

Differentiated Instruction in Today's Classroom and Social Media Differentiated Instruction: The Background

One fundamental premise of constructivism is that all students learn differently (von Glasersfeld, 1995). Many researchers called for adapting educational approaches to diverse learners' needs (Grant & Spencer, 2003; Parchoma, 2003). As a result, adaptive educational theories, principles, and practices have sprouted during the past decade, e.g., individualized instruction, personalized learning and differentiated instruction, etc. This chapter does not intend to thoroughly review or distinguish between these different approaches, but DI to stand for the conglomerate of those educational approaches. Such approaches generally provide multiple means of representation, engagement, and expression, and allow multiple entry points, pathways, and varied modes of assessment (Looi et al., 2009).

According to Tomlinson (2005), three elements of instruction should be adapted to achieve DI based on learners' readiness, interests, and learning profile—(a) content, (b) process, and (c) product—to maximize students' growth and individual success. Differentiating content means the customization of what students will learn—the curricular materials. To differentiate processes, the instructor usually needs to adjust the learning activities through which students make sense of the content in response to students' needs. Differentiating product refers to the different means by which students demonstrate the result of their learning, in other words, the summative assessment of learning. Besides flexibility, the interwoven and interdependent process of assessment and instruction is greatly emphasized as an important hallmark of DI (Tomlinson, 2005). Assessment in DI usually includes formative and summative assessment. In this chapter, we also discuss the whole spectrum of assessment types needed in DI: (a) pre-assessment to discover students' interests and learning styles prior to teaching or instructional decision, (b) on-going formative assessment to constantly gauge their learning progress, and (c) summative assessment to ensure students have met the curricular standards as well as their individual learning goals. The remainder of the chapter describes assessment designs for DI. Due to the dual nature of assessment, this discussion inevitably transcends both the *process* and *product* aspects of DI. Table 11.1 shows the assessment elements and considerations for DI.

TABLE 11.1 Assessment Elements and Considerations of DI

Type of Assessment	*Elements and Considerations*
Pre-Assessment (completed prior to teaching by teachers)	• Background characteristics of target group/student • Prior knowledge in one particular area or domain • Student's readiness, interest, learning style, etc. • Student's language ability
Formative Assessment (constantly conducted *during* the instruction by teachers and/or students)	• Personal learning goal • Check points on student learning progress • Difficulties or hurdles • Frequent feedback • Modification of instruction
Summative Assessment (performed at the end of DI)	• Varied performance measures to check whether learner has met both the curricular standards and individual learning goal

Social Media in Education

During the first decade of the Web's prominence in the early 1990s, it was used as an information sharing tool, and the majority users were consumers of content created by Web publishers (Cormode & Krishnamurthy, 2008). From the early 2000s, it has evolved into a participatory information sharing design, and *user-generated content* has become increasingly popular. More users, especially the younger generations, participate in content creation or interaction with others rather than as a passive viewers. In response, teachers began to take advantage of students' high level interest and motivation of social engagement by redesigning their instruction and assessment to engage students in social construction of knowledge beyond mere social networking.

Web 2.0 stands for a group of Web technologies encouraging constructive information creation and communication (O'Reilly, 2005). Such technologies include weblogs (online journal systems, e.g., blogger.com), wiki (collaborative websites editable by a community of users, e.g., Wikipedia.com), video-sharing sites (e.g., YouTube.com), social-networking sites (e.g., Facebook.com), podcasts or videocasts (a series of digital media content downloadable from webcast or syndication), etc. The major characteristics of social media include user participation (users are no longer consumers of information, but creators of Web-based content) and collaborative interaction (interchange of user-generated content in real time using the Web as the platform) (Solomon, Harrison, & Duce, 2011).

These social media technologies are also rapidly changing the educational horizon. If incorporated into a class, face-to-face, blended, or completely virtual, such technologies could dramatically change how students communicate, collaborate and learn. For example, the social media technologies greatly encourage self-expression and sharing of ideas. With these freely available, collaborative websites, students can easily create and post their own images, video and text information and then share these with others. Such tools allow students and instructors to discuss information in a much more efficient way than traditional communication methods like emails. Most importantly, the collaborative features of these tools, if appropriately implemented, could abundantly increase the depth of interactions among students, the instructor and the content, which will in turn promote sense of learning community among students. In the following section, the potential use of social media for DI is discussed.

Differentiated Instruction and Social Media

Through DI, students participate in learning activities adaptive to their readiness, interests, and learning styles. However, it is important to note that DI does not mean secluded individual learning without collaborative activities. In fact, DI advocates collaboration and learning with and from peers while retaining individual autonomy to chart their learning paths. Vygotsky (1978), an influential social constructivist, highlighted the role of social mediation in cognition and meaning making, stated that the mind is socially constructed and all higher level meaning making originates from a social level. Any educational experience is about engagement, including interaction, collaboration and reflection (Garrison & Vaughan, 2008). Rudd (2008) stresses that the gist of the adaptive educational approach is to enable greater diversity, participation, and responsibility for different learners with different learning styles.

The advent and development of social media technologies can offer many pedagogical benefits for designing DI because of the social and constructive nature of these technologies. According to Rudd (2008), learners prosper from DI allowing individual learning pathways and more room for creativity, collaboration, communication, content creation, multi-modal learning, and problem solving. With these social media technologies, students have more platforms to demonstrate wide-ranging skills and knowledge beyond traditional assessment techniques. In addition, these technologies offer additional avenues for informal and formal communication among students, peers, and instructors, and, therefore, facilitate formative assessment within instructional processes. In the following sections, we first present summaries of two exemplary cases. Then, we identify a number of instructional design factors and recommendations for employing social media technologies to design assessments for DI.

Successful Cases of Assessment for Differentiated Instruction Using Social Media

In a differentiated class, the teacher uses a variety of assessment options and tools to accommodate students' various learning styles, needs and capabilities. The following two exemplary projects or cases, illustrate how a teacher uses social media for both formative and summative assessment in DI in the classrooms.

Case 1: Podcasts in K-4 Social Studies

Koch, Misook, Kush, and Carbonara (2009) used podcasts with 20 students in a K-4 Social Studies and Language Arts class. The 20 participants included Gifted, Attention Deficit Disorder (ADD), Title I Reading, and Regular Education students. Podcasting was employed to promote reflective practices and DI. In order to prepare students for a museum field trip, the teacher created a podcasting episode that emphasized particular details and historical facts. Compared to traditional learning, podcasting offered an array of pedagogical advantages, including the ability to replay, to develop vocabulary and language skills, to maintain attention, as well as to learn in multi-modality (Craig & Paraiso, 2007). The use of this podcast episode created a differentiated learning opportunity because students could learn at a different pace and various occasions they had felt fit. After the field trip, students researched the topics they experienced at the museum and wrote a story from a foreigner's point of view.

Finally, podcasting was employed again as a tool for deeper reflection, with the students recording their own reflective episodes as podcasts.

This instruction employed both formative and summative assessments. Informal and constant one-on-one discussions with the students, as formative assessments, checked student understanding and project progress. Also, through the discussions after the museum trip, the instructor scaffolded students in the editing process of the written portion of the students' heritage story, the construction of the framework for the Podcast, and the listening to the Podcasts of others. While implementing the informal discussions with the students, the instructor used a checklist and anecdotal notes as checkpoints for the final assessment. The categories for formative assessment included Completion of Individual Tasks, Ability to Work Independently, Level of Participation, Ability to Discuss, Explanation of Plan, Making Connections, Retelling Stories, and Descriptive Interpretation of the Project. Although students were not graded on any points in this formative assessment, levels of achievements were marked as Basic, Proficient, or Transformative. In addition, the anecdotal notes included personal notes on how the student was learning and if the student was moving ahead. A variety of assessments besides student-created podcasts included comprehension, expression, and recall of facts to gather information about student achievement. These summative assessments utilized a rubric, which also guided the students as they developed their projects.

Podcasts in this class mainly served two purposes: (a) delivering instruction in a manner that students could listen to on demand, and (b) gauging students learning and reflection as one type of summative assessment. For the first purpose, the researchers of this study attested that all students were highly focused while listening to the podcasting episode in the museums and the technology created an avenue to provide DI to students of multi-literacy skills. In addition, the use of podcasts for the second purpose was exceptionally successful too. The results showed that the students were actively involved in their individual knowledge building by conducting historical research. The increased depth of their work also indicated outstanding learning performance. Since students had plenty of time to experiment with the technology at their own pace, teacher support was hardly needed when they were creating the podcasts. In summary, the use of Web 2.0 technology such as podcasting promoted student-centered constructivist learning through active interaction and promoted a sense of ownership of learning while accommodating individual differences.

Case 2: Using Vodcast-Embedded Blogs in a Science Class

Colombo and Colombo (2007) described how blogs were used in a seventh grade science class to improve DI. This class had about 20 students. Some of the students were identified as gifted and talented, whereas a few others were ESL (English as Second Language) students with reading levels between fourth and fifth grade. In order to accommodate these students with different prior knowledge and learning abilities, the instructor used blogs to extend class time. In these blogs, the teacher provided study guides, introduced new topics and concepts, reviewed important class points for tests, and provided enrichment. More specifically, the teacher created vodcasts (video on demand) by narrating PowerPoint files and uploading the vodcasts to the blog site. These vodcasts were designed to provide additional support for the ESL learners so that they had an additional opportunity to learn the scientific vocabulary. In addition, the teacher created questions to promote inquiry-based learning and useful links to advanced materials in the blog posts. Students were also encouraged to communicate with the instructor on the blog with the comment feature.

The formative assessment used in this class was student journals. Students were asked to record notes in journals both during and after class. Then, the instructor held conferences with each individual student to discuss his/her journals. For the ESL students, the instructor also used individual conferences to bring them up to speed about scientific language by giving them a chance to discuss scientific concepts and verbally expressing understanding with scientific terms. For the gifted students, the instructor discussed the advanced content available on the blog. The teacher used group work and individual projects as summative evaluation of students' learning in the course.

In this class, traditional face-to-face lectures were still used to deliver the course content because the teacher found lectures efficient in conveying large amounts of information in a short time period. However, the teacher could not differentiate instructions to each student's needs because during the class time the teacher needed to lecture to the whole group of students. As a supplemental method, a blog site was set up to extend the instruction and communication needed for DI. The teacher used vodcasts to provide remedial instruction for the less advanced students while offering additional inquiry-based materials and activities for the gifted. In this case, the blog tool was mainly used to deliver instructional materials to learners with different needs and capabilities, increase the dialogues and informal communications between each learner and the teacher, and provide scaffolding support for inquiry activities when necessary. In addition, the teacher also adjusted the assignments based on each student's needs and interests. In this class, although students did not create artifacts with these Web 2.0 technologies, with the podcasts and additional just-in-time information on the blogs, students were found to be actively engaged in learning. The teacher reported that compared to students in other classes, most of the students in this class showed higher learning performance in science.

As shown in the case above, Web 2.0 technologies using an online journal, such as a blog, would be very helpful for students to communicate with the instructor. The teachers are also able to formatively assess students' progress retrospectively by tracking/reviewing students' journals. If the teachers wish to create more flexible and student-centered learning environments with a variety of social media tools, they can conduct formative assessment with student-led blogs, classroom response systems, anonymous online surveys, or Twitter to evaluate students' understandings about scientific in concepts real time. In this way, teachers will learn about the areas in which students need help and additional resources to be created accordingly. The following sections discuss more practical strategies to design effective assessments for DI with a variety of social media technologies.

Assessment Strategies for Differentiated Instruction with Social Media

The design of an assessment can be a significant factor affecting the quality of instruction, especially in DI. This section provides some guidelines to design effective assessments by addressing a series of issues related to creating assessments with social media. These issues include (a) aligning assessment with learning objectives, (b) developing an assessment schedule, (c) incorporating social media for assessment activities in DI, (d) designing assessment and grading guidelines, and (e) additional issues and concerns related to the use of these technologies.

Aligning Assessments with Learning Objectives

To develop any instruction and assessment, it is crucial to align learning goals and objectives with learning standards set forth in a discipline while considering each individual student's needs. In order to meet learning standards and students' needs, teachers should use a variety of techniques and multiple forms of assessments that are engaging and intellectually challenging. Table 11.2 shows some examples of performance assessments that are aligned with learning objectives derived from the 21st Century Learning Outcomes by the Partnership for 21st Century Skills (see Table 11.2).

The table does not intend to provide a comprehensive list of assessment types for these learning goals. Yet, it offers some practical suggestions for teachers to tap into the possibility of assessment measures in various types of instruction. Specifically, in DI, an array of flexible assessment measures is necessary due to students' needs and interests. Some assessments in the table can serve both the formative and/or summative purposes because of the on-going nature of the tasks, such as discussions and journal writing. Assessments like problem solving and group projects can also fall into this category as long as the instructor properly tracks students' progress. In fact, social media, as discussed below, could be a useful tool for user participation and progress tracking. Nonetheless, other types of assessments could probably only work for summative assessment purposes, such as role-play. Once the teacher decides on the assessment types, taking both formative and summative purposes into account, he or she needs to carefully lay out the assessment schedule.

TABLE 11.2 Alignment between Learning Objectives and Assessments

Learning Objectives	Types of Assessment
Creativity and Innovation	• Writing stories, songs, journals • Developing artwork by utilizing a variety of media • Formulating a model
Critical thinking and Problem solving	• Developing solutions to problems by critically analyzing information and integrating the ideas from a variety of sources • Defending a position or evaluating a situation by appraising the context and major aspects of the issue comprehensively
Communication and Collaboration	• Communicating effectively with others with multiple media and technology • Working effectively with diverse people • Making necessary negotiations to achieve common goals in a team
Information, Media, and Technology skills	• Critically judging information delivered through media • Skillfully producing/creating media messages/products using appropriate technology tools • Using information, media and technology in a safe, ethical, and responsible manner
Flexibility and Adaptability	• Applying knowledge and skills to real-life contexts • Transforming skill sets to different environments or situations • Responding to criticism and critical feedback amiably
Initiative-taking and Self-direction	• Demonstrating motivation and willingness to work • Proactively engaging in activities for learning and self-improvement after conducting self-assessment • Managing time and workload effectively
Social and Cross-cultural Competence	• Demonstrating awareness, knowledge, and understanding toward cultural differences • Working effectively and respectfully with others from different cultural/ethnic backgrounds
Productivity and Accountability	• Producing quality work in a timely manner • Setting up goals realistically and managing work effectively • Demonstrating willingness to accept responsibility
Leadership	• Effectively guiding self and others to achieve common goals • Demonstrating great vision

Developing Assessments Schedule

As mentioned earlier, DI is guided by the constructivist or student-centered approach to teaching and learning. Some assessment strategies use various forms of assessment in multiple points during student learning process. Unlike test-based assessment in traditional classrooms, differentiated instruction usually uses performance or authentic assessment such as discussion, reflection, self-monitoring/assessment, and project work, etc. With these assessment types, students learn and are evaluated by participating in these tasks while demonstrating their learning achievements in an on–going assessment process.

If performance assessments are selected in differentiated instruction, it is important for the teacher to plan checkpoints in multiple places during the span of the course. The checkpoints could be on a weekly basis or set up to mirror the milestones of the course. In either case, students need to be informed of the assessment schedule so as to ensure constant teacher-student communication that is essential for performing formative assessment. Social media technologies can assist teachers to provide instant feedback and keep track of student learning—these technologies appear in detail in the following section. In addition, some social media can also keep students informed about the assessment schedule. For example, with Google Calendar, teachers can share a calendar with short- and long-term due dates to remind students to focus on their work. An assessment calendar using Google Calendar can also include key components of assessment tasks and be embedded into another website or blog (see Figure 11.1 for the html code to be copied and pasted into another website to show Google calendars).

Incorporating Social Media for Assessment Activities in DI

To provide valuable opportunities for students to maximize their learning based on their needs and backgrounds, teachers should plan instruction and assessments with a variety of tools in differentiated instruction. Assessment planning should take into account individual student's needs and learning objectives so that necessary accommodations can be made with the assistance of appropriate technology tools. However, it can also be challenging to find tasks that are of equal or similar complexity for each individual or team. Whenever possible, teachers need to provide assessment options that allow students to demonstrate their learning while utilizing their strengths and interests. Hence, in

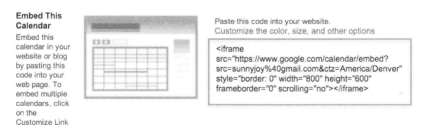

Embed This Calendar
Embed this calendar in your website or blog by pasting this code into your web page. To embed multiple calendars, click on the Customize Link

Paste this code into your website.
Customize the color, size, and other options

```
<iframe
src="https://www.google.com/calendar/embed?
src=sunnyjoy%40gmail.com&ctz=America/Denver"
style="border: 0" width="800" height="600"
frameborder="0" scrolling="no"></iframe>
```

FIGURE 11.1 This screenshot shows an example of how to embed Google Calendar in your website or blog. To embed it, select the option under "Calendar settings" and "Calendar details" at the calendar list after you sign in. Retrieved from: http://www.google.com/intl/en/googlecalendar/about.html

DI, students should have more choices to learn, participate, and express. Social media allows them to easily present and share their work in a variety of media formats such as image, audio, video, music, and animation. In addition, social media helps to broaden the learning context and extend the class time as needed by DI. Moreover, while students in traditional classrooms learn about other cultures or countries mostly in books, social media gives students opportunities to actually connect with people all over the world. With the ease of participating and sharing on social networks, learning is no longer limited to a classroom setting. These social media can create an open and amply expressive learning environment that both facilitates individualized learning and engages them in quality and authentic activities. In the following section, we introduce some examples of social media tools that can be used for assessment tasks in differentiated instruction.

Diagnostic Assessment: Pre-assessment

In order to ensure effective teaching and learning, pre-assessment investigating students' prior knowledge, interest, and readiness, provides fundamental feeds for the later differentiation of instruction. The teacher should use the results of pre-assessment to differentiate the content, process or product to better meet the needs of all students. To explore students' existing conditions, observe some strategies and tools below.

Free Survey Tool.   Google docs (Figure 11.2 & Figure 11.3) provides a form tool, which can be used to survey students' prior knowledge, interest, background, and learning preference. Once created, one can send the link in an email to all students to fill out. Besides pre-assessments, an on-going survey can be established to gather information about students' self-assessed learning progress.

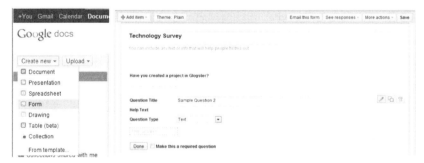

FIGURE 11.2 This image introduces how to create a form in Google Docs. To create a survey, after you sign in on your Google account and inside Google Docs, go to "New" and then click on "Form." Retrieved from: http://www.google.com/google-d-s/forms/

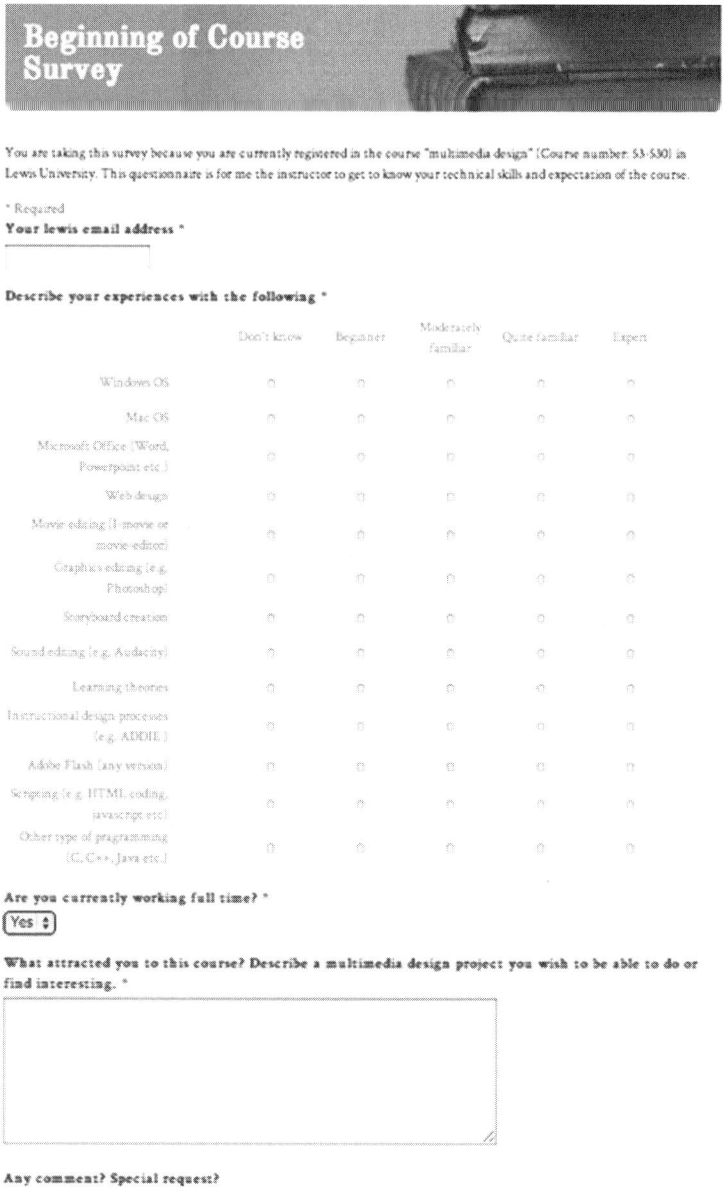

Beginning of Course Survey

You are taking this survey because you are currently registered in the course "multimedia design" (Course number: 53-530) in Lewis University. This questionnaire is for me the instructor to get to know your technical skills and expectation of the course.

* Required

Your lewis email address *

Describe your experiences with the following *

	Don't know	Beginner	Moderately familiar	Quite familiar	Expert
Windows OS					
Mac OS					
Microsoft Office (Word, Powerpoint etc.)					
Web design					
Movie editing (I-movie or movie-editor)					
Graphics editing (e.g. Photoshop)					
Storyboard creation					
Sound editing (e.g. Audacity)					
Learning theories					
Instructional design processes (e.g. ADDIE)					
Adobe Flash (any version)					
Scripting (e.g. HTML coding, javascript etc)					
Other type of programming (C, C++, Java etc.)					

Are you currently working full time? *

Yes

What attracted you to this course? Describe a multimedia design project you wish to be able to do or find interesting. *

Any comment? Special request?

FIGURE 11.3 This image is an example of the student view of the survey using Google Docs. After you have created your survey, a link to your survey will appear at the bottom of your screen. You can then copy and paste that link into your website or blog.

Concept Mapping. Novak (1998) suggested that concept maps might be one efficacious method for capturing and utilizing knowledge because concept maps allow students to analyze information and speculate on the relationships among pieces of information. Concept maps were found effective for knowledge retention and transfer (Nesbit & Adesope, 2006). Concept mapping used to be a one-shot activity, usually performed at the end of the course. Yet, the online concept-mapping tools such as Mindmeister (http://www.mindmeister.com/) or Google Drawing (found in Google Docs) allow students to keep building their concept map for a long time (see Figure 11.4). These tools can be used to analyze each individual student's prior knowledge or a group's collective prior knowledge for an active student-based pre-assessment. In addition, if students are required to keep building their concept map throughout the semester, the teacher can gauge the learning progress of each student/team. If teachers use concept mapping as a summative assessment at the end of instruction, the initial and final maps can be compared to show students' learning progress.

OnlinePhoto Sharing. Flickr (http://www.flickr.com). Students can upload and manage their photos with a story and make comments about other people's photos. They also can use Flickr for educational purposes such as learning about different places through a virtual field trip or exploring photos on specific

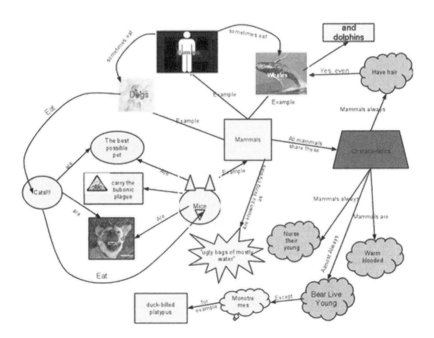

FIGURE 11.4 This screenshot is an example of a concept map in Google drawing created by the students in the EDLT 6616 class at Idaho State University to access a group's collective knowledge in multiple forms.

topics. With Flickr, a teacher may ask students to upload/post the pictures containing arguments/issues or provide their beliefs and understanding about the pictures to assess student's prior knowledge. As the course unfolds, students can keep adding photos and pictures to express their understanding of the topics. By carefully examining the pictures, the teacher can find gaps in learning and provide additional support as needed.

Process-Based Learning and Assessment: Formative Assessment

Many social media technologies support evolution of products or artifacts before they can be turned in for summative assessment. Some technologies not only allow the teacher to monitor individual student or a team's progress but also provide an opportunity for the teacher to scaffold students' learning based on the observed progress. These technologies might include the following.

Wiki-Assisted Group Projects. Such sites include Wikispaces (http://www.wikispaces.com/) or PBWorks (http://pbworks.com/). The educational benefits of students working in groups have been well documented (Wagner & Gooding, 1987). Recently, wikis have been widely used to support group projects (Robertson, 2008; Zorko, 2009). Group projects can also be an effective strategy for differentiated instruction. In the process of collaborative group work, students learn from each other about different strategies and perspectives and enhance their learning through discussion and rehearsal with peers. In addition, group work can also take advantage of each individual student's strengths. For example, in a class (face to face or online) students can be put into groups to solve a problem or complete a project. If the problem or project takes extensive research and analyses of materials, then wikis can be incorporated to facilitate the group work. The wiki project is also advantageous because the assignments can be differentiated in terms of content whilst the teacher can provide similar kinds of support in wiki templates with scaffolding questions created by instructor. However, many learners who experienced group working have also indicated common challenges such as grading system, inequity of contribution, lack of responsibility, or diverse reaction to group projects. To ensure quality group work, educators should establish explicit guidelines for instruction and assessment. Educators may also use the tracking feature embedded in most wiki tools to assess each individual student's learning progress in groups. Here is an example of a tracking system in a wiki tool (Figure 11.5). In Figure 11.6, the tracking feature in the tool generates reports highlighting the changes between selected versions.

Folksonomy. This is also referred to as social tagging or social bookmarking, standing for a method to annotate and categorize content by collaboratively creating and managing tags (Peters, 2009). For example, Del.icio.us (http://www.delicious.com/) is one of the most popular social bookmarking services

FIGURE 11.5 This image is an example of a tracking system in a wiki tool. You can review each individual student's activity on wiki using the Page history button after you sign in to your wiki account/page. Retrieved from: https://plans.pbworks.com/academic

and is a powerful research and knowledge community. One can store the bookmarks online, access them from any computer, and share the interesting links with others. This tool can be employed in DI in several different ways. For example, based on each individual student's interest and learning progress, a teacher can gather links, classify and tag them with keywords related to students' needs. Then, the teacher can direct students to the sites and point out the tags for each individual student or group. The teacher may encourage the group to work together to gather links about a specific topic to achieve collective knowledge sharing and building. Such social tagging sites can also be used for inquiry-driven research projects. Having a separate research topic, each student can work with the instructor individually by creating bookmarks and annotating the bookmarked content.

Private Journal and Public Blog. Penzu (http://penzu.com/). Students can write their own personal journal online and share a journal entry including specific questions or ideas. They can insert photos and manage their entries by using search, sort, filter, rename, and trash options. If students want to share their individual entries, they can do it via email or a public link, like any other

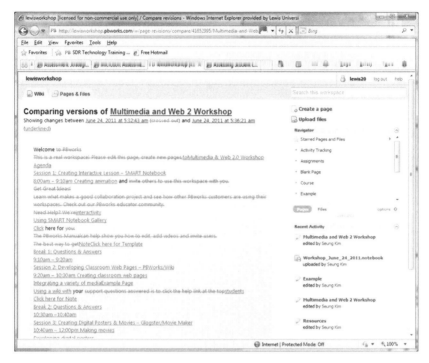

FIGURE 11.6 The screenshot demonstrates the tracking feature in the tool which generates reports by highlighting the changes between selected versions.

blog site (http://blogger.com). As discussed in Case 2, the teacher had the students keep journals and designated a particular time slot every week to discuss the journals with each student. Keeping journals/blogs is a relatively private and non-threatening approach for fostering teacher-student two-way communication, which is imperative for differentiated instruction. Moreover, most blog tools provide functions to embed media and RSS feeds so that the students have many tools at their disposal to express themselves (e.g., creating videoed blogs etc.) and to keep the instructor posted.

Product-Based Assessment: Summative Assessment

In the section above, we discussed using the social media tools to track students' work so that teachers can be consistently informed of the evolution of their learning progress. Such formative assessment does not aim to assign grades but to feed for a teacher's decision-making process for further learning. Nonetheless, social media technologies are power tools for summative assessment as well. These tools offer a vast variety of methods for students to express themselves and demonstrate their learning by employing pertinent materials in diverse formats. The employment of versatile assessment strategies can greatly accommodate differentiated learner styles, strengths and interest, without requiring mastery of sophisticated technical skills.

Podcasting/Vodcasting. Podcast or vodcast (or video podcast) (e.g., http://www.podomatic.com/) allows one to create podcasts/vodcasts by uploading audio/video files, or by live capturing audio/video from a microphone or web-cam. Because of the real-time syndication nature of the technology, podcasts could help the formative assessment with a careful design. For example, students could be encouraged to talk aloud to record their voice on comprehension, points of interests, their discovery, etc. and load onto podcasting sites when recording was completed. These techniques would allow the instructors to "catch the moment" of each student's learning and therefore address their concerns or challenges in a relatively timely manner. While podcasting tools can be used for pre-assessment and formative assessment, podcast or vodcast projects can also be utilized for summative assessment, as discussed in Case 1 above. For example, students can create a book report using pod/vodcasting to demonstrate their understanding of concepts and embedded misconceptions or explain what they learned from the book assigned. Through audio/video sharing, students can demonstrate how to solve a specific task/problem, along with sharing their findings and conclusions. An audio/video recorder and a flip camera can be used for classroom learning activities because of their portability and ease of use from recording to downloading.

Digital Storytelling. Digital storytelling is the practice of using Web-based tools to tell stories with a mixture of digital images, text, recorded audio narration, video clips, and/or music. The topics are only limited by imagination: personal tales, historical events, life exploration, self reflection, anthropological research, and scientific findings, etc. Due to the variety of topic selection, it could be a useful way to engage students in differentiated summative assessment projects. Many tools can support digital storytelling activity, such as MS Photo Story, Movie Maker, and iMovie. Storybird (http://storybird.com/) is a free online site where students can create a collaborative visual storytelling product. Examples of the projects include memorable moments in their lives, a project for advertisement or virtual field trip, a photo story of an interview with experts, etc. In addition, Animoto (http://animoto.com/education) is a Web application that produces stunning videos, using images, video clips, text, and music that you select or upload for auto-editing. An educator's account (a free Animoto Plus account) allows teachers and their students to create unlimited videos. Students can share their videos via email or on a blog/website, export to YouTube, or download to a computer for use in presentations.

Online Presentation. Glogster (http://edu.glogster.com/) allows teachers with an account to share class projects with other students in the class and with other teachers in the school and beyond. The students create non-linear projects with text, images, videos, photos, graphics, music, and more, to demonstrate their knowledge and skills (see Figure 11.7). Dynamic and multi-sensory learning activities, with Glogster, can be used for collaborative cross-curricular projects. Teachers can create and share their own dynamic instruction and monitor student assignments through social networking. Similarly, Prezi (http://prezi.com/your/) allows you to create nonlinear presentations by using the simple editor and include text, images, videos, and paths to show sequences/relationships. Students can share their prezis with others for collaboration or send the presentations to non-prezi members. Teachers can design assignment tasks that allow students to present their ideas in a variety of manners and modes using different visual forms and provide individualized feedback indicating each student's learning performance.

The discussion above shows that social media technologies, due to their innate features, offer various ways for differentiating the learning process and assessments to cater to individual differences. Measuring the growth of

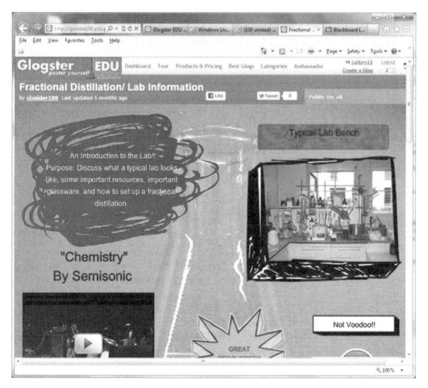

FIGURE 11.7 This screenshot is an example of a student's Glog project in the Technology and Teaching and Learning class at Lewis University. The Glog project demonstrates his knowledge and skills in a non-linear form with text, images, videos, photos, graphics, music, and more.

individual students in a differentiated classroom would be a challenge for teachers whose schools still depend on a test-based, traditional grading system. In the section below, we discuss how teachers can design some alternative assessments and grading guidelines for high quality learning in DI.

Designing Assessment and Grading Guidelines

There are a variety of ways to differentiate each student's learning progress. Instead of standardized tests, teachers have used alternative techniques such as rubrics, portfolios, authentic assessment or performance-based assessment for assessing a student's performance on a process, product or group effort in DI. For instance, an invaluable tool with the differentiated activities is a holistic and performance-specific rubric. When the teacher develops a grading rubric in DI, the criteria should be developed differently according to varied learning styles and activities, but an equal amount of points need to be given for the same type of assessment. As an example, the teacher needs to develop rubrics to evaluate the students' understanding of the main concept/topic by the level of performance on certain criteria. The teacher should clearly define what is expected in different learning situations with different tools/projects. The rubrics need to be shared with students prior to their learning process for self-assessment and peer evaluation and for communicating expectations of high quality of work. The students should also have an opportunity to understand, discuss and even provide input to refine the rubrics to better fit their specific learning tasks.

Additional Issues and Concerns

Privacy and Security. Because of the sharing nature of these social media technologies and the ever-increasing popularity of these tools, privacy-related issues (such as cyber bullying, online attacks, identity theft, etc.) are becoming

TABLE 11.3 A Generic Rubric Table for DI assessment

Category	Criteria
Content (materials and resources)	The teacher states what content need to be to learn.
Process (learning activities)	The teacher explains different activities in which students can be engaged.
Product (learning outcome)	In order to evaluate the product, the teacher lists various performance indicators for students to demonstrate as evidence of learning. As an example, the teacher should clearly define what is expected in different learning situations/tasks aligned with the learning outcomes. It needs to be shared with students prior to their learning process for self-assessment and peer evaluation and for communicating expectation of high quality of work.

a growing concern for teachers, students, and parents. For example, a few students expressed fear of being attacked on a blog when anybody could respond to a blog post (Sharma & Xie, 2008). Yet, most of the students did not think of privacy as a big concern as long as they kept their online sharing on the academic and professional level. Most of the Web 2.0 tools discussed above provide mechanisms for administrators to define/control the access level. However, it is imperative for teachers to inform students of the potential risks of online sharing and publishing before any work is created. Students should also learn and practice common cyber security rules and communicate with their teachers and guardians about any discomfort or threat they might feel.

Plagiarism.   With the help of modern search engines, students have information at their fingertips. As a result, academic integrity is inevitably another critical issue. For students' works created on Web 2.0 technologies, the problem exasperates dramatically. That is because the plagiarism detection software such as turnitin.com is usually designed to check papers that can be uploaded to the site. Yet, most of the projects students create with Web 2.0 technologies (e.g., prezi) naturally reside on those websites. Therefore, those projects cannot be reformatted for the plagiarism detection software. Researchers and practitioners have proposed many ways to combat this problem. For example, Harris and Rea (2009) mentioned that giving a Google search demonstration to locate the "lifted" work could deter plagiarism to a certain degree. In addition, teachers can consider assessments that are of personal interest, contextual, and complex instead of factual or informational in nature. Asking students to provide the sources of their information would also be a good idea to reduce occurrences of plagiarism.

Conclusion

Social media technologies offer numerous opportunities for differentiated instruction and assessment. For example, social media tools allow for student-centered learning, rich and flexible learning with multiple media, and collaborative interactions within a class or outside the classroom. Social media tools also facilitate self and peer assessment in DI and reinforce students' critical thinking and communication skills through online interactions. While the teachers can publish class resources such as class notes, worksheets, or assignment guidelines on social media networks, parents can remain involved in the student's learning process. In addition, many social media tools allow the teacher to control the access levels such as reader, writer, editor or administrator on specific pages to meet the learning purpose and secure student learning activities and information online. With the tracking system in some social media, teachers can improve their understanding of students' needs and learning progress in DI.

In conclusion, social media technologies have great potential to significantly impact differentiated learning by providing a richer and more flexible learning environment. Today's educators should develop effective pedagogical practices to differentiate learning for extremely varied students through collaborative learning and problem solving processes. Teachers should continuously make meaningful changes to content, processes, products and learning environments to meet the needs of diverse students in today's classrooms with emerging social media.

Acknowledgment

The authors of the chapter would like to thank the pre- and in-service teachers in the technology classes at Lewis University (spring, 2011) and the EDLT 6616 class at Idaho State University (fall, 2011) for their creative work and letting us use their collaborative concept map in this chapter.

References

Colombo, M. W., & Colombo, P. D. (2007). Using blogs to improve differentiated instruction. *Education Digest: Essential Readings Condensed for Quick Review, 73*(4), 10–14.

Cormode, G., & Krishnamurthy, B. (2008). Key differences between Web1.0 and Web2.0. *Computer and Information Science, 13*(6), 1–30.

Craig, D., & Paraiso, J. (2007, March). *E-Literacy and literacy: Using iPods in the ESL classroom.* Presentation at the Society for Information Technology and Teacher Education International Conference, San Antonio, Texas.

Garrison, R., & Vaughan, N. D. (2008). *Blended learning in higher education: framework, principles, and guidelines.* San Francisco, CA: Jossey-Bass.

Grant, L. K., & Spencer, R. E. (2003). The personalized system of instruction: Review and applications to distance education. *International Review of Research in Open and Distance Learning, 4*(2), 1–12.

Harris, A. L., & Rea, A. (2009). Web 2.0 and virtual world technologies: A growing impact on IS education. *Journal of Information Systems Education, 20*(2), 137–144

Koch, A., Misook, H., Kush, J., & Carbonara, D. (2009. July). *Active learning with digital media: The use of podcasting in reflective learning for elementary social studies instruction.* Paper presented at the International Conference on e-Learning (ICEL), Toronto, Canada.

Looi, C., Wong, L., So, H., Seow, P., Toh, Y., Chen, W., … & Soloway, E. (2009). Anatomy of a mobilized lesson: Learning my way. *Computers & Education, 53*(44), 1120–1132.

Nesbit, J. C., & Adesope, O. O. (2006). Learning with concept and knowledge maps: A meta-analysis. *Review of Educational Research, 76*(3), 413–448.

Novak, J. D. (1998). *Learning, creating, and using knowledge: Concept maps as facilitative tools in schools and corporations.* Mahwah, NJ: Erlbaum.

O'Reilly, T. (2005). *What Is Web 2.0: Design patterns and business models for the next generation of software.* Retrieved December 10, 2011, from http://oreilly.com/web2/archive/what-is-web-20.html

Parchoma, G. (2003). Learner-centered instructional design and development: Two examples of success. *Journal of Distance Education, 18*(2), 35–60.

Peters, I. (2009). *Folksonomies. Indexing and retrieval in Web 2.0.* Berlin: De Gruyter Saur.

Robertson, I. (2008). Learners' attitudes to wiki technology in problem based, blended learning for vocational teacher education. *Australasian Journal of Educational Technology, 24*, 425–441.

Rudd, T. (2008). *Learning spaces and personalisation workshop outcomes.* Bristol, UK: NESTA Futurelab. Retrieved from http://www2.futurelab.org.uk/events/listing/learning-spaces-and-personalisation-workshop/outcomes

Sharma, P., & Xie, Y. (2008). Students' experiences of using weblog: An exploratory study. *Journal of Asynchronous Learning Networks, 12*(3–4), 137–156.

Solomon, B. S., Harrison, R., & Duce, D. (2011, August). *Methodologies for usng social media collaborative work systems.* Paper presented at the 19th IEEE International Requirements Engineering Conference, Trento, Italy.

Tomlinson, C. A. (2005). *How to differentiate instruction in mixed-ability classrooms* (2nd Ed.). Upper Saddle River, NJ: Pearson/Merrill Prentice Hall.

Von Glasersfeld, E. (1995). *Radical constructivism: A way of knowing and learning.* London: The Falmer Press.

Vygotsky, L. S. (1978). *Mind in society.* Cambridge, MA: Harvard University Press.

Wagner, J., & Gooding, R. (1987). Shared influence and organizational behavior: A meta-analysis of situational variables expected to moderate participation-outcome relationships. *The Academy of Management Journal, 30*(3), 524–541.

Zorko, V. (2009). Factors affecting the way students collaborate in a wiki for English language learning. *Australasian Journal of Educational Technology, 25*(5), 645–665.

12

VOICETHREAD® AS A FACILITATOR OF INSTRUCTIONAL CRITIQUE

Jamie Smith and Teresa Franklin

Introduction

As technology advances and our conception of formal learning evolves, increasing emphasis is placed on new and relevant resources for the emergent world of hybrid, online, and virtual instruction. With the transition to these partially, if not wholly, Web-based learning environments comes a need to reconstruct opportunities for interaction. Early attempts at Web-based learning were often highly instructor-focused and could easily leave individuals feeling isolated in their learning. Humans are social beings, however, and the Web, as a reflection of this, has become a vastly social phenomenon. Now virtually any action executed online can become a social opportunity. Shopping, watching TV, reading the news—all of these tasks—have morphed into social experiences when carried out in an online environment. More specifically, and arguably more important, is the social phenomenon of personal participation.

The Web has become a participatory environment. Individuals can publish, share, re-mix, and provide feedback via an innumerable array of options. The Web is changing the construct of literacy in our world. In modern times, it takes more than the ability to read, write, and understand the written language to be literate; new media literacies encompass a range of necessary skills. The New Media Literacies Project (n.d.) inventories and details these essential competencies, which include the ability to navigate various online environments, problem-solve issues through exploration and troubleshooting, sample and re-mix media and generally understand, negotiate and contribute to the online world.

At the heart of this notion of participation is interaction. What was once a fairly static mode of delivery of information is now a dynamic and constantly changing space. This is a positive development for instructional designers and practitioners searching for approaches to learner-centered, Web-based instruction. No longer bound to merely presenting information, the potential of these interactions for learning are immense. As our teaching and learning endeavors migrate to this arena, we are now able to maintain, if not elevate our traditional classroom expectations for student interaction and participation. What's more, we have at our disposal an increasingly diverse and dynamic array of means of facilitating these interactions with the additional benefit of reinforcing critical new media literacies (Schrum & Solomon, 2007).

Interactions in Evaluation

In the evaluation of learning or assessment of artifacts produced to demonstrate learning, interaction can be a crucial provision for understanding and individual growth. Interaction between instructor and learner reinforces expectations and meaningful discourse aids in clarity of feedback as well as the formation of new goals for continuous learning and improvement. In a learner-centered approach to evaluation, it is common to ask students to self-evaluate and/or assess their peers. These approaches to evaluation can be highly rewarding for the learner. Self-reflection encourages personal ownership of learning and peer assessment or critique reinforces understanding of one's own learning for the student while providing a fresh perspective to the individual whose work or performance is being evaluated (Akyol & Garrison, 2008). All of these approaches are accomplished best through interaction.

Interaction, particularly in the context of a virtual setting, does not always occur synchronously (Hrastinski, 2008). It is important to note that this factor is not in itself a reflection of the quality of the interaction. Just as we can have more or less meaningful interactions in face-to-face settings, these possibilities also exist in an online setting, regardless of timing. The charge of the instructional designer or practitioner is to harness the opportunities for the interactions and structure them for optimal success and value. One overarching criticism of online interactions is the lack of human quality, or social presence. This concept involves the degree of perceived reality in interactions. Text-based interactions are fairly common online and may be perceived as impersonal as compared to having a conversation with someone in person. However, just as there is a range of quality of interactions on this level in a traditional setting, there are ways to improve the social presence in online settings (Aragon, 2003).

As an example, consider two face-to-face scenarios: In scenario A, student work is displayed and everyone in class has a standardized evaluation form to complete and submit to their peer. In scenario B, students present and explain their work to peers, who are then encouraged to contribute constructive feedback as part of an open discussion. In comparing the two approaches, scenario A may seem highly impersonal. Similarly, in an online setting, scenario A may involve students providing text-based feedback via a form, while scenario B may involve students presenting and explaining their work to their classmates who will then provide video and audio feedback describing their perceptions. In the former scenario, students may be identified by a heading with their name, an online ID, etc., whereas in the latter, the peers can be seen and heard as if talking to them in person. This type of interaction affords participants increased social presence.

This situation can occur synchronously through the use of voice/video chat; however, especially in distance learning, it is often difficult to have students meet online at the same time. Technical considerations and personal schedules can be barriers to this type of activity, which negates a major affordance of anytime, anywhere online learning (Ally, 2004). Luckily, the same objectives and level of social presence may be achieved asynchronously through an application like VoiceThread®.

Why? Affordances for Instruction

Technology should be a thoughtful and deliberate integration, not a novel addition, to instruction (Ertmer, 1999). It is true any situation that the application should be selected for its alignment with purposeful and intentional learning activities. As these factors are particular to each unique situation, the broader affordances of VoiceThread® as a teaching tool will be discussed here.

Social Presence

As online learning becomes increasingly prevalent in formal education, research efforts have focused on assessing and analyzing the differences between traditional and online environments. Unique variables have been pinpointed, and efforts to maximize the effectiveness of these variables for online learning have been synthesized and evaluated. One such variable is social presence. The impact of distance, particularly between teacher and learner, is at the root of most early research into online learning environments. Moore's explanation of transactional distance theory specifies the distinction between physical distance and the implications of the distance for interaction and relationships between teacher and learner (Moore, 1993). From this perspective, the significance of distance is arguably far more psychological than physical (Garrison, 2000).

So and Brush (2008) note that it is important to investigate how learners perceive this distance, what factors affect perceptions, and how these perceptions affect learning. Given the increased potential for isolation in online learning, a prominent research trend is to examine strategies for increasing interaction, affording the learner a voice and perceived social presence. Social presence theory was borne out of a focus on media long before widespread computer-based instruction (Short, Williams, & Christie, 1976). The concept involves the degree of perceived reality across technology-mediated interactions. Gunawardena (1995) explains that two key factors, immediacy and intimacy, have been identified to significantly impact individuals' perceptions of social presence. These factors can be related not simply to the types of media used, but how it is used to facilitate interactions.

Ever-growing support for constructivist learning bolsters the advocacy for enhanced social presence in formal online learning environments. A review of the research reveals that social presence is a significant predictor of student retention (Boston et al., 2010; Liu, Gomez, & Cherng-Jyh Yen, 2009), learning (Ke, 2010; Liu et al., 2009), and learner satisfaction (Akyol & Garrison, 2008; Hostetter & Busch, 2006; Ke, 2010; Lin, Lin, & Laffey, 2008). Social presence is extended beyond user names and text with the ability to see and hear participants within the context of VoiceThread®.

Accessibility and Differentiated Instruction

Accessibility is a necessary consideration in online instruction. VoiceThread® addresses accessibility issues and presents a transparent explanation of their efforts to continuously improve the accessibility of the application for a population of users with a range of abilities. The Voluntary Product Accessibility Template details the application's compliance with Section 508 of the Rehabilitation Act (VoiceThread LLC, 2011b). The company is clear about listening to users and openly calls for user feedback to help make the product accessible for everyone (VoiceThread LLC, 2011a). VoiceThread Universal®, the screen-reader friendly version of the application, is entirely accessible by screen-reading software.

The range of options available for learners to contribute to and navigate a VoiceThread® makes it more approachable than strictly text-based online content. Much communication in formal online learning scenarios is text-based. This can pose difficulties for dyslexic students, students with attention deficit disorders, learning disabled students, and others who may find it challenging to read and comprehend or type computerized text. VoiceThread® makes communicating far more approachable for these individuals by extending the format of online communication to audio and video. Audio commenting provides opportunities for enhanced context through inflection or sound effects. Video provides visual and aural cues for understanding and connection. Hand gestures, body language, facial expression, and tone can all be perceived through the use of video, aspects lacking in text-based exchanges. Actions can be modeled and demonstrated via video, as will be addressed in the example case in the following section. This application yields greater opportunities for understanding by providing prospects for differentiated instruction, creating the potential for meaningful engagement for visual, aural and kinesthetic learners.

Lack of Content Specificity

That VoiceThread® is not in and of itself educational software suggests that it was not designed specifically for instruction. As such, it is not bound to one particular content area or purpose. VoiceThread® can be used to present, communicate, and collaborate through a variety of media formats. For example, the software may be used to display individual work with the intent to simply present material or to set up a gallery of student work and ask learners to offer critique, emphasizing the communicative aspect of the application. Learners may develop a VoiceThread® that demonstrates particular concepts in a lesson, requiring students to add media, discuss and annotate via commenting features, determine which artifacts to keep and which to discard, thereby acting as collaborative curators of the VoiceThread®.

The diversity of media formats available to integrate into VoiceThread® suggests that the presentation, communicative, or collaborative objectives can center on virtually any topic. VoiceThread® lends itself just as well to science-, grammar-, and math-focused learning objectives as it does to goals for a physical education, art, or music lesson. Subject matter is of no particular consequence in considering the usefulness of the application, allowing practitioners and instructional designers to utilize the tool when it aligns with goals for presentation, communication or collaboration in any subject area. Further examples of the use of VoiceThread® for various content areas will be discussed later in the chapter.

What? About VoiceThread®

VoiceThread® is a Web-based application which allows individuals to create multimedia slideshows containing any combination of images, videos, and documents. Authors can narrate and annotate this media through the use of commenting and markup tools. They have the ability to share these slideshows by making the VoiceThread® available in the site's public gallery, providing access to an established group of users, sharing a link via e-mail, web posting, or other social media or by embedding the VoiceThread® in a webpage. VoiceThreads® can be opened up for individual text, audio and video comments from other users. The use of a doodling tool allows users to visually markup the included media during audio and video commenting. Comments can be moderated by the creator of the VoiceThread® if the author wishes to monitor feedback. Users have the ability to upload an image to their account that is displayed with their comment in the sidebar of the application (VoiceThread LLC, 2011a). The creation of a VoiceThread® need not be an individual endeavor, as contributing permissions can be extended to other users, providing a collaborative opportunity that can vary in scope from peer groups to a global context.

Anatomy of a VoiceThread®

The software has a number of features that provide a media-rich, accessible environment in which users share and interact. Figure 12.1 depicts various aspects of the interface. These elements will be detailed in the following sections.

Media Content

VoiceThread® allows users to incorporate a variety of media via various integration methods. Document formats supported by the application include PDF, Microsoft Word, Excel, and PowerPoint. Images and video can be uploaded from the user's computer, integrated by providing a URL (e.g., to a YouTube video or image stored online), copied from another VoiceThread®, or captured via webcam. VoiceThread® has Flickr and Facebook integration, allowing users to load content directly through these resources. The application provides access to over 700,000 images via the New York Public Library. Each piece of media receives its own 'slide' in the VoiceThread® (see element A, Figure 12.1).

Author Identity

Individuals' identities are displayed to acknowledge their contributions. Users can add multiple identities to their account, making it easy to participate in various roles. For example, one might wish to participate with different identities when navigating a class VoiceThread® versus one created for friends, family, or

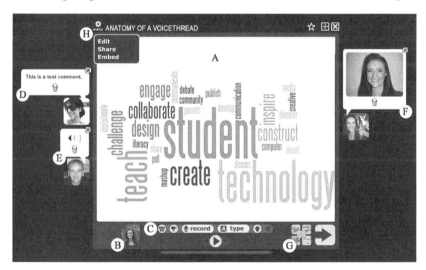

FIGURE 12.1 This screenshot depicts various aspects of the VoiceThread® interface, including the main media content area (A), author identity (B), commenting options (C), text comments (D), audio comments (E), video comments (F), slide thumbnails (G), and menu options (H).

individuals sharing a particular hobby or interest. Author identities are always displayed in the lower left corner so that viewers of the slide can see who contributed the main media content (see element B in, Figure 12.1). The identities of comment contributors are displayed on the side of the main media content.

Commenting Options

There are a number of ways to comment. Options are displayed at the bottom of the application and include text-based, audio or visual markup feedback. Should the main media content be a video, comments can be added while the video plays. The user can control the video while commenting as well, pausing to explain, or skipping to specific points of interest. All comments can be reviewed before being posted to the VoiceThread®. If the user decides to delete the comment and start over, it is no longer accessible. Comments may be deleted by the author of or the individual who posted the comment by clicking the trashcan icon (see elements D, E, and F in Figure 12.1).

Visual Feedback

There are two options for providing visual feedback within VoiceThread®. The type button in the commenting options allows users to create a text-based comment. This comment will be displayed above the individual's identity on the side of the main content area (see element D in Figure 12.1).

The doodling tool, which allows the user to select a color and draw on the main content, can be used in conjunction with text, audio, and video feedback to identify specific talking points. The markup added with the doodling tool will not overwrite the original main media content; rather, it will be displayed only when viewing an individual's comment.

Audio Feedback

There are several different methods available for users who wish to leave audio comments, including recording within the VoiceThread® application, leaving a telephone message, and uploading externally created audio either MP3 or WAV format. An audio comment is displayed above the identity of the user who left it (see element E in Figure 12.1).

Arguably, the simplest method for leaving audio feedback is to record the comment within the VoiceThread® environment. To do this, the user simply presses the record button and speaks, creating a live recording of their comment that can be reviewed before posting. The telephone feature is useful in the event that a computer microphone is not accessible. The user can click the telephone commenting button and enter a phone number. VoiceThread® will instantly call the number and allow the user to leave audio feedback. The Voice-Thread® can be navigated through use of the dialing buttons on the phone, allowing the user to leave comments across all slides in the VoiceThread® in one phone call. When the user hangs up the phone, the audio feedback is posted to VoiceThread®.

Video feedback

Video commenting extends social presence to its fullest potential within the VoiceThread® environment by allowing users to both see and hear each other. This can increase understanding through expression and body language cues. Examples can be demonstrated via video feedback. Video feedback is created by clicking the camera icon in the commenting options and utilizing a webcam. Video comments are displayed above the identity of the user who created them (see element F in Figure 12.1).

Additional Slides

The VoiceThread® slideshow can contain multiple pieces of media. The interface is arranged so that the content being viewed is displayed in the center of the VoiceThread®, and the navigation controls below can be used to progress to the previous or next slide. In the lower right corner of the interface (see element G in Figure 12.1), the thumbnail grid can be clicked to view an extended thumbnail display of all slides. New, unviewed comments are denoted with a yellow callout icon.

Menu Options

In the upper left corner of the VoiceThread®, the menu button (see element H in Figure 12.1) can be selected to view options for sharing and editing. Authors and users with the appropriate permissions can edit the VoiceThread® by adding, removing, and reordering slides (see main media content above). Playback and sharing options can also be selected.

User Permissions

VoiceThreads® can range from very public, highlighted on a browse page on the website, to highly restricted or private settings. Authors can decide whether to make public VoiceThreads® available on the web page for visitors to search and scan. Authors can also determine how freely other users can interact with these VoiceThreads®. Private VoiceThreads® can be made available to the author or to selected users who are added as contacts to the author's account and granted access by invitation. Authors may choose to moderate, displaying comments only after author approval. Individual invited users can be assigned any combination of three capabilities: viewing, commenting, and editing the VoiceThread®.

Sharing

There are various sharing options available for authors and permitted users. Links to a VoiceThread® can be sent via e-mail or via instant message or posted to a webpage as a URL. When links are shared, individuals are transferred to access the application within the VoiceThread.com site. They can also be embedded as an object anywhere that allows custom HTML to be displayed. This embedded format maintains the interactive qualities of VoiceThread®, providing opportunity for communication and collaboration within the context of any website. There is even a plugin for Moodle users to incorporate VoiceThread® into their open source Learning Management System (LMS), and VoiceThread® has announced that further development efforts will focus on integration for other LMSs (VoiceThread LLC, 2011a). VoiceThreads® may be distributed through a number of integrated social media quick share options, including Facebook, Twitter, Yahoo, Blogger, and the like. Archival versions of a VoiceThread® can be exported in either .mov or .mp4 formats and include the original media as well as all comments and markup viewable as one continuous video.

How? A Case for Instructional Critique

The following lesson will provide supporting evidence that the application can facilitate various aspects of instructional critique. The content focus of this case is musical conducting, but the principles and methods can be extended to any peer critique scenario. VoiceThread® was utilized for self-reflection, peer feedback, and instructor critique in a beginning musical conducting lesson. An online survey was used to solicit learner feedback regarding perceived affordances and constraints to the use of this tool for critique; these results will be presented and discussed to help inform future implementation.

Lesson Plan

The lesson was intended to introduce learners to the basics of instrumental musical conducting through engaging face-to-face and Web-based learning activities. Learning goals included the following assessable actions. The learners will be able to demonstrate: conducting in readable 2 and 4 patterns, stylistic contrast, dynamic contrast, and gradual dynamic change; learners will also be able to assess conducting for clarity and effectiveness of techniques.

Prior to class, participants were asked to register for a free VoiceThread® account and were added to a class VoiceThread® with the permissions to edit and comment. Participatory learning activities included instructor modeling of conducting patterns followed by learner matching and independent learner demonstration. Individuals were given time to practice and then partnered to record guided demonstrations of their musical conducting. Netbooks with internal microphones and webcams were used to record the demonstrations directly into the main content area of the VoiceThread®.

After the conclusion of this face-to-face portion of the class, learners were asked to use VoiceThread® to critique their peers' conducting. Guidelines were provided focus feedback on the learning objectives of the lesson. Participants were given the option to use any commenting format(s) they wished. Instructor feedback was provided via video commenting and the doodling tool. Learners were asked to review the feedback reflect on their own performance.

After the lesson, participants were asked to complete an online questionnaire regarding the use of VoiceThread® for self, peer, and instructor critique. Additional insight into learner perceptions was gained via reflective blog posts and post-lesson conversations with participants.

Literature-Base Rationale

The ARCS model for motivational design (Keller, 1987) provided a framework for lesson structure. Attention strategies, such as visual representations, examples, variability in interaction, and participation were utilized. Responsiveness, need matching, and modeling were employed to demonstrate relevance. Confidence was promoted through clearly stated learning requirements, self-evaluation, scaffolding, appropriate attributions of success, and increased independence on tasks, and low risk conditions where learners may enjoy the activity and be unconcerned with failure. Strategies to increase satisfaction, such as verbal reinforcement, peer assistance, personal attention, and motivating feedback were incorporated into the lesson.

Psychomotor taxonomy consists of imitation, manipulation, precision, articulation and naturalization (Dave, 1967); this taxonomy provided domains with which to align instructional goals, scaffold activities, and derive assessments. Learners began with imitating what was modeled by the instructor, then reproduced the action individually and worked toward a state of precision in which they could execute the action without assistance. Dickey (1992) explains, "Conducting is an imitative form of communication utilizing patterns of movement that have evolved into a series of conventionally understood gestures" (p. 1). Cognitive taxonomy (Bloom & Krathwohl, 1956) supports the goals, activities, and assessments, as learners progress through knowledge, understanding, applying, and analyzing the content of this lesson.

The use of VoiceThread® in this lesson allowed learners to view their performances from an external perspective. While this could be accomplished via practicing in front of a mirror, the use of video allows learners to further detach themselves from the action of performing the skill and enables them to more critically assess their own demonstration. Further, VoiceThread® enables users to produce visual markups on their videos, allowing them to trace the conducting patterns for increased visual clarity. The use of video for self-evaluation has been demonstrated to produce more accurate assessments than other means (Rapee & Hayman, 1996).

Peer assessment provided two benefits to the learners—it reinforced learning and provided a deeper level of understanding (Ertmer et al., 2007). Learners not only benefited from the feedback provided on their own performance, but through the process of assessing their peer's performance as well.

Results

Learners were asked to complete an online questionnaire regarding the use of VoiceThread® for self, peer, and instructor critique. Following is a discussion of the results.

Specific Features

Specific features of the application were addressed, including the text, audio, and video commenting, as well as the doodling function and video playback capability. Text was by far the most frequently utilized commenting option, with 88% of participants using this feature. Audio and video commenting were used equally by 38% of participants, while only 25% tried the doodling function. Convenience was cited by 62.5% of respondents as a rationale for the use of text commenting, explaining it was "quick and easy."

Participants rated these features on a 5-point Likert-type scale on their usefulness for learning. It was noted in the survey that this rating was not specific to those used by participants themselves, but included consideration of the features for peer and instructor feedback as well. While no feature was rated somewhat or highly ineffective, text commenting had the lowest score, with 37.8% of respondents showing they were neutral in their perception of its usefulness. Both the doodling and audio commenting were rated as somewhat to highly effective by 87.5% of participants, and all participants rated video commenting as somewhat to highly effective. This demonstrates a clear disconnect between perceived usefulness of the commenting features and what participants actually utilized in their commenting, discussed later in the implications section.

Affordances

All participants responded that they "somewhat" or "highly" agreed that VoiceThread® allowed them to assess their own performance, assess the performance of others, and learn from instructor feedback. Participants were able to learn from peer feedback and observation as well as their own performances.

Levels of overall usefulness, ease of use, motivation, interest, engagement, social presence, and level of reflection produced were rated on a 5-point scale from Low to High. The highest levels were reported for usefulness and engagement, at 75%, followed by social presence and level of reflection at 62.5%; 50% indicated the highest level of motivation and interest, and all participants indicated the ease of use was "moderately high" to "high." In open responses addressing the affordances of VoiceThread® for instructional critique, participants offered enthusiastically positive feedback (see Table 12.1).

Constraints

Technology requirements were cited as potential constraints (e.g., the need for Internet access, the need for microphone or phone for audio commenting and webcam for video commenting). Technical requirements must be considered if asking students to utilize the application outside of a scenario where the instructor can provide technological necessities. Particularly the use of video and streaming audio comments require adequate Internet capability and can be a frustrating experience for individuals attempting to use slower or less dependable connection.

TABLE 12.1 Responses Regarding Affordances of VoiceThread for Critique

I can watch back my own performance, listen to isntructor's feedback while watching my performance, and see my peers' performance feedback and their performance easily just back moving back and forward. it 's pretty neat!
I really like instructor critique, especially (the instructor) provides us all video feedback for all of us. She talks the problems of ours and uses doodle to circle the places that the problem occurs. peer critique is fun. Someone said I am deadly serious :) By looking at the critique people left me on VT, I can see my problem that I would never notice.
It makes sharing easy. I am able to see everybody's performance and comments, which lead to a high level of social presence. The doodling function has made it easy for the instructor to point out what students did wrong or did well.
It is really good for instructor feedback. I don't see any other way to give this audio and visual feedback without using voice-thread.
I love this tool. I think it would be very useful for taping presentations and then provide specific feedback to the student on what he did well and what he missed. In a systems analysis class, it could be used to tape students practicing their interaction with a client. You could then provide feedback and suggest other tactics. It's rare to get an opportunity to view yourself performing and I think it could be very powerful.
I believe that Voice Thread can offer an amazing coaching opportunity for anyone actually "doing" something. It could be used for facilitators, athletes, conductors, and others who could take the videos and the feedback and be able to see the behavior that someone is commenting on.
It's easy to use and made me more willing to give feedback to others. And also, I think the instructor's video feedback was very helpful to me.
Using VoiceThread let me watch myself and peers outside of the action, so I didn't have to think about what I was doing and try to reflect at the same time. It was so much easier for me to see what I was doing on VoiceThread and separating the action from reflection helped me understand peer and instructor feedback better.

Privacy and data security were also cited as possible concerns. Although VoiceThread® allows control over the level of access to content and commenting capabilities, privacy could remain a concern amongst learners. Individual comfort levels with sharing personally identifying information, such as a photo for the VoiceThread® identity or videos of oneself, vary among students. Thoroughly explaining the privacy controls, including detailed information regarding who can access the slideshow and sharing limitations, is crucial to optimizing comfort level with sharing this type of information. It may be necessary to increase privacy by reducing the level of accessibility to the slideshow or to offer alternatives for individuals who do not wish to publish personally identifiable information online, such as using a generic icon as an identity, a user id in lieu of real names, or utilizing only text or audio commenting. Ideally, the instructor should attempt to create a scenario where privacy settings are strict enough that all individuals feel comfortable participating with optimal social presence.

While participants in this case reported a high ease of use, the level of comfort in navigating new technologies will also vary among students. A brief walk-through during class can go a long way in increasing student familiarity and comfort with a new application. It is recommended based on the authors' prior experience that a VoiceThread® is created and students are added before class. This will provide learners an opportunity to peruse the site before the walk-through; they can then quickly log in during class to practice navigating the application with the support of the instructor before they are asked to use it individually. This will likely be easier for students than troubleshooting the application on their own. In the event that a synchronous walk-through is not a possibility, useful resources can be found on the VoiceThread® website (http://www.voicethread.com).

Comfort level with the use of video (in reference to their own appearance in videos) was cited by some participants as a potential personal constraint. This is discussed further with the implications as it is likely a key factor in the discrepancy between what was perceived as the most useful form of commenting and what was most widely utilized by participants.

Implications

Learners' self-reported perceptions of ease of use and usefulness support high prospects for the adoption of this application in educational endeavors as prescribed by the Technology Acceptance Model (Davis, 1989). A high level of enthusiasm for the application was indicated by participants in survey responses, blog reflections and one-on-one interviews.

Enhanced self-reflection was supported. Several participants noted, as shown in the comments in Table 12.1, that they were able to see potential areas of improvement that they would not have otherwise noticed. Possible attributions to this may be the ability for participants to see themselves from a third person perspective as well as the lightening of cognitive load (i.e., learners need not concentrate on performing the actions while self-reflecting).

Peer critique process was also facilitated, but it should be noted that scaffolding for peer critiques is advisable to optimize the usefulness of feedback. One participant noted in the survey that "Sometimes people don't say many helpful comments in critique—they just say good job, but this is more related to things outside of VoiceThread." This reflects pedagogical implications for the employment of peer critique. While some general guidelines were provided to help guide peer feedback, recommendations for future applications include the provision of specific assessment points for learners to address. Modeling appropriate and effective critique would also likely prove highly beneficial in promoting valuable peer feedback.

A noteworthy finding is the disconnect between the frequency of use and perceived usefulness of specific commenting features. While text commenting was perceived to be the least useful and video commenting was reported to be the most useful, the number of participants who chose to use the text feature (88%) greatly outnumbered those who utilized video commenting (38%). One frequently cited rationale for using text was that it was easy and quick to use. Some participants mentioned location as a reason for not using these features (e.g., background noise was a problem for one learner, and another mentioned recording audio comments would have been disruptive to the environment that she/he was in). Lack of essential hardware was also noted as a rationale for not leaving audio or video comments. One participant reported, "For me, the biggest problem is that I don't want to be on camera. But I really like others' video." This issue was mentioned by a few participants in one-on-one interviews.

These issues warrant consideration for future applications. Instructor feedback was provided solely via video commenting and doodling. After discussions with the students, it was concluded that had instructor feedback been presented as an example prior to peer feedback, learners would have been more apt to utilize the video commenting feature. This may have also yielded higher quality critiques.

Recommendations for future use include utilizing the application with diverse instructional media in order to investigate the potential affordances and constraints for various objectives. While video was perceived to be the most useful format for feedback in this instance where demonstration of a skill was integral, audio commenting may be sufficient in cases where the objective is critique of a visual artifact. The current case clearly demonstrates a great deal of potential for this application in the facilitation of self, peer, and instructor critique, but there are many potential applications.

Who, When, and Where? Using VoiceThread®
across Diverse Contexts

VoiceThread® can be used in virtually any instructional scenario. It is free from the constraints of a target audience or typical learner, content-specificity, and optimal contexts. While the case provided demonstrates the use of this application for critique in an adult learning scenario, ease of use makes VoiceThread® highly approachable for K-12 students and teachers as well (Educause Learning Initiative, 2009).

VoiceThread® is not subject specific. It can be implemented just as usefully to promote higher order thinking in hypothesizing for simulated scientific experiments as it can for promoting empathy through role playing (Burden & Atkinson, 2008). While it could be used for more teacher-centered presentation strategies (Holcomb & Beal, 2010), the application's true potential is its ability to provide learners a voice and an opportunity to contribute and take ownership of the educational experience (Pallos & Pallos, 2011). Appropriate use of this application is a question of instructional goals, but possibilities for constructivist learning endeavors are obvious.

VoiceThread® can be utilized in various locations and formal learning scenarios. The case presented a hybrid format as an example where learners used the application both in class as well as outside of a traditional face-to-face environment. VoiceThread® could be used completely within a traditional setting and is easily incorporated into fully online learning settings, as it can be used within the native environment, embedded into other external sites, and integrated fully into Moodle. VoiceThread® mobile has recently been introduced and will be extended to a broader range of devices, making it usable from virtually anywhere (VoiceThread LLC, 2011a). Educause Learning Initiative (2009) highlights the use of the application in distance learning courses for art history and art appreciation at Sierra College, Rocklin, California, where VoiceThread® was used to establish a sense of community and increase instructor social presence (Educause Learning Initiative, 2009). Public VoiceThreads® can offer opportunities for global collaboration and communication and can transcend physical classrooms and cultural boundaries (Yildiz, 2010).

In the context of evaluation, videos of experiential learning can be utilized for modeling and reflection (McCormack, 2010). Students can use the application to evaluate, discuss, and debate exemplary works (Lofton, 2010). In such cases, the application can be used to gather documented evidence for evaluation of the students' ability to verbalize course concepts (Mandernach & Taylor, 2011). It can be used to evaluate student work or as a portfolio to demonstrate progress through artifacts across a period of time (Holland, 2010). The authors have utilized the application for evaluation of movie projects, demonstrated skill performance and visual mockups of websites. VoiceThread® naturally lends itself to the analysis and creation of texts in the media classroom (Rodesiler,

2010). The range of media available to use in the application makes it extremely versatile in terms of instructional objectives. The potential of VoiceThread® to empower learners by supporting their voice and presence in learning contexts is great and the use of this innovative and user-friendly application is limited only by your own creativity.

References

Akyol, Z., & Garrison, D. R. (2008). The development of a community of inquiry over time in an online course: Understanding the progression and integration of social, cognitive and teaching presence. *Journal of Asynchronous Learning Networks, 12*(3–4), 3–22.

Ally, M. (2004). Foundations of educational theory for online learning. In T. A. Anderson & F. Elloumi (Eds.), *Theory and practice of online learning* (pp. 3–31). Alberta, Canada: Athabasca University.

Aragon, S. R. (2003). Creating social presence in online environments. *New Directions for Adult and Continuing Education, 100,* 57-68. doi:10.1002/ace.119

Bloom, B., & Krathwohl, D. (1956). *Taxonomy of educational objectives: The classification of educational goals. Handbook I: Cognitive domain.* New York, NY: Longman.

Boston, W., Díaz, S. R., Gibson, A. M., Ice, P., Richardson, J., & Swan, K. (2010). An exploration of the relationship between indicators of the community of inquiry framework and retention in online programs. *Journal of Asynchronous Learning Networks, 14*(1), 3–19.

Burden, K., & Atkinson, S. (2008). Evaluating pedagogical 'affordances' of media sharing Web 2.0 technologies: A case study. In *Hello! Where are you in the landscape of educational technology? Proceedings ascilite Melbourne 2008.* Retrieved from http://www.ascilite.org.au/conferences/melbourne08/procs/burden-2.pdf

Dave, R. (1967). *Psychomotor domain.* Berlin: International Conference of Educational Testing.

Davis, F. D. (1989). Perceived usefulness, perceived ease of use, and user acceptance of information technology. *MIS Quarterly, 13*(3), 319–340.

Dickey, M. R. (1992). A review of research on modeling in music teaching and learning. *Bulletin of the Council for Research in Music Education*, (113), 27–40.

Educause Learning Initiative (2009). 7 things you should know about VoiceThread. Retrieved from http://net.educause.edu/ir/library/pdf/ELI7050.pdf

Ertmer, P. A. (1999). Addressing first- and second-order barriers to change: Strategies for technology integration. *Educational Technology Research and Development,47*(4), 47–61. doi: 10.1007/BF02299597

Ertmer, P. A., Richardson, J. C., Belland, B., Camin, D., Connolly, P., Coulthard, G., Mong, C. (2007). Using peer feedback to enhance the quality of student online postings: An exploratory study. *Journal of Computer-Mediated Communication, 12*(2), 412–433. doi:10.1111/j.1083-6101.2007.00331.x

Hrastinski, S. (2008). Asynchronous and synchronous E-learning. *EDUCAUSE Quarterly, 31*(4). Retrieved from http://www.educause.edu/EDUCAUSE+Quarterly/ EDU CAUSEQuarterlyMagazineVolum/AsynchronousandSynchronousELea/163445

Holcomb, L. B., & Beal, C. M. (2010). Captializing on web 2.0 in the social studies context. *Tech Trends, 54*(4), 28–32.

Holland, J. (2010). Cross discipline technology integration. *International Journal for Cross-Disciplinary Subjects in Education, 1*(4), 208–215.

Hostetter, C., & Busch, M. (2006). Measuring up online: The relationship between social presence and student learning satisfaction. *Journal of Scholarship of Teaching and Learning, 6*(2), 1–12.

Garrison, R. (2000). Theoretical challenges for distance education in the 21st century: A shift from structural to transactional issues. *International Review of Research in Open and Distance Learning, 1*(1), 1–17.

Gunawardena, C. N. (1995). Social presence theory and implications for interaction and collaborative learning in computer conferences. *International Journal of Educational Telecommunications, 1*(2), 147–166.

Keller, J. M. (1987). Development and use of the ARCS model of motivational design. *Journal of Instructional Development, 10*(3), 2–10.

Ke, F. (2010). Examining online teaching, cognitive, and social presence for adult students. *Computers & Education, 55*(2), 808–820.

Lin, Y.-M., Lin, G.-Y., & Laffey, J. M. (2008). Building a social and motivational framework for understanding satisfaction in online learning. *Journal of Educational Computing Research, 38*(1), 1–27. doi:10.2190/EC.38.1.a

Liu, S. Y., Gomez, J., & Cherng-Jyh Yen. (2009). Community college online course retention and final grade: Predictability of social presence. *Journal of Interactive Online Learning, 8*(2), 165–182.

Lofton, J. (2010). Using VoiceThread for online communication. *The School Librarian's Workshop, 30*(3), 9–10.

New Media Literacies Project. (n.d.). The new media literacies. Retrieved from http://www.newmedialiteracies.org/the-literacies.php

Mandernach, J., & Taylor, S. S. (2011). Web 2.0 applications to foster student engagement. In R. L. Miller, E. Amsel, B. M. Kowalewski, B. C. Beins, K. D. Keith, & B. F. Peden (Eds.), *Promoting student engagement, Volume 1: Programs, techniques, and opportunities* (pp. 220–229). Retrieved from http://teachpsych.com/ebooks/pse2011/vol1/volume1.pdf#page=220

McCormack, V. (2010). Utilizing VoiceThread to increase teacher candidates' reflection and global implications for usage. In J. Yamamoto, J. C. Kush, R. Lombard, & C. J. Hertzog (Eds.), *Technology implementation and teacher education: Reflective models* (pp. 108–123). doi:10.4018/978-1-61520-897-5.ch007

Moore, M. G. (1993). Theory of transactional distance. In D. Keegan (Ed.), *Theoretical principles of distance education* (pp. 22–38). London: Routledge.

Pallos, H., & Pallos, L. (2011). Evaluation of Voicethread© technology to improve Japanese graduate students presentation skills in English in a blended learning environment. In S. Barton, J. Hedberg, & K. Suzuki (Eds.), *Proceedings of Global Learn Asia Pacific 2011* (p. 1078).Sydney, Australia: AACE.

Rapee, R. M., & Hayman, K. (1996). The effects of video feedback on the self-evaluation of performance in socially anxious subjects. *Behaviour Research and Therapy, 34*(4), 315–322. doi:10.1016/0005-7967(96)00003-4

Rodesiler, L. (2010). Voices in action: The potential of VoiceThread in the media classroom. *Screen Education, 59,* 72–74.

Short, J., Williams, E., & Christie, B. (1976). *The social psychology of telecommunications.* London: Wiley.

So, H.-J., & Brush, T. A. (2008). Student perceptions of collaborative learning, social presence and satisfaction in a blended learning environment: Relationships and critical factors. *Computers & Education, 51*(1), 318–336.

Schrum, L., & Solomon, G. (2007). *Web 2.0: New tools, new schools.* Washington, DC: International Society for Technology in Education.

VoiceThread LLC. (2011a). VoiceThread overview. Retrieved September 26, 2011 from http://voicethread.com/about/features/

VoiceThread LLC. (2011b). VoiceThread voluntary product accessibility template. Retrieved from http://cdn.voicethread.com/media/misc/VoiceThread-Accessibility-Whitepaper.pdf

Yildiz, M. N. (2010, October). Multicultural and multilingual youth projects from Turkmenistan: *Developing 21st century skills through global connections and teaching beyond borders.* Paper presented at the annual meeting of the Northeastern Educational Research Association, Rocky Hill, CT. Retrieved from http://digitalcommons.uconn.edu/nera_2010/14

13

IS THERE (STILL) A PLACE FOR BLOGGING IN THE CLASSROOM?

Using Blogging to Assess Writing, Facilitate Engagement, and Evaluate Student Attitudes

Tricia M. Farwell and Matthew Krüger-Ross

Introduction

In 2011 prominent educator Will Richardson, who is most well-known for his educational blog weblogg-ed, announced that after 10 years of blog authorship he was stepping back from blogging and embracing more real-time social media along with other professional activities. This announcement may have been seen, by some, as a sign of the final days of blogging in education as it appeared to confirm the viewpoint that blogs have become passé (Machlis, 2009). As teachers and students migrate to newer technology, a noticeable shift away from blogs and wikis, which are often seen as being part of the first wave of Web 2.0 and web-based technologies, towards newer social media outlets, including Twitter and various other real-time social media applications, is apparent.

Blogs are online journals used to explore thoughts and feelings regarding various topics. In a more advanced form, blogs become the central hub for businesses' web offerings (Scobel & Israel, 2006), connecting with others, sharing ideas, and fostering discussion. Blog entries, commonly called posts, are organized chronologically with the newest addition at the top of the page. Users can add keywords and tags as descriptors to enable others to easily find content. The commenting function on each post allows readers to reply to what was written enabling engagement with the author and other readers. This allows for online discussion and feedback with and for the writer.

Blogs can function in a similar way when added to classroom activities. They can serve as a forum outside the classroom while giving educators another outlet to assess engagement with topics and evaluate student learning. While it may seem odd to discuss blogging in terms of assessment due to their link to journaling, blogs may present a more up-to-date and meaningful method to encourage students to write class reflections and develop viewpoints stemming from class discussion. Depending on the topics covered, blogs may alert educators to potential problems that students may not mention in class or that the students may not be able to identify themselves.

However, there are some drawbacks to incorporating blogs into the curriculum. Despite the common belief that today's students are more tech savvy than in the past, there are still many who have never used a blog or are in need of technical assistance when beginning blogging (McCabe-Remmell, 2004). Alternatively, some educators have found some students to be so significantly more advanced with blogging that they outpace their peers and educator (McCabe-Remmell, 2004). Beyond student skill level issues, blogging has also been faulted for being too conversational in ways that are not as effective as other electronic platforms (Krause, 2004). Finally, and perhaps most concerning, actual student engagement with blogs has been questioned as they do not post consistently, abandon the blog once the course is over, and discuss posts superficially (Krause, 2004).

Despite the drawbacks, this chapter envisions a place for blogging in the classroom as a way to evaluate student learning and engagement. Through incorporating blogs in the classroom, communities may be formed which deepen student engagement with the subject, improve writing styles and encourage learning beyond the classroom. Since blogging can help students identify issues they may be having and assist students in processing and synthesizing what happens in the classroom, blogging should remain at the forefront regarding evaluating student learning.

Literature Review

Blogging, and more generally social media, is a hot topic within educational scholarship as academia scrambles to keep up with the technological advances. A quick Google Scholar search in mid-2011 using the search-string "social media" revealed more than 2.9 million hits on the topic. The impact of social media is further seen in the regular reports and data summaries chronicling the influence of new media and a variety of other technologies on any number of users (e.g., teens, youth, older adults) by the Pew Internet & American Life Center. Given the rapid rise of new technologies in social media, it is understandable that educators want to stay at the forefront in order to engage students. This desire to incorporate the newest technology may have educators jumping from older technologies, such as blogs, to newer platforms such as Twitter, Tumblr, and others. However, these newer platforms may not offer the same benefits as blogging. In fact, the newer tools may encourage instant responses over deeper engagement, a higher learning curve with the technology and, in some cases, a heavy reliance on graphics over text. Although there is a place in education for this type of interaction, when assessment needs to be based on depth of engagement, these platforms may not provide adequate information with which educators can evaluate students.

Despite the fact that blogs may be dropping in stature, many are still creat ing and interacting with them on a consistent basis. Lenhart and Fox (2006) found that 8% (12 million) of American users regularly update their own blog and 39% (54 million) regularly read and consult blogs. While the data is somewhat dated, it still demonstrates that a strong group of Internet users make up the so-called blogosphere, the name given to denote the metaphori- cal space that includes and encompasses bloggers and their respective blogs. More recently Hampton, Sessions Goulet, Rainie, and Purcell (2011) found that when looking at blogs by gender divisions, women were more likely to use blogs than men.

With generations coming into the classroom expecting interconnectedness, educators must find a way to work within student expectations or fear their stu- dents becoming disconnected from education. Millennials, 90% of whom use the Internet for convenience, may experience this interlinked web of associa- tions more strongly than other generations as their world revolves around shar- ing knowledge, connecting, and being connected through technology (Pew, 2010). Millennials are also the leaders when it comes to using social networking sites with 75% of them reporting to have created social networking profiles and 29% visiting social networking sites several times a day (Pew, 2010). Younger age groups are not just fascinated with social networking profiles, but also have experience with blogging. A 2007 Pew Center report regarding teens' use of blogs found that usage from 2004 to 2007 increased from 19% to 28% (Lenhart, Madden, Macgill, & Smith, 2007). As with previous studies, this one found that female teens were more likely to blog than male teens. So, at least as of 2007, blog usage among younger audiences had been on the rise.

Research specifically concerning blogging in educational settings remains inconclusive (Kim, 2008) and this may be a contributing factor to its lack of popularity in higher education. Halic, Lee, Paulus, and Spence (2010) orga- nize existing research on blogging and education into four broad categories: blogs in higher education, perceived learning, sense of community, and col- laborative constructivism. Within these categories it is evident that while there are perceived learning benefits, increased sense of community and a goal of generating shared knowledge, these cannot always be expected or counted on when incorporating blogging. What this research may be showing is that there is a feeling of community and discussion surrounding bloggers that can be capitalized upon for classroom use. It is this sense of community and freedom for constructive collaboration established through commenting on posts that allows for participants to feel a stronger connection (Halic et al, 2010). This connection, perhaps, allows learners to be more open to constructive feedback and reaching a shared knowledge. Comments made on blog posts are seen as individualized, personal, and targeted to the specific post to which they are attached rather than sweeping statements issued in a classroom.

One promising area for learning why the use of blogging may be beneficial for college students is the impact on students' perceived learning. Perceived learning, as noted in the terminology, describes a phenomena described by students whereby students identify their awareness of their learning through reflecting on their experiences (Caspi & Blau, 2008). Used as a research tool beginning with immediacy and perceived cognitive learning (Richmond, Gorham & McCroskey, 1987), blogging is known to contribute to perceived learning, regardless of context (Churchill, 2009; Ducate & Lomicka, 2008). Thus, blogging may provide an ideal intersection for evaluating student learning both by educator and student.

In addition to expanding the classroom, blogs can serve as a writing sample with which to evaluate student writing. As such, blogs could function as journal writing that enables educators to evaluate student writing over time, targeting a variety of audiences and answering Massé's (1999) call for extended use of journals for evaluation. In exploring the viability of using student journals from a media writing class as an assessment tool, Massé's examination of common themes in a semester's worth of journals revealed themes were neither linear nor mutually exclusive. As elements are introduced to the students' writing, the themes changed from confidence to apprehension or vice versa.

Blogging may provide students with a form of evaluation they feel is more valuable than traditional feedback. Ellison and Wu (2008) found that while students may believe that peer comments were ineffective in aiding learning, the same students believed that blog comments were beneficial. Thus, there seems to be some perceived lack with peer evaluation that does not exist with blog comments. The increased perceived credibility from blog comments may stem from the concept that blogging does build a feeling of community. As Leslie and Murphy (2008) point out, the two main streams of thought regarding blogging research are that blogs are catalysts for group interaction and blogs have the ability to promote building knowledge through social channels. As such, blogs become ideal channels for feedback and engagement.

Given the inconclusive nature of the research regarding blogging (Kim, 2008), this chapter enters the discussion by asking: Can blogs (still) be used effectively in classroom settings? In examining this question, the authors will discuss subquestions including:

- How effective are blogs in facilitating student learning experiences?
- How effective are blogs in facilitating student engagement?

To answer these questions, the authors draw upon their own experiences using blogging in their courses. While the experiences may not be able to be generalized, they may provide a starting place for others considering using blogs for evaluation in their classrooms.

Courses Involved

Together, the authors have experienced blogging in the classroom across a variety of courses, topics, and learning approaches. This expanse goes to show that this technology can be used as an evaluation platform that is not subject specific. Rather than ordering and classifying chronologically, the courses have been listed arbitrarily.

Perhaps the most obvious course in which to incorporate blogging was a social media and advertising course. Throughout the semester, students were asked to experience a variety of social media platforms from the perspectives of end-user and advertiser. At the beginning of the course, students were asked to start, maintain, and interact with class bogs on WordPress. The educator selected WordPress because it was the industry standard at the time and had more credibility with those in social media than other sites. Students were asked to write two posts per week. One entry was to focus on how a company used social media for a product or service and the other entry was to focus on any topic. No word length or other content restrictions were placed upon the students to allow them some editorial freedom.

A less self-evident course that used blogging was an advertising campaigns course. While the primary task of this course was for students to devise an advertising campaign for a client, blogs were used as reflection journals for the students to comment on their progress, their team's progress and any other items related to the experience they wish to share. Reflection journals are key elements in the course because they ask students to think beyond just completing tasks. They may also assist students by helping students focus on the process of learning, not just the grade at the end of the class (Kolb, 1984). Due to the nature of the course, students did have the option of sharing their journals with only the professor. Students were also given the option of blogging via a platform of their choosing, journaling by hand, or submitting their journal via D2L, the university's online learning environment. These options were provided because often students may need to critique their team members' contributions and skill-levels. In order to keep harmony, the educator felt that students may not feel comfortable making such critiques open. Although a 100-word minimum was placed on each entry, students were encouraged to go beyond the minimum requirements.

The third and final course was a graduate-level class in web design in educational technology that was taught via distance education. Taught primarily by utilizing the blogging platform WordPress and the social networking site Ning, students in this course were required to select either WordPress or Blogger to chronicle their participation throughout the semester. Other than the base requirement of creating and sharing the link to their blog, there were no additional specific requirements for students. In addition, no word length or other content restrictions were mentioned. In order to facilitate course interaction among students, they were grouped purposefully based on their prior knowledge of the subject area and comfortableness with new media. Each group consisted of members with varying levels of ability and comfort with technology that included expert/experienced to novice/intermediate users. As a component of their group work they were strongly encouraged to follow along with their group members' blogs by reading and posting comments. While participation with their peers via their individual reflective blogs was assessed as a subset of their participation score, it was weighted relatively equal to any of the other weekly course assignments. Students were also given the option to submit their course assignments via their reflective blog from time to time.

For all the courses, the blogs were evaluated on a variety of levels. While content expressed as depth of engagement was deemed to be the most important element of the grade, students were also evaluated on mechanical aspects such as meeting deadlines and minimum requirements, when provided. In two of the courses, the blogs served as part of the class participation and engagement grade. In the remaining course, the blogs were a stand-alone grade category. No rubrics were used to evaluate the blogs as the instructors felt that rubrics were unable to accurately accommodate the levels of engagement and content they expected in the blog posts.

Overall, the authors' course selection not only crosses topics ranging from advertising to web design, it also crosses educational levels and delivery methods. This gives a relatively wide range of experiences when presenting the successes and failures of using blogging in practice for evaluation purposes.

Blogging as Evaluation Tool

As a refresher, the following question drives the examination of using blogging in the aforementioned courses: How effective are blogs in facilitating student learning experiences and student interaction? This section begins by addressing using blogs to evaluate student engagement and then move to discussing using blogs to evaluate student learning.

Blogs as Evaluation of Engagement

No discussion of using blogs to evaluate engagement can exist without a discussion of the concerns surrounding the question of where to host the blogs. While this operational concern may seem to be relatively simple, it is significantly deeper than just selecting platform A or platform B. One of the main trade-offs educators will encounter is freedom of platform choice vs. ease of connectivity. While emphasizing ease of connectivity, educators may experience students complaining about lack of choice and/or difficulty of using the platform. Emphasizing freedom of platform choice, however, may make it more difficult to build a community among class members. The classes selected for this chapter represent a range of platform selection from complete freedom of choice, to required platforms. In fact, it appears that platform selection may have the strongest influence upon building a community outside of the classroom.

Despite all the considerations for selecting the proper platform for the class, some student resistance was encountered. One student wrote, "I am doing this blog mainly because my professor is [making me]." Student resistance, in the initial phases of the assignment at least, may be strong or educators may find themselves faced with confronting a student's online image which is not necessarily the student's in-person image. Students with experience in blogging may also share their previous successes or failures, such as this student comment, "I had tried creating blogs in the past, but they ultimately failed. I'm not a big fan of keeping stuff updated." Therefore, educators must work to facilitate student engagement with the platform and process of blogging.

When students were allowed to select their preferred platform, such as in the advertising campaigns course, no clear consensus emerged. However, student choice is important and limiting the blogging platform that students can use is best when considering the whole learning experience. If building an online community is essential to the learning experience, the authors recommend against an emphasis on student freedom of choice. The benefits of a required platform outweigh the benefits of choice in this context. In addition, removing any barriers to student feelings of comfort with particular technologies should always be a best practice. Therefore, it may be best, where there are a large number of students who are inexperienced with blogging platforms, to select the easier of the platforms under consideration. This may reduce capabilities, but students need to be able to easily access, post and comment.

On the whole, blogging was found to be most successful in facilitating learning and interaction when students were given a single platform, minimum word limits for posts, the opportunity to use RSS feeds, and autonomy in determining the content of their posts. The single platform allowed students to only need one set of log-on credentials and a single landing spot. Additionally, having one platform made it easier for students to learn and master the platform, compare notes, and assist classmates with their posts. The single platform may make students feel more comfortable with the application so they can focus upon other issues that not only provide for interesting blog posts, but also assist in building a community.

The two courses that required a specific platform were the social media and advertising course and the web design course. In the former course, the professor also created a blog that linked all the student blogs through a listing function called a blogroll. This aided the students in finding their classmates as WordPress has a rather steep learning curve. Students unfamiliar with blogging platforms did not express any distaste with the required platform selection until they had issues with posting. However, students who were already comfortable with blogging and being online expressed distaste for the requirement; their experience made them wish for more freedom of choice. In the web design course, students were limited to two platforms: WordPress or Blogger. Knowing the varying technical ability of the students, the instructors chose to limit student choice to two options giving students the opportunity to select the appropriate platform for their skill-level. To assist in organizing and streamlining student blog posts, a RSS feed was created using Google Reader that collected and correlated all of the students' posts into one centralized location. While this did solve the concern regarding locating student blogs, there remained a concern when commenting and resolving other technical difficulties.

Both courses also approached blog comments from different perspectives. Students in social media and advertising were not paired, but were told to read and comment on at least one class blog a week. This requirement was to facilitate community building among the class. However, the way the community was built did not fit expectations. Instead of using the professor's blog as a launch page to the classmate's blogs, students mostly commented on the professor's posts. Even with this centralized commenting, however, the students interacted with each other's comments along with the professor's original post. The web design course encouraged groups to visit and comment on their fellow group members' posts each week. It was also suggested that students occasionally visit the blogs of their other classmates to identify common challenges and concerns. Most students were easily able to maintain a presence with their group members on their respective blogs while overall not as many students truly utilized the blogging platform beyond their groups.

When using blogs to build community, the authors recommend encouraging students to use RSS technology via a Reader to help ensure student success. RSS or Really Simple Syndication creates a centralized online location for users to enter a feed specific to a website that includes changing content (Herndon, 2007). When new content is posted on the linked websites, the Reader notifies the user of the posted content. By collecting and marking their peers' RSS feeds, students in the course were easily able to keep current on their peers' writing and reflections. This increased interactivity as well as their overall learning experience while also introducing students to a foundational technology. This also created an opportunity for students to become aware of the writings of all class members beyond their groups.

One additional thought regarding evaluating blogging for building community includes the dreaded the question of "How long does this have to be?" The authors found that setting minimum word requirements to be most helpful for both the student authoring the blog and the student commenting on the post. The minimums give the student enough flexibility to interact with the topic while making sure they actually engage with the theme. It also generally provides a post with substance. The authors recommend considering adding minimum word counts to comments as well. This would remove the generic

"I agree" that some students may post when they are just going through the motions of reading their peers' writing. The recommendation of word limits resolves the font, size, and spacing concerns of traditional writing assignments and assists students in keeping their writing and reflections within specific, set boundaries. Additionally, it helps students conform to blogging standards.

Blogs as Evaluation of Learning

While it may seem self-evident, the simplest way of incorporating blogs in courses to assist in evaluating student learning is to use them as journals. In doing this, educators are returning to the foundations of the application to be used as a tool for communicating personal experiences. This approach can allow educators to use the posts as writing samples across the entire semester, depending on course requirements. Student blogs in the social media and advertising course provided an outlet for writing throughout the semester on topics relevant to the course and of the blog author's choosing. While the initial posts for the majority of the students were similar to "welcome to my blog that I'm writing for class," they quickly evolved into more in-depth commentary on course specific topics. Despite this quick progression, many of the introductory posts expressed thoughts that the blog may not live up to expectations (such as "we shall see what happens with this"). Some of this hesitation may have stemmed from the students' uncertainty regarding the audience of a public blog.

The advertising campaigns course did not have the same uncertainty towards blogging. Each journal entry was written with a single audience member in mind, their professor. Students often skipped the introductory post, delving directly into discussing their expectations and experiences. The content of the posts filled with ups and downs throughout the semester as student journals reflected the interactions of their group and their progress. In some cases, the posts reflected on how impressed the author was with some skill or how frustrated the author was with something going wrong.

The addition of individual course blogs in the web design for educators' course was implemented not only to incorporate an alternative to traditional forms of web design but also to create the space for students to openly and publicly reflect on the progression of their learning. Students were purposefully required to have their blog posts public in the spirit of the philosophy of Web 2.0 and web-based technologies that includes such values as sharing, openness, and transparency. In this way the instructors were encouraging open reflection and collaboration beyond the classroom, reaching out and connecting with other bloggers, educators, and designers interested in concepts surrounding web design. Student posting evolved naturally over the course of the semester from novice and tentative to more comfortable and knowledgeable. Each student's blog marked a personal journey through the course readings and activities and ultimately served as a key component in course assessment. Both of these aims, to chronicle student growth and build a greater sense of community, are noted frequently in the research literature as benefits of blogging. This provided information with which to evaluate engagement throughout the semester, rather than just at specific checkpoints.

One of the more interesting results of incorporating blogging into classroom activities is the approach the students took towards the work. Instead of dreading writing, the students looked towards the blogging homework as fun and low- to no-stress. Several students thought of blogging as a type of non-homework. As one student commented in writing the blog posts, "I'm doing something that is technically homework to take a break from other homework." In seeing the blogs as a break from traditional homework, students may find it easier to be engaged. While they understand the posts are still graded and for class, there appears to be an element of freedom associated with writing them. The students did not feel as restrained to be as formal with their content either due to the platform they were using or the fact that they believed that the educator was just another member of their audience, not the only member. In fact, one student even felt comfortable enough to playfully challenge the professor as part of a post and objecting to the notion that the class was going to be "easy" because of the subject matter.

Essentially, through blogging the boundaries between more traditional roles such as expert and student become muddled. Although the educator may start the course as the perceived expert, as students gain confidence in their posts and community knowledge, they move closer to the role of expert. This also allows for educators to evaluate student writing in terms of content. As those who give advice for successful blogging will attest, content is key. Students will not be able to fake their knowledge on a subject as more than one reader eventually serves as a check. The emphasis on content for successful blogs should also prompt educators to view content as key in their evaluations of student blogging. From the educators' perspective, blogging was most successful when grading included appropriate depth within posts and themes throughout posts.

Given these examples, it is relatively obvious that the intended audience will play a larger role in student blog posts than, perhaps, in traditional essays or work written specifically for the instructor. Not only will this audience impact how the students write, but also the content. Due to the notion that the posts were not "real" homework, educators may need to approach blogging with a more flexible set of expectations when using them for evaluation purposes. This is not to say that they should disregard all traditional expectations in areas such as grammar, punctuation, and content. One need only look at the criticisms that abound online where people are scorned or mocked for spelling and grammar mistakes in blogs and on other platforms. While excessively correcting posts to reflect formal grammar marks one as a "grammar troll" in the blogosphere, being too lax becomes a sign of ignorance and a lack of commitment to the content.

Thus, it is essential when using blogs as a form of writing assessment to be aware of the writing challenges posting may present. While one of the most appealing aspects of using blogs to evaluate student writing is the fact that they allow educators to watch students develop over time, educators may have to relinquish some control to the intended audience and subculture. This change in mindset is in line with what many recommend as proper blog etiquette to encourage readers. While there are numerous websites that offer advice on how to cultivate regular readers, thus build the blog community, they all reiterate some common traits of a good blog. Among those traits are having good content, finding a voice, knowing the audience and posting on a regular schedule. These become the factors which educators may need to consider when beginning their evaluations.

The authors are not recommending a total disregard of grammar and spelling rules, just a reconfiguration to fit the medium. Common chat speak, emoticons, and even leetspeak may be appropriate for posts, depending on the audience, in ways that would be deemed unacceptable in academic writing. For those unfamiliar with chat and leetspeak, the words are often shortened or spelled using a combination of letters and numbers. For example 1337 translates to "leet" and cul8r is "see you later." Obviously, educators do not want to see that kind of writing in more formal documents, however for the web, the approach may be fitting for the target audience. In fact, depending on the audience, not using common web speak may mark the blogger as an outsider or, even worse, an uninformed fraud. Thus, educators should be open to more informal modes of writing and students demonstrating their part of the subculture they are targeting.

What blogs do offer students and educators looking to evaluate writing is an expanded pool of contributors for feedback. As mentioned in previous studies (see Hsieh, 2011; Kolb 1984; Lewin, 1951; Mory 2003), feedback enhances student learning and performance. While most educators believe that feedback is essential, they also may find themselves writing the same comments repeatedly. This repetition may show that while students may read the feedback, they may not be truly thinking about applying the comments. However, with more than just the educator providing the feedback, students may be more open to fixing errors in future writings. Perhaps even comments from the educator may take added importance if additional community members comment that they agree with what the educator posted.

Often, students want and need feedback about their work, ideas, and reflections. Students' blogs should be examined within the context of depth of thought and for themes that guide, support, or are threaded throughout the student's post. This does come with the drawback of an increased investment of time and energy, but it also best meets student needs and can lead to more meaningful feedback for students. Also, it may at times be necessary for educators to set specific parameters on certain posts when feedback is the primary concern for the post. In the experience from the web design class, giving students free reign also gave them the freedom to rise to expectations, and their writing reflected the depth of their thinking and understanding.

As with using blogs to evaluate student writing, it seems relatively self-evident that blogs can allow for educators to evaluate student perceived learning relatively easily. On one side, students will provide feedback to educators through their reflections. This feedback can range from "Our [final project] is awesome! I can't wait for you to see it" to "I know we went over it in class, but I still can't figure out how to install the WordPress Twitter widget." The students' perceived learning progress is easily tracked depending on the content and frequency of the posts. Even in posts that do not focus solely on their reflected experiences may contain elements that can be used to assess learning. For example, when students are posting a critique of a website, their critique can reflect the application of knowledge, much as a traditional paper would. Themes can also emerge from multiple students' blogs to alert the instructor to a lack of clarity on an assignment or student frustration with solving a required course activity.

A more involved way to evaluate individual student learning through blogs is to examine the recurring themes throughout the semester. While this can be done using other methods, such as periodic, anonymous course evaluations, face-to-face meetings and other methods, the consistent and repetitive schedule of blog posting makes feedback more available to educators on a post-by-post basis. In this way, blogs may provide educators with resources to evaluate learning and course progress in a timelier manner. Thus, educators may be able to adjust the course schedule quicker to alleviate possible problems and future concerns.

The theme analysis proved to be an essential aid for group projects as it alerted the professor to which students were possibly slacking or struggling with content. Students who may not feel comfortable speaking out about another's contribution in traditional settings may feel more comfortable speaking out via their blogged reflection journal. Additionally, the fact that the blog may be semi- or completely public may make the student rely more on factual evidence than feelings. Student comments were no longer just "I wish [Sally] would do more." Instead, they showed a deeper connection to the tasks. The comments became "[Bobby] was assigned to research and analyze the product. Instead, he showed up to class with a list of links. If we wanted links, we could have done that. Where was the analysis?" Thus the students move beyond complaints based on personality issues to elements which have more substance to the group function.

Blogs can also be a valuable tool to facilitate learning through peer evaluation. In the web design course, students were encouraged to post drafts of their course activities and projects on specific dates throughout the semester. This provided a window for their peers into their process and progress while also serving as a resource for themselves and a useful tool for the instructors in evaluating student understanding of core course concepts. Student reflections were also paramount in evaluating the course as a whole and are being utilized in the latest revision of the course. For example, one of the themes that emerged from student blogs was their lack of clarity in some of the basic structures and requirements. While this feedback was made available through official university-sponsored evaluations, the instructors were able to elicit and analyze students' critical feedback early on in the semester and made attempts at remedying some of the student concerns.

Conclusion

Based on the experiences of the authors, blogging can still be used effectively in classes to assess student writing, foster a learning community both in and out of the classroom and evaluate student learning. However, incorporating blogging is not something to be done on a whim. Instead, course objectives, student outcomes, and evaluation expectations need to be firmly established, communicated and in-line with what blogging can deliver. With these thoughts in mind, the authors recommend the following best practices for using blogs in the classroom for evaluation purposes.

Best Practices for Evaluating Engagement

- Consider requiring students to use a single platform to host all student blogs.
- Make sure students post on a regular schedule so that educators and other readers know what to expect and when.
- Encourage students to utilize a reader to collect new posts.

Best Practices for Evaluating Learning

- Set aside time to read and engage with the text and subtext of the blogs through leaving comments or finding points to discuss in class.
- Look for feedback not just from open statements of success or struggles, but also in terms of theme and specificity.
- Communicate writing expectations to students in terms of grammar, spelling, word counts and formatting.
- Remain flexible in expectations, making adjustments for audience, sub-culture, and the need to show membership.
- Remember that content is king in the blogosphere. Evaluation should incorporate an element of depth of engagement.
- Remain open to the blurring roles between student and learner, expert and student.

Although there is no quick and easy approach to using blogging to assess student engagement and learning, the authors believe there is a place for the application within evaluation of student progress and understanding. In order to successfully use blogging as an evaluation tool, educators may need to rethink their approach to evaluation, becoming more fluid in terms of sources for feedback. Also, traditional writing prompts and evaluation rubrics and guidelines may need to be revamped to account for the opportunities for which blogging allows.

The blogosphere is alive and well and doesn't show any sign of stopping. So, at least for the authors of this chapter, there is still a place for blogging in their classes.

References

Caspi, A., & Blau, I. (2008). Social presence in online discussion groups: Testing three conceptions and their relations to perceived learning. *Social Psychology Education, 11,* 323–346.

Churchill, D. (2009). Educational applications of Web 2.0: Using blogs to support teaching and learning. *British Journal of Educational Technology, 40*(1), 179–183.

Ducate, L. C., & Lomicka, L. L. (2008). Adventures in the blogosphere: From blog readers to blog writers. *Computer Assisted Language Learning, 21*(1), 9–28.

Ellison, N. B., & Wu, Y. (2008). Blogging in the classroom: A preliminary exploration of student attitudes and impact on comprehension. *Journal of Educational Multimedia and Hypermedia, 17*(1), 99–122.

Halic, O., Lee, D., Paulus, T., & Spence, M. (2010). To blog or not to blog: Student perceptions of blog effectiveness for learning in a college-level course. *The Internet and Higher Education, 13*(4), 206–213.

Hampton, K. N., Sessions Goulet, L., Rainie, L., & Purcell, K. (2011, June 16). Social networking sites and our lives. Pew Internet & American Life Project. Retrieved from http://www.pewinternet.org/~/media//Files/Reports/2011/PIP%20-%20Social%20networking%20sites%20and%20our%20lives.pdf

Herndon, J. G. (2007). *RSS for educators.* Eugene, OR: ISTE.

Hsieh, P-A. J. (2011). Comparing e-learning tools' success: The case of instructor-student interactive vs. self-paced tools. *Computers & Education, 57*(3), 2025–2038.

Kim, H. K. (2008). The phenomenon of blogs and theoretical model of blog use in educational contexts. *Computer & Education, 51,* 1342–1352.

Kolb, D. A. (1984). *Experiential learning: Experience as the source of learning and development.* Upper Saddle River, NJ: Prentice-Hall.

Krause, S. D. (2004). When blogging goes bad: A cautionary tale about blogs, email lists, discussion and interaction. *Kairos 9.1.* Retrieved from http://english.ttu.edu/kairos/9.1/binder.html?praxis/krause/index.html

Lenhart, A., & Fox, S. (2006). Bloggers: A portrait of the internet's new storytellers. Pew Internet & American Life Project. Retrieved from http://www.pewinternet.org/Reports/2006/Bloggers.aspx

Lenhart, A., Madden, M., Macgill, A. R., & Smith, A. (2007). Teens and social media. Pew Internet & American Life Project. Retrieved from http://www.pewinternet.org/~/media//Files/Reports/2007/PIP_Teens_Social_Media_Final.pdf.pdf

Leslie, P., & Murphy, E. (2008). Post-secondary students' purposes for blogging. *International Review of Research in Open and Distance Learning, 9*(3), 1–17

Lewin, K. (1951). *Field theory in social science: Selected theoretical papers.* New York. Harper and Row.

Machlis, S. (2009). Blogging is over with. *PC World*. Retrieved from http://www.pcworld.com/article/167568/blogging_is_over_with.html

Massé, M. (1999). Evaluating students' progress by reading their journals. *Journalism & Mass Communication Educator, 54*(3), 43–56.

McCabe-Remmell, P. (2004). Falling out of love with blogging. *Kairosnews*. Retrieved from http://kairosnews.org/node/4003

Mory, E. H. (2003). Feedback research revisited. In D. H. Jonassen (Ed.), *Handbook of research for educational communications and technology* (2nd ed., pp. 745–783). Mahwah, NJ: Erlbaum.

Pew Internet & American Life Center. (2010). Millennials: Confident. Connected. Open to change. Retrieved from http://pewsocialtrends.org/assets/pdf/millennials-confident-connected-open-to-change.pdf

Richardson, W. (2011, June 20). 10 years of blogging: Time for a chance and a book. Retrieved from http://weblogg-ed.com/2011/10-years-of-blogging-time-for-a-change-and-a-book/

Richmond, V. P., Gorham, J. S., & McCroskey, J. C. (1987). The relationship between selected immediacy behaviors and cognitive learning. In M. L. McLaughlin (Ed.), *Communication yearbook 10* (pp. 574–590). Newbury Park, CA: Sage.

Scobel, R., & Israel, S. (2006). *Naked conversations: How blogs are changing the way businesses talk with customers*. Hoboken, N J: Wiley.

INDEX

21st century community 104
3D 34–35

access 20, 24–25, 27, 29–30, 32
achievement 20
age 20
analysis 5, 19, 21, 25, 31, 35
assessment 35, 38–39, 169–70
audio 47
    audio journal 51, 57
audio recording 50
audio reflection 49, 52–53
Australian university 155
avatar 4–5, 7–8, 10–16, 34, 38–40, 42–43, 62

blended learning 152
blogs 51, 103–04, 106–07, 207–10

case study 87
class discussion 123
cognitive presence 150, 156, 161, 164
collaboration 88, 194, 198, 204
collaborative learning 188
collective intelligence 80
communication 171–72, 174, 176–77, 183, 187
communicative actions 99–100
communities 64, 78
Community of Inquiry (CoI) 147–48, 150, 164
computer-mediated communication 98
Concerns-Based Adoption Model (CBAM) 82–83

constructivism 169
context 5–7, 16–17
co-presence 10
cultural considerations 42

delivery mechanism 35, 37–40, 43
differentiated instruction 169, 171–72, 175
digital natives 20, 32
digital technology 30, 32
discourse 98, 100, 110–112

eBusiness 155
educational experience 150–51
emerging technology 41
engagement 170–72, 193, 200–01
English as a foreign language 34, 36
evaluation 191, 204

feedback 47, 51, 53–55, 106–07, 199–203

gaming 7–9, 14–17
gender 5, 7–9, 14–16
gestures 42

hashtag 153–57, 160–61, 164
Heads-Up Display (HUD) 67
higher education 117, 147, 150–51, 209
higher level learning 42

identity 3, 7, 10, 12–13
immersive technology 41
individualized instruction 170

instructional design 5–6, 17, 19–21, 172
instructional designer 35, 38, 42–43
interaction 190–93, 199, 201
interpersonal distance 41, 43
inventory 69, 73
in-world 65, 67, 74–75
island 34, 41

journal 53, 57

land 74
language learners 41, 43
learner characteristics 3, 5–7, 9
learning management system (LMS) 148–50
Learning and Teaching as Communicative
    Actions (LTCA) 100
lesson planning 22, 26
limitations 24, 26, 30
listening guide 9

micro-blogging 117, 119, 147–50
Millennials 19, 20
modeling 198–99, 203–04
multimedia 48–49, 52–53, 194

native speakers 38, 41–42
new media literacies 190–91

online collaboration 19, 22
online learning 83, 192–93, 204
online social media 19–21
online videos 132, 134, 139, 144–45
open source software 82–88

participatory learning 198
peer critique 198, 201, 203
performance context 42
personalized learning 170
podcasts 47, 50–51
potential 19
preparation time 41
presence 4, 7, 10
prims 69
privacy 119–20, 122, 125–29
problem solving 172, 175–76, 188
problem-based learning 81–82
production 19–20
psychological behavior 43

real life 63–66, 69, 76

real-time tweeting 117, 121, 123–124, 127
residents 74–75
risks 38, 40–41
role play 85–86, 97

safety concerns 40–41
scripting 69, 75
Second Life® 4–7, 34–35, 62–66
self-evaluation 199
social interaction 4, 6, 12
social media 3–5, 9, 47, 49, 100, 106, 111,
    118–20, 148, 150, 169, 171–72, 207–08,
    211, 213–15
social networking 80, 87–88, 209, 211
social presence 99, 105, 108, 110, 112,
    149–52, 156, 161, 164, 191–93
Sociology 132–34
standards 21, 23, 26, 28
student-centered learning 174

teacher resistance 20, 27, 32
teacher roles 32
teaching presence 150–51, 157, 162–64
technical difficulties 39
technical skill 6, 8–10, 12, 14
technical support 6, 10, 17
tertiary education 149, 152, 160
text chat 72
timeline 38–39
TweetDeck 153, 164
Twitter 101, 117–20, 148–50

virtual reality 36–37, 40, 43
virtual world 4, 34, 42–43, 67
virtual world beliefs 16
voice 13,16, 50
VoiceThread® 192–95
voice board 52, 54
    voice inflection 49–51
voice reflection 53

Web 2.0 19–20, 47, 50–51, 59, 84–85, 171,
    173–74, 187
web-based technologies 207, 215
Wiki 80–81
Wimba Voice Tools® 51
workload 123–24

YouTube 132–35